*1974*

# Modern Latin American Literature

D. P. GALLAGHER

# Modern Latin American Literature

1973
Oxford University Press
New York and London

For Alegría

# Preface

I HAVE not attempted, in this book, to compete with the considerable number of histories of Latin American literature now available. I have not therefore aimed to be encyclopedic, and have chosen rather to concentrate on the few writers that seem to me exceptionally important. Many will quarrel with my choices. Needless to say, I am guilty of many no doubt regrettable omissions.

With the exception of translations from Borges in chapter 8, from García Márquez in chapter 10, and from Cabrera Infante in chapter 11, for which sources are given in the footnotes, all the translations are mine. I have deliberately made them literal, in order that they serve efficiently to illustrate my discussions of the various writers concerned.

# Acknowledgements

THE author and publishers gratefully acknowledge permission to reprint copyright material.

Jorge Luis Borges: from *A Personal Anthology*, edited by A. Kerrigan. Copyright © 1967 by Grove Press, Inc. Reprinted by permission of Jonathan Cape, Ltd., and Grove Press, Inc.

Guillermo Cabrera Infante: from *Tres Tristes Tigres (Three Trapped Tigers)*, translated by D. Gardner and S. J. Levine. Copyright © 1965 by G. Cabrera Infante. English translation copyright © 1971 by Harper & Row, Publishers, Inc. Reprinted by permission of the author and publishers.

Gabriel García Márquez: from *One Hundred Years of Solitude*, translated by Gregory Rabassa. Reprinted by permission of Jonathan Cape, Ltd., and Harper & Row, Publishers, Inc.

Pablo Neruda: from *Odas elementales* (copyright © 1954 by Editorial Losada), *Residencia en la tierra* (copyright © 1958 by Editorial Losada), and *20 poemas de amor y una canción desesperada* (copyright © 1944 by Editorial Losada). Reprinted by permission of Editorial Losada.

Octavio Paz: from *Ladera este* (copyright © 1962) and *Salamandra* (copyright © 1958). Reprinted by permission of Editorial Joaquín Mortiz. From *Libertad bajo palabra*. Copyright © 1960. Reprinted by permission of Fondo de Cultura Económica.

César Vallejo: from *Poemas humanos*. Copyright © 1939. Reprinted by permission of Mrs. Georgette Vallejo. From *Los heraldos negros* (copyright © 1919) and *Trilce* (copyright © 1922). Reprinted by permission of Editorial Losada.

# Contents

# 1

## Introduction : The Nineteenth Century

NINETEENTH-CENTURY Latin American literature has certain fundamental limitations. With the exception of the Brazilian novelist Machado de Assis (1839–1908), Latin American writers in the nineteenth century were usually too immature and too derivative to merit the serious consideration of anyone not specifically interested in the Latin American context as such. There was no lack of Romantics, Realists, Naturalists, Parnassians, or Symbolists but the European model was always more impressive and anyway the Great Movement tended to arrive too late, when its original inspirational impetus had long been jaded. There were some splendid failures—but failures they were simply because their authors lacked the technique, the application, and the language to make them otherwise.

Language indeed was one of the central shortcomings of Latin American writing in the nineteenth century. The language had been inherited from a rejected colonial power. Like the English of Irish literature, it had to find itself and liberate itself in order to carry conviction—and it did not. Many writers in the nineteenth century attempted to grope their way to an authentic language in which to write—a language they could feel was their own—but they never really managed to. The most conspicuous attempts were perhaps those of such Argentinian *gauchesco* poets as Hilario Ascasubi (1807–75) and José Hernández (1834–86). They endeavoured to appropriate the language of the *gauchos* in an effort to lay the foundations of an authentically national literature. Their poems were a spectacular improvement on the neoclassical odes they inherited but their endeavour was too self-conscious: they aimed too strenuously to *imitate* a language which they did not speak themselves, and consequently their poetry was too much of a charade, too little an expression of their own identity.

However, the fine literature that has emerged from Latin America in the twentieth century owes a great deal to its nineteenth-century antecedents. Many contemporary obsessions can be traced to them and it must not be forgotten that even contemporary Latin American writers were brought up at school on nineteenth-century texts, with the result that they are deeply embedded in their consciousness. Moreover, the fact that so many of the central topics of Latin American literature have not significantly altered—they have merely come to be investigated with greater skill and with greater attention to their complexity— suggests that there are certain deeply rooted habits of thought which are specific to the continent. An understanding of Latin American literature in the twentieth century cannot be complete therefore without at any rate a cursory glance at the century that preceded it.

To begin with, one can discern in the literature of the nineteenth century the same perplexity with regard to the continent's heritage and identity that, we shall see, is to be so basic to the work of Pablo Neruda (1904– ), Octavio Paz (1914– ), or Miguel Angel Asturias (1899– ) say. Where is the writer to look in order to discover his real identity? Where is the continent to find an acceptable heritage? Few Spanish American nineteenth-century writers do not adopt as a starting-point in their answer to these questions an *a priori* rejection of Spain. For the poets of independence Spain is of course primarily the enemy in battle, but already it is something worse: it is the country that has deployed a Dark Age over a whole continent, an age of 'Blood, swift lead, and chains' for the Ecuadorian poet José Joaquín de Olmedo (1780–1847)—all in the guise of 'Holy Sacraments'. The first Spanish American novel moreover, *El Periquillo Sarniento* (1816), by Fernández de Lizardi (1776–1827), turns out to be a ferocious indictment of Spanish administration in Mexico: ignorance, superstition, and corruption are seen to be its most notable characteristics.

Yet if three hundred years of Spanish heritage are to be rejected, what is to replace them? Sometimes, writers turn to Enlightened

France for help. French models prevail in many Argentinian Romantic novels for instance, and they are central to the work of Esteban Echeverría (1805–51) and José Mármol (1817–71) there. Yet France, too, frequently disappoints, as does Europe in general. For the influential Venezuelan poet of the independence, Andrés Bello (1781–1865), Europe very quickly becomes the scene of mere fashionable affectation and unconstructive frivolity.

In Mexico, where the Indian past had been a grand one and where, unlike Argentina or Chile, for example, the population remained predominantly Indian, writers sought to revamp history with the aim of reinstating the country's *indigenous* heritage. An indigenous national consciousness burgeoned most conspicuously there after the liberal revolution of 1854. Under the aegis of the novelist Ignacio Altamirano (1834–93) a spate of historical novels were written in Mexico that asserted the conquered Indian to be idyllically wise and noble, the colonizing Spaniard being presented in contrast as a voracious savage. If Mexico had an identity and a heritage, they were to be found therefore not only in the rejection of the Spanish colony but also in the rediscovery of a pre-Columbine past.

In general, the urge to discover and assert a national identity necessitated a great deal of uncompromising aggression on the part of Latin American writers. Unfortunately, such aggression precludes many of the qualities that we normally take for granted in the more lasting monuments of literature. For most nineteenth-century Latin American writers the issues are so urgent that there is no room for instance for detachment in their treatment of them and there is no room for attention to their potential complexity. Most of the writers are politicians, generals, or lawyers, and their novels or poems are merely useful means for divulging a point of view. Their aim is didactic; there is no room for argument. The characters are either good or bad—unremittingly so. No opportunity is lost to spell the issues out. A novel like *Amalia* (1851–5) by José Mármol is written with the sole intention of overthrowing a dictator, Rosas. The more it can damage him, the better it is; there is no other criterion to judge it from. This, for contemporary Latin American Maoists, was no doubt the Golden Age!

Occasionally, writers unwittingly escape their rigid dichotomies and their black-and-white vision is undermined by a genuine, unconscious artistic impulse. Thus for Domingo Faustino Sarmiento (1811–88), Rosas is a *barbarian* who has savaged all that is *civilized* in Argentina. The dichotomy is rigid, and Sarmiento allows himself no opportunity to examine its respective categories analytically, no time to ask himself for instance if civilization, epitomized by 'elegant manners, European clothes, tails, and frock-coats', is necessarily so universal a panacea as he takes it to be. Yet now and then, in describing the savagery of Rosas's *gauchos*, he is so overwhelmed by it that he becomes a *gaucho* himself. His language becomes so gloriously 'barbaric' that it unexpectedly undermines its 'civilizing' purpose. In initiating a dichotomy that is to remain a central topic of Latin American writing up until now, that of 'civilization' and 'barbarism', Sarmiento becomes in spite of himself, one of the continent's first literary barbarians. He becomes one of the first Redskins in a continent which, like the United States, is to have its own long line of literary Redskins and Palefaces.

There is, maybe, no nineteenth-century writer more widely disseminated in schools than Andrés Bello, and one can surmise that his influence has been felt, consciously or unconsciously, by a vast majority of Latin American writers up until now. Certainly, one can find in his work many of the most reiterated concerns of Latin American writing. Thus in 'Alocución a la poesía' (1823) he urges that poetry abandon 'cultured Europe' and turn instead for inspiration to 'the vast scene of Columbus's world'. And he recognizes a task that many Latin American writers are subsequently to consider central to their endeavour: the basic one of describing a continent and landscape that have *never* before been described. The task is not to be an easy one. One hundred and forty-four years later, in *Quarup* (1966), a novel by the Brazilian writer Antonio Callado, a group of characters are to be confronted by a jungle full of hundreds of different species of orchids, not one of which they can name!

In Bello too one gets a sense, typical of subsequent Latin American writing—and typical of Whitman in the North—of the grandeur of the continent, of the urgent necessity to show it forth on a vast, epic scale. His 'Alocución a la poesía' foreshadows many subsequent epics of the continent and most notably it foreshadows Pablo Neruda's *Canto general* (1950).

Yet if the continent is a grand, promised land, it is also one whose promise has turned sour. Bello is the first of many Latin American writers significantly to express the feeling that the auspicious promise of their continent has been frustrated. He could not help doing so, for he was able to witness the euphoric promise of independence very soon degenerating into fratricidal Civil War. Many nineteenth-century Latin American novels, and most expertly those of Machado de Assis, are, indeed, like their counterparts in the twentieth century, to be imbued with a tragic sense of *waste*.

Society—what is given, what the hero of the novel or the poet is confronted with—is rotten. Either they rot too in the confrontation or they rise in rebellion. One of the most successful works of literature written in Spanish America in the nineteenth century, José Hernández's vast poem on the gauchos, *Martín Fierro* (1872–9), is a violent aggression on society, a desperate attempt at rebellion. It was intended as an attack on a specific society, on the presidency of Sarmiento in fact and on its exploitation of the *gaucho* as cannon fodder in the wars against the Indians. But it deploys a more generally anarchic spirit which is perhaps best exemplified in one splendid scene. Martín Fierro is guilty of murder and desertion and one day the rural militia surround him. He fights with exemplary courage. Then, suddenly, the man in charge of the militia, Sergeant Cruz, cannot stand it any longer. He shouts that 'Cruz will not permit the crime of killing a brave man', and joins sides with Fierro.

What greater rejection of society could there be than this blatantly *approved* spectacle of a policeman joining a bandit and murderer in mid-battle?

Now if the given society is to be rejected, what is to be put in its place? Something somewhat airy, usually. It is a curious fact that whereas in the nineteenth century many writers, such as Ascasubi, Echeverría, or Mármol were capable of the most aggressive naturalism in their depiction of what they rejected, they all tended to adopt a somewhat ethereal spectral language when depicting anything they approved of. Thus in Echeverría's *El matadero*, or Mármol's *Amalia*, Rosas and his supporters are described with an almost grotesque—or Goyesque—realism. Yet any mention of the liberal cause that Rosas has supplanted precipitates a language that is in contrast idyllically Romantic. The liberal heroine Amalia is thus not a *woman* ('Amalia no era una mujer'), but rather 'a goddess'. In general the adjectives and metaphors used by these writers would seem to be unwittingly asserting that the ideal was impossible, because it had no real or human basis.

Having set out, at the beginning of the century, to celebrate the happy reality of independence, and the magnificent reality of the continent's landscape, Latin American poets indeed finish the century celebrating goddesses and marble statues. There is a brief discussion of this culminating movement—*modernismo*—in the next chapter.

**2**

# Poetry, 1880–1925

THE *modernista* movement that burgeoned in the 1880s, and whose most notable exponent was the Nicaraguan poet Rubén Darío (1867–1916), derived its inspiration mainly from French Parnassian and French Symbolist poetry. There is not a great deal in its imagery and in the topics it seeks to express that cannot be found in some French poet or other, or in Poe or the English Pre-Raphaelites.

*Modernista* poetry is frequently populated, at any rate in its early stages, with ethereal *princesas* or *marquesas* lasciviously reclining upon velvet divans. The setting if often enough an eighteenth-century palace. 'Sweet violins of Hungary' play 'galant *pavanes*, fleeting *gavottes*'. Champagne flows, and outside the palace, there is an impeccable French garden. Metaphors and similes refer anything at hand to an ideal realm of regal splendour. Even the water of a fountain (a marble one of course) is 'like a girl scattering her pearl necklaces in a regal palace'.[1] Roses are like 'Persian shawls of bejewelled silk'.[2] April is 'prince April'[3] and rhymes are so rich that they are made of 'silver and crystal'.[4]

The *modernistas* may not have invented many of these images, but the fact that they chose to imitate them and not others is symptomatic of an escalation of that cult of an ethereal ideal we

[1] Manuel Gutiérrez Nájera, 'Ondas muertas', in *Spanish American Modernista Poets*, ed. G. Brotherston, Oxford, 1966, p. 42.

[2] Gutiérrez Nájera, 'A la Corregidora', ibid., p. 46.

[3] Ibid.

[4] José Asunción Silva, 'Un poema', ibid., p. 60.

discerned in writers of a previous generation. In referring the already idyllic subjects of their poems to a realm of mystical splendour the *modernistas* may of course have been implicitly protesting against the grim realities of their respective countries, protest taking the form of escape into idyll. Yet in a way they were also echoing current aspirations. Several countries were beginning to enjoy a considerable export boom in raw materials in the 1880s, and the new élites that were benefiting from it were beginning to spend their newly acquired sterling on imported luxuries. The velvet furniture, the silky and embroidered clothes, and the snow-white princesses of *modernista* poetry thus maybe echo the dreams of a new élite that longed to be the equal of the European aristocracy.

A fundamental unauthenticity belies *modernista* poetry. There is something strange and sad about a humble Nicaraguan like Rubén Darío yearning for 'diamonds upon white necks',[5] or about a Bolivian like Ricardo Jaimes Freyre (1868–1933) blindly immersing himself in Nordic mythology. Also, one rarely gets the feeling reading a *modernista* poem that the poet *had* to write it. There is no sense of urgency, no tension. Occasionally *modernista* poets—and notably the Colombian poet José Asunción Silva (1865–96)—actually write about their own experiences, and then we get a sense of what they really might have achieved had they not clung so strenuously to foreign models.

Yet the *modernista* movement did a great deal for poetry in Spanish, not only in Spanish America but also in Spain. The *modernistas*, and Darío in particular, greatly enriched Spanish versification. They learnt a great deal from the French Symbolists about the musical potential of poetry, and consequently wrote verse which, though weak in content, was richly melodious. They wrote erotic poetry, thus removing an unhelpful Hispanic taboo, and they asserted the right of Latin Americans to be cosmopolitan. This may sound paradoxical, in view of my criticism of their very cosmopolitanism in the preceding paragraph. But the problem is not that Latin American poets have no right to immerse themselves, for example, in Nordic mythology. They have as much right to do so as D. H. Lawrence did to depict Mexican mythology. What is important is that they should do it with assurance. The fact that the *modernistas* lacked the assurance and maturity to be

[5] Rubén Darío, 'Epístola', ibid., p. 93.

cosmopolitan convincingly does not mean that they did not pave the way for their successors to be so. Poets like César Vallejo (1892–1938) and Neruda, who could put the trials and short-comings of the *modernistas* behind them, were able, when they started writing in the 1920s, to write poetry that for the first time in Latin America was triumphantly not at all circumscribed by the limitations of a local context, although—and this is per-haps where the lesson lies—it was deeply rooted in one too.

As will become evident when we discuss them in detail, Vallejo and Neruda served their literary apprenticeship in the context of *modernismo*. Vallejo was particularly influenced by Leopoldo Lugones (Argentina, 1874–1938) and Julio Herrera y Reissig (Uruguay, 1875–1910), two late *modernistas* whose poetry success-fully revitalized the clichés of their predecessors, and who de-ployed a new intensity of expression in their work. They were both masters of the violently surprising image, and their poetry is free of the jaded air of fatigued mimicry that many *modernista* poems had come to display. Yet it must be admitted that neither Lugones nor Herrera y Reissig had a great deal to say. There is no urgency underlying their poetry either.

After the First World War the ideas and habits of the con-temporary European *avant-garde* began to be transmitted to Latin America. In February 1922 a Week of Modern Art was celebrated in São Paolo, thus heralding the burgeoning of Brazilian *modern-ismo*, a movement that had little in common with the Spanish American one of the same name. Brazilian *modernismo* was in fact a calculated reaction against the work of such Parnassian or Symbolist Brazilian poets as Raimundo Correia (1869–1911) and João Cruz e Sousa (1861–98). Its early manifestos were influenced by Italian Futurism. They urged that poets be hectically con-temporary, that they abandon the decadence of Parnassus, and be sensitive to the conditions of modern life. Some Brazilian *modern-istas* were often blatantly nationalist, and they enthused about the future greatness of Brazil. Others, such as Oswald de Andrade (1890–1954) and Mário de Andrade (1893–1945), believed that Brazilian poetry had to find its way back to the origins of Brazilian culture in order to rediscover an authentic national identity which Portuguese domination had uprooted. Such a concern we saw was present in nineteenth-century writing in Spanish America. We shall see, moreover, that it foreshadowed the determination of Pablo Neruda and Octavio Paz to recover a supposedly edenic past.

The Brazilian *modernistas* proclaimed the gospel of free verse, and sought to find their way to a specifically Brazilian language. They preferred to write badly than to write like the Portuguese, or than to ape the stilted literariness of the Parnassians. Their quest was for a colloquial, spoken language. Their manifestos and discussions crystallize the principle worries and hopes of twentieth-century Latin American literature in general. Their influence outside Brazil was admittedly not great—there has never been a great deal of cultural contact between Brazil and the rest of the continent—but the ferment of ideas that burgeoned during the Week of Modern Art in São Paolo in 1922 produced some of the finest poets in the Portuguese language—the most impressive of all being perhaps that sardonically wise observer of human folly, Carlos Drummond de Andrade (1902– ).

The ideas of the European *avant-garde* entered Spanish America through other channels. A notable disseminator was the Chilean poet Vicente Huidobro (1893–1948). Of considerable importance too was the *ultraísta* movement. The *ultraístas* were a Spanish group of poets who eclectically imbibed practically every *-ism* current in Europe at the time—Futurism, Cubism, and Expressionism in particular. Jorge Luis Borges (1899– ), who had collaborated with them in Spain, championed the *ultraísta* creed in Argentina on his return from Europe in 1921. But Borges soon discarded *ultraísmo*, and there was no impressive *ultraísta* poet as such. *Ultraísmo* served rather to disseminate current ideas about poetry, and consequently to create a stimulating climate for young poets to operate in. Yet because poetry in Latin America was beginning to achieve an unprecedented maturity and self-assurance, poets felt free at last to use foreign ideas only if they really wanted to, and then discard them at will. It was their own experience, their own sensibility, and their own vision that were ultimately to matter.

Two poets began writing around 1920 who notoriously started to express a sensibility that was very much their own. They are César Vallejo and Pablo Neruda. They each merit detailed and separate treatment.

# 3
# César Vallejo (Peru, 1892–1938)

VALLEJO'S first book of poems, *Los heraldos negros* (1918), is at first sight a derivative work, and one or two poems in it could easily have been written by Rubén Darío, others by Herrera y Reissig or Lugones. Take the opening stanza of 'Nochebuena' ('Christmas Eve'):

> Al callar la orquesta, pasean veladas
> sombras femeninas bajo los ramajes,
> por cuya hojarasca se filtran heladas
> quimeras de luna, pálidos celajes[1]

—a purely decorative description that parades all the portentous hush, the hectically contrived mystery of fleeting feminine presences, the subtly filtered light effects, the delicate pallors of *modernista* rhetoric. Silk appears predictably in the next stanza, deployed for an equally predictable synaesthesic effect:

> Charlas y sonrisas en locas bandadas
> perfuman de seda los rudos boscajes.[2]

In fairness 'Nochebuena' is an exception, the only poem in the book that could have fitted easily in Darío's *Prosas profanas* (1896). More common are the poems that imitate Herrera y Reissig, whom we noted as the exponent of a more intense, more imagistic *modernismo* who was, however, equally affected, equally

---

[1] César Vallejo, *Los heraldos negros*, Buenos Aires, 1961, p. 16. 'When the orchestra falls silent, veiled / female shadows stride beneath the branches / through whose foliage are filtered / frozen whims of moon, pallid skyscapes.'

[2] 'Chats and smiles in wild flocks / perfume the rugged woods with silk.'

a concocter of literary exercises wholly lacking in emotional urgency. These poems, like Herrera y Reissig's, are almost obligatorily set in a pastoral dusk. Portentous poplars, 'like imprisoned hieratic bards',[3] decorate a landscape charged too conspicuously with idyllic significance. Even the supposedly innovatory poems about the Indians of the Peruvian sierra where Vallejo was born read in parts like mere exercises in exotic decoration, and the fact that the landscape is one Vallejo knew well, unlike the Basque country which was so dear to Herrera y Reissig although he never visited it, seems quite accidental:

> La aldea ... se reviste
> de un rudo gris, en que un mugir de vaca
> se aceita en sueño y emoción de huaca.
> Y en el festín del cielo azul yodado
> gime en el cáliz de la esquila triste
> un viejo coraquenque desterrado.[4]

Dreamy sounds, a melancholy that feels very self-imposed, a contrived wistfulness all add up to a meekly derivative literary exercise, not an authentic description of the sierra and its Indians. The cycle of poems called 'Nostalgias imperiales', from which the above passage is quoted, and another one called 'Terceto autóctono', also about the sierra and the Indians, have, in general, the glossy feel of exotica set up for the tourist, much as do the Indians that Darío occasionally evoked.

The *modernista*—especially the late *modernista*—roots of much of *Los heraldos negros* have been expertly charted by André Coyné in his *César Vallejo y su obra poética*.[5] We should not, of course, be surprised by them. They are present in the first efforts of all the best poets of Vallejo's generation, in Neruda and Borges for instance, who felt the call of duty to describe the dusk as assiduously as Vallejo did. What is remarkable about *Los heraldos negros* is the sense one gets now and then of a personal voice emerging, far more assertively than it does, say, in Neruda's *Crepusculario* (1923). In many of the poems, Vallejo's own ex-

---

[3] p. 18.
[4] p. 49. 'The village ... is decked / in rugged grey. The bellowing of a cow / is annointed in dreams and the emotion of a *huaca* tomb. / And in a feast of blue, iodic sky / an old exiled *coraquenque* groans from the chalice of a cattle-bell.'
[5] Lima, *c.* 1950.

periences, his own personality, begin confidently to express themselves, and with them there tentatively burgeons a new language,
the beginnings of maybe the most original voice in Latin American poetry.

The most predominant type of poem in *Los heraldos negros* is
the love poem—the setting and the idiom are very often *modernista*, but the poems are already beginngin to tell a personal story,
the story of Vallejo's own attitudes, fears, and hopes. Thus whereas
their religious-cum-erotic imagery has strong *modernista* overtones, it begins to take on connotations that are not purely
decorative.

Vallejo was born and brought up in an intensely Catholic environment in the primitive Andean town of Santiago del Chuco,
in the north of Peru. It is indeed said that he was sometimes under
pressure from his family to become a priest. It is not surprising,
therefore, that when sexual experience is seen in some of his
poems in a religious context, a personal dilemma is being worked
out far removed from any mere literary influence:

> Linda Regia! Tus pies son dos lágrimas
> que al bajar del Espiritu ahogué,
> un Domingo de Ramos que entré al Mundo,
> ya lejos para siempre de Belén.[6]

Throughout his work, the erotic is treated by Vallejo with
ambivalence, and he shifts back and forth from sheer disgust with
it to a hope that it will stimulate some sort of spiritual fulfilment.
Either way, its points of reference are spiritual, he will not allow
himself any sheer physical *enjoyment* from it.

The ambivalence is stressed in a punning line from 'Nervazón
de angustia' ('Nervous gust of anguish'). A 'sweet Hebrew girl'
to whom the poem is addressed (echoing the biblical tone that
was dear to Herrera y Reissig) is asked to '*unnail* his nervous
tension'. Then 'Tus lutos trenzan mi gran cilicio / con gotas de
curare'—'Your mourning braids my great hairshirt / with drops
of curare.'[7] She is thus either the poison that magnifies and final-

---

[6] p. 12. 'Gorgeous girl! Your feet are two tears / which I drowned when I
descended from the Spirit / one Palm Sunday that I entered the World /
already distant, for ever, from Bethlehem.'
[7] p. 13.

izes his agony, or its cure, the ultimate executioner, or the re-
deemer. Or both, because that fundamental conceit of the Spanish
mystics, that life is the beginning of death and that death is the
beginning of life, is central to Vallejo's early poetry. And copulation consequently implies both annihilation and rebirth, crucifixion (which its posture resembles) and resurrection. Thus in
'Ascuas' ('Embers'):

> sangrará cada fruta melodiosa
> como un sol funeral, lúgubres vinos,
>     Tilia tendrá la cruz
> que en la hora final será de luz.[8]

Each noun ('fruit', 'sun', 'wine') suggests achievement; each verb
or adjective ('will bleed', 'funereal', 'gloomy') suggests the struggle
involved in its path, the blemishes that still mar it, until the final
struggle, the crucifixion, leads to an ultimate light. Similarly
in 'El poeta a su amada' ('The poet to his beloved'), the 'sacrifice' involved in love-making 'sobre los dos maderos curvados
de mi beso' ('upon the two curved beams of my kiss') is a mere
prelude to a more satisfactory relationship that will follow death,
where

> ... ya no habrán reproches en tus ojos benditos;
> no volveré a ofenderte. Y en una sepultura
> los dos nos dormiremos, como dos hermanitos.[9]

Death thus purifies a relationship which during life has been sin-
fully profane, and sets him free from his sanctimonious fear of
copulation. 'Love, come to me fleshless', he asks in 'Amor',

> y que yo a manera de Dios, sea el hombre
> que ama y engendra sin sensual placer.[10]

---

[8] p. 17. 'Each melodious fruit will bleed / like a funereal sun, gloomy
wines, / Tilia will have the cross / which in the final hour will turn to light.'
N.B. Tendrá suggests tenderá: 'will stretch out' or 'unfold' the cross.

[9] p. 32. 'There will be no more reproaches in your blessed eyes; / I shall not
offend you again. And in a tomb / the two of us shall sleep, like a little
brother and sister.'

[10] p. 95. 'And may I, in the manner of God, be the man / who loves and
begets without sensual pleasure.'

In the poem 'Deshora' ('Untimely moment') he hankers after a

> Pureza amada, que mis ojos nunca
> llegaron a gozar. Pureza absurda—[11]

a pre-pubertal purity 'en falda neutra de colegio' ('in a neutral
school skirt'). This ideal is frequently contrasted to a more lustful
form of sexual experience of which his memories are always
guilty ones, memories of masculine violence imposed on a female
whose purity is thereby irrevocably savaged. Thus in 'Heces'
('Dregs'), amidst the dreary rain of Lima, he remembers

> las cavernas crueles de mi ingratitud;
> mi bloque de hielo sobre su amapola
> más fuerte que su 'No seas así.'[12]

One of the central obsessions within this very personal statement that thus begins to emerge from the poems of *Los heraldos
negros*, and which is developed with a far more eloquent anguish
in his next book, *Trilce* (1922), is the memory of one single
traumatic act: Vallejo's departure from his family up in Santiago
del Chuco, and his consequent initiation into worldliness. Like
the idyll of a pure, fleshless love, the idyll of the rural home is
evoked in poems like 'Idilio muerto' in deliberate contrast to
Lima or 'Byzantium', a stifling Babylon where it rains drearily,
where the air asphyxiates and the blood goes to sleep. Not only
does he regret the fact that he has lost a pastoral paradise for the
sake of a rotten city; he feels guilty about it:

> Hay soledad en el hogar; se reza;
> y no hay noticias de los hijos hoy.
> Mi padre se despierta, ausculta
> la huída a Egipto, el restañante adios.
> Está ahora tan cerca;
> si hay algo en el de lejos, seré yo.[13]

[11] p. 41. 'Beloved purity, which my eyes never / managed to enjoy. Absurd
purity.'
[12] p. 36. 'The cruel caves of my ungratefulness; / my block of ice upon
your poppy / more potent than your 'Don't be like that.'
[13] pp. 101–2. 'There is loneliness back home; they're praying / and there's no
news of the children today. / My father wakes up, listens for / the flight into
Egypt, the staunching farewell. / He is so near now. / If there's something far
in him, it must be me.'

Yet always the memory of the home town, in particular of the archetypally beautiful mother is summoned as a consolation, as something to latch on to even now, and the home town and family elicit from Vallejo his first wholly genuine poetry, underivative, untainted by literary postures. In 'Canciones del hogar' ('Home songs'), a cycle of five poems that closes *Los heraldos negros*, a wholly new idiom emerges, only glimpsed at in most of the other poems of the book, and such as had not been seen before in Latin American poetry. For one gets a sense reading these final poems that they really had to be written, and that the sentiments they need to convey are really more important than the style in which they are expressed. It is as if Vallejo for the first time felt he no longer needed to enlist the aid of Darío or Herrera y Reissig, felt he could manage on his own. And the deeply felt emotions unwittingly produce a new language: directly simple, free of posturing decoration, yet always under strict control, with the result that the poems often risk reaching the brink of sentimentality yet yet hold back and are able, as few poems can, to be moving about the most ordinary things without bathos. Thus Vallejo remembers playing hide-and-seek with his brother Miguel ('A mi hermano Miguel'), who is now dead:

> Miguel, tú te escondiste
> una noche de agosto, al alborear;
> pero, en vez de ocultarte riendo, estabas triste.
> Y tu gemelo corazón de esas tardes
> extintas se ha aburrido de no encontrarte. Y ya
> cae sombra en el alma.
>
> Oye, hermano no tardes
> en salir. ¿Bueno? Puede inquietarse mamá.[14]

There are a few other poems here and there which are written in this direct, unpretentious manner. Usually they are poems that express a genuine confused awkwardness, a sense that life is somehow bigger and more elusive than he had bargained for. Thus the title poem that opens the book:

[14] pp. 103-4. 'Miguel, you hid / one August night, at daybreak; / but instead of laughing you were sad. / And your twin heart of those faded / evenings has grown weary of not finding you. And already / a shadow is falling on my soul. / Listen brother, hurry / out. All right? Mother might start worrying.'

Hay golpes en la vida, tan fuertes ... Yo no sé!
Golpes como del odio de Dios; como si ante ellos,
la resaca de todo lo sufrido
se empozara en el alma ... Yo no sé![15]

Or the poem 'Agape' where a sense of pain and loneliness is kept
this side of self-pity with the occasional mocking irony: 'Per-
dóname Señor: qué poco he muerto' ('Lord forgive me: how little
I've died').[16]

Vallejo is, indeed, always effective in *Los heraldos negros* when
shouting sardonic defiance at God, as though in liberating himself from his devotional guilt he were liberating himself too from
the clogging postures of an inherited idiom:

Dios mío, si tú hubieras sido hombre.
hoy supieras ser Dios;
pero tú, que estuviste siempre bien,
no sientes nada de tu creación.
Y el hombre sí te sufre: el Dios es él![17]

It should be remembered that *Los heraldos negros* was written
by a very young man indeed, by a young provincial, moreover,
who had nothing but the limited *modernista* tradition to fall
back on. Even so, and even in his blatantly *modernista* poems, he
is able to surpass the *modernistas*. The book, of course, must have
been useful anyway as a literary exercise, as an apprenticeship.
Most of the metres that the *modernistas* introduced into Spanish
poetry for the first time are mastered with assurance. All of the
poems are written moreover with a discipline rare before then in
Spanish American poetry: within the limitations of the idiom in
which they are written, the poems perpetrate very few redundant
lines.

And yet *Los heraldos negros* is a paltry work in comparison
with the book that followed it in 1922, *Trilce*. What happened
to Vallejo in the three or four years that separated the two
volumes? What developments explain his passage from the

[15] p. 9. 'There are blows in life that are so heavy ... I don't know! / Blows
like the hatred of God; as though in face of them / the dregs of all suffering /
were stagnating in the soul ... I don't know!'

[16] p. 66.

[17] p. 90. 'God, if you'd been a man / you'd know how to be God; / but you
who were always all right / have no feeling for your creatures. / Yet man
must endure you: *he* is God.'

elegant correctness of *Los heraldos negros* to the utterly unprecedented innovatory power of the new book?

Certainly a few experiences enriched that unpromising background to *Los heraldos negros* which had consisted merely of a quiet life in Santiago del Chuco, a thesis on 'Romanticism in Spanish poetry' in Trujillo, soul-searching conversations with provincial intellectuals there, and a perhaps marginally more fruitful impecunious loneliness in Lima.

In 1918 his mother died, with the consequence that there could no longer be any hope of recovering the forsaken idyll. Definitely on his own, the fragile balance that seemed to hold his neuroses just about at bay in *Los heraldos negros* began to crack. He returned to Santiago del Chuco in 1920, yet became involved almost immediately in a local political dispute which culminated in the burning down of the town's general store. Vallejo's role appears to have been merely conciliatory, yet he managed to get himself imprisoned in Trujillo for some three and a half months, accused of being the 'intellectual instigator' of the incident.

One can safely imagine that conditions in a Trujillo prison in 1920 were not congenial. Certainly, both the injustice of the sentence and the rough loneliness of the cell appear to have left a marked impression on Vallejo, who was obviously a most hypersensitive man. And it is important to note that many of the poems in *Trilce* were in fact written in prison, the circumstance contributing greatly, no doubt, to their sometimes frenzied anguish.

*Trilce* is so different a book from *Los heraldos negros* that it is hard to believe it was written by the same man. Whereas *Los heraldos negros* is either politely literary or, at best, starkly direct, *Trilce* is an intensely difficult work. For in freeing language from the received rhetoric of *modernismo* or even of colloquial directness Vallejo presents us the word in the raw, disconnected, thrust upon us in isolation or, more often perhaps, under the guise of a syntax which, though deceptively conventional, appears, at first sight anyway, to add up to no recognizable meaning. All the decorative aspects of *Los heraldos negros* are, moreover, abandoned. There is no question any longer of Vallejo allowing himself to sit back and describe a landscape. Indeed he allows himself nothing in *Trilce* that does not appear to be urgently important personally, just as he grimly shuns all temptation to indulge in a 'beautiful' turn of phrase.

There is a revealing poem in the book—poem LV—that suggests how he now thinks his poetry should be behaving:

> Samain diría el aire es quieto y de una
> contenida tristeza.
>   Vallejo dice hoy la Muerte está soldando
> cada lindero a cada hebra de cabello perdido,
> desde la cubeta de un frontal, donde hay algas,
> toronjiles que cantan divinos almácigos en guardia,
> y versos antisépticos sin dueño.[18]

Thus the delicate cadences and preciously fragile melancholy of a French Symbolist like Samain (who was a decisive influence on Lugones and Herrera y Reissig) are dismissed, replaced by a self-parodying effusion of harsh 'antiseptic' contradictions, 'verses without an owner', without the spurious backing of received ideas or a received idiom. Moreover, the announced lack of 'ownership' underlines the extent to which the poetry of *Trilce* involves a 'letting the language speak'. The man gives way to the words that are unsuspectedly buried within him, the words more than the images, for Vallejo's enterprise is not, fundamentally, a surrealist one. Vallejo seems to be seeking to find himself not in the *images* of his unconscious, but rather in the *language* of his unconscious. He is perhaps the first Latin American writer to have realized that it is precisely in the discovery of a language where literature must find itself in a continent where for centuries the written word was notorious more for what it concealed than for what it revealed, where 'beautiful' writing, sheer sonorous wordiness was a mere holding operation against the fact that you did not dare really say anything at all. The summoning of unprecedented, raw language involves in Vallejo a process of self-discovery, therefore, a fact worth noting all the more simply because Vallejo's frequently cited debt to Mallarmé can thereby be put into perspective. The reason is that for Vallejo a poem is never a mere verbal object, a cluster of sparsely connected words that seek to refer to nothing but themselves. For Vallejo a poem is essentially a state-

---

[18] *Trilce*, Buenos Aires, 1961, p. 90. 'Samain would say the air is quiet, of a / composed sadness.
Vallejo says Death today is welding each limit to each thread of lost hair; from the cask of a frontal, where there is sea weed, balm-gentle singing divine vigilant seedlings and antiseptic verses without an owner.'

ment about Vallejo or about the human problems of which Vallejo is a microcosm. Language is not wrenched in order to achieve a new, unprecedented decorativeness, but rather in order to discover the man that has been hitherto hidden behind its decorative façades. The discovery is not a pleasant one, and the noise the poems make is consequently aggressive and not beautiful.

Let us take the love poems, almost as predominant in *Trilce* as in *Los heraldos negros*. Much the same sexual ambivalence as was displayed in *Los heraldos negros* can be found, yet again, in *Trilce*. Again there is a hankering after a pure, innocent love which may have been possible in the past and which is now out of reach:

> ... Es el rincón
> donde a tu lado, leí una noche,
> entre tus tiernos puntos,
> un cuento de Daudet. Es el rincón
> amado. No lo equivoques.[19]

One notes that there is no need felt here to complicate the language. Indeed there are one or two things that Vallejo appears to be so sure of—a pure forsaken love, his family, his mother—that he does not have to grapple with their meaning within himself, and he expresses them therefore unabashedly in the direct language of 'Canciones del hogar'. But where the erotic becomes tortured, guilt-ridden, the language becomes contorted, as though Vallejo felt that he could maybe get to the complex truth of his experience if only he could find the right idiom to define it.

Clayton Eshleman has written that 'In Vallejo the amount of physical suffering is the alteration that it seeks.'[20] This is indeed so, the main problem being worked out in the erotic poems in *Trilce* being therefore that his dissatisfaction with sexual experience is usually a direct result of the great deal he expects from it. The splendour that he hopes to extract from copulation always runs aground against the inevitable limitations of copulation it-

---

[19] p. 28. 'It's the corner / where at your side I read one night / amidst your sweet polka dots / a Daudet story. It's the beloved / corner. Don't mistake it.' *NB. Puntos* is somewhat enigmatic in this context. 'Knitting' might also be a plausible translation.

[20] Foreword to *Poemas humanos. Human Poems*, edited and translated by Clayton Eshleman, London, 1969, p. xv.

self. In poem LIX his vast hopes are mirrored by the 'Pacific, immobile, glass, bulging / with all the possibles',[21] only to be coun-
tered by the great wall of the 'Andes, cold, inhumanable,[22] pure'.
The vastness of his expectations would seem, therefore, to be the
cause of his ultimate disgust with 'aquel punto tan espantable-
mente conocido' ('that point so horrifierly[23] known'—presumably the vagina?) and the cause in general of his failure to obtain
satisfaction:

> Y me retiro hasta azular, y retrayéndome
> endurezco, hasta apretarme el alma![24]

Now and then the erotic poems start hopefully. Thus IX:

> Vusco volvver de golpe el golpe.
> Sus dos hojas anchas, su válvula
> que se abre en suculenta recepción
> de multiplicando a multiplicador,
> su condición excelente para el placer,
> todo avía verdad.[25]

A hectic effort is, indeed, announced in the first line, but there
seems no reason why it should not be rewarded. Then:

> Busco volvver de golpe el golpe.
> A su halago, enveto bolivarianas fragosidades
> a treintidós cables y sus múltiples,
> se arrequintan pelo por pelo
> soberanos belfos, los dos tomos de la Obra,
> y no vivo entonces ausencia,
>                 ni al tacto.[26]

[21] *Trilce*, p. 97.

[22] and [23] Vallejo is most fond of using adjectives and adverbs that are only
just neologistic, only just off centre.

[24] p. 98. 'And I retire until I'm blue, and in the act of withdrawal / I
harden, until my soul grows tight'.

[25] p. 19. 'I vish to retturn* the blow by blow. / Its two broad leaves, a valve
/ that opens in succulent reception / from multiplied to multiplier / its excellent ability to please / everything promises truth.'

* Note the eccentric forms *vusco* and *volvver* for *busco* and *volver*. This
hectic arrangement of v's conjures a sense of almost impossible effort.

[26] 'I wish to retturn the blow by blow. / In its honour I impose mountain
sickness* on Bolivarian crags / at thirty-two cables and their multiples, / hair

Craggy Andean heights worthy of Bolívar and enigmatic cables of probably very high tension are dizzily deployed on (presumably?) a receptive vagina whose lips are no less than the two volumes of *the Book*, and the enterprise succeeds in abolishing 'absence'.

But the poem ends with a characteristic statement of failure, despite the effort and initial optimism:

> Fallo bolver de golpe el golpe.
> No ensillaremos jamas el toroso Vaveo
> de egoísmo y de aquel ludir mortal
> de sábana,
> desque la mujer esta
>     ¡cuánto pesa de general!
>
> Y hembra es el alma de la ausente.
> Y hembra es el alma mía.[27]

The failure—indeed the horror ('that mortal rubbing of the sheet')—looks as if it is about to be explained, even blamed on the woman ('desque da mujer esta . . .'). Yet what is the explanation? An exclamation which seems to be a *non sequitur* (unless he is blaming her for a sort of contingent weightiness, for having too much *body* and not enough soul), followed by two lines which are surely merely enigmatic, offering the appearance of explanatory meaning, but remaining ultimately irreducible.

Most of the poetry in *Trilce* is indeed ultimately too irreducible for it to have been fair even to have offered the sort of exegesis I have attempted to offer of this poem, which may, after all, not have been intended to have the sexual connotations suggested at all. One thing though, is I think clear: the poem is about effort of some kind, effort to surpass some sort of limitation, marred in the end by failure.

---

by hair, there is a contraction / of glorious blubber-lips, the two volumes of the Book, / and I live no absence then, / not even touching.'

   * *Enveto* is an invented transitive form of a Peruvian verb *envetarse*, 'to suffer mountain sickness'.

   [27] pp. 19–20. 'I fail to zepay [*sic*] the blow by blow. / We shall never saddle the robust shlabering* / of selfishness and of that mortal rubbing / of the sheet / ever since this woman here / how much she weighs of general!† / And the soul of the absent woman is female. / And my soul is female.'

   * I take *Vaveo* to be *Babeo* (slavering), on analogy with *vusco* for *busco*.

   † 'In general' would be *en general*, or *por lo general*: another example of gentle distortion.

The gap that separates aspiration from execution is indeed the central concern of *Trilce*, whatever form it takes. Always Vallejo is bashing his head against some limit, trying to wrench himself through what is given, trying to free himself, in general, from the limitations imposed by time and by space. The man who can write that 'La muerte está soldando cada lindero a cada hebra de cabello perdido' (LV) and that men are 'the corpses of a life that never was' (LXXV) is also the man who announced that we must 'fight to thread ourselves through the eye of a needle', or who declares:

> ... traspasaré mi propio frente
> hasta perder el eco
> y quedar con el frente hacia la espalda.[28]

Impressive though it is to manage to pass through one's own forehead, it is maybe no improvement to end up with one's forehead turned towards one's back, and indeed very often Vallejo's efforts to surpass limits end with him falling flat on his face. Very often Vallejo introduces a sort of nightmare arithmetic to dramatize the battleground. Numbers, of course, have their own relentless logic, and for Vallejo they symbolize the relentlessness of fate and of time. If only we could change the rules of arithmetic, maybe we could also change our destiny! Thus in LIII he seems to be hoping that by dint of a 'cabezazo brutal' (a brutal blow of the head) he might convert eleven into an even number:

> Como si las hubiesen pujado, se afrontan
> de dos en dos las once veces.[29]

In the end, the enterprise is marred by an inability to surpass the 'eternal three hundred and sixty degrees', and by the return of a menacing 'frontier', which interposes itself, like an 'itinerant conductor's baton' ('ambulante batuta') between ambition and its fruition. Vallejo in the end is always being cut down to size by frontiers, by demarcation lines in general (*fronteras, linderos*), and none are more definitive than the four walls of his cell in Trujillo. Like all his frontiers, they too are relentlessly numerical:

[28] p. 18. 'I shall pass through my own forehead / until I loose the echo / and end up with my forehead turned towards my back.'

[29] p. 87. 'As though they'd been pressured the eleven times / confront each other two by two.'

Oh las cuatro paredes de la celda.
Ah las cuatro paredes albicantes
que sin remedio dan al mismo número.[30]

Whereas to grapple with the limitations of numerals and spaces may seem a somewhat abstract enterprise, the cell does indeed give Vallejo good reason to feel cut down to size. Similarly, whereas it is somewhat abstract to aspire to thread oneself through the eye of a needle, Vallejo has some very tangible ambitions too, and they often relate to his mother, first abandoned, and now dead and buried in Santiago del Chuco.

In *Los heraldos negros* mere separation from the mother gave Vallejo the sense that he had become an orphan. In *Trilce*, where the mother is finally dead, we get a sense of his growing resentment at having to cope on his own with a hostile environment that holds no promise any longer of a potential return to the cosy security of the family fold. Yet this anguished orphanhood is not set up self-pityingly as a merely personal problem. It is to become—it had already begun to in *Los heraldos negros*—the orphanhood of mankind in general abandoned by God, or more specifically of the toiling masses abandoned by their employers. And the sense of 'orphanhood' felt by the man from the sierra in a hostile Lima is of course not one on which Vallejo need have a monopoly. The drama of the *serrano* emigrating to Lima in the hope of making good there, and finding instead exploitation, unemployment, and homelessness, is one that has long bedevilled Peru. Vallejo summarizes the intimidated feelings of the *serrano* who arrives in Lima in a poem (XIV) in which he expresses his awe at 'that manner' the *limeño* has 'of walking on trapezes'.[31] And in another poem (VI) he wistfully evokes the absence of a washerwoman (his mother?) who used to wash his clothes. The objects on his bedside table are no longer his. If only, in his loneliness, he knew that one day she would return:

a entregarme las ropas lavadas, mi aquella
lavandera del alma. Qué mañana entrará
satisfecha, capulí de obrería, dichosa

[30] p. 31. 'Oh the four walls of the cell. / Ah the four bleaching walls / which give the same number without fail.'
[31] p. 27.

de probar que sí sabe, que sí puede
¡COMO NO VA A PODER!
azular y planchar todos los caos.[32]

Life is now ordinary, automatic, full of mere 'loving and carry-
ing on', of mere 'this and that' (LVII).[33] 'Every day I wake up
blind / to work for a living: and I have breakfast / without
tasting a drop of it, every morning' (LVI).[34] Food without his
mother is not worth tasting, even if he shares it with another
happy family. What's the use when it is not *his* family?

> El yantar de esas mesas así, en que se prueba
> amor ajeno en vez del propio amor,
> torna tierra el bocado que no brinda la
>           MADRE,
> hace golpe la dura deglusión; el dulce.
> hiel; aceite funéreo, el café.[35]

Such are the rewards of the 'futile coming to age of being a man'
—'esta mayoría inválida de hombre' (XVIII).[36]
Throughout *Trilce*, Vallejo contrasts the drabness, the limitations, the loneliness he has landed himself in with the forsaken
paradise of the sierra. Sometimes he allows himself desperately to
conjecture that nothing has happened at all, that he has not left,
or otherwise that he is returning to find everything the same as
before. In these poems Vallejo drops linguistic complications
once more and achieves a tone similar to that of 'Canciones del
hogar', only it is more effective now because the fragile idyll is
seen to be on the point of cracking.

> Las personas mayores
> a qué hora volverán?

---

[32] pp. 14–15. 'To hand over the washed clothes, laundress / of my heart. What
morning will she enter all satisfied, a good job done, happy / to show that
yes, she knows how, she can / HOW COULD SHE NOT! / bleach and iron
all the chaoses.'

[33] p. 94.

[34] p. 92.

[35] p. 49. 'Having supper at tables like that, where you taste / the love of
others instead of your own / turns the mouthful that the MOTHER hasn't provided to dirt / and the painful swallowing becomes a slap; the sweet / becomes
icy; the coffee, a funereal oil.'

[36] p. 32.

> Da las seis el ciego Santiago,
> y ya está muy oscuro.
>
> Madre dijo que no demoraría. (III)[37]

In another poem, after evoking his family desperately, as though by writing about them he could bring them back to life, he eventually gives in and opts instead for a sort of bravado irony:

> Todos están durmiendo para siempre,
> y tan de lo mas bien, que por fin
> mi caballo acaba fatigado por cabecear
> a su vez, y entre sueños, a cada venia, dice
> que está bien, que todo está muy bien. (LXI)[38]

In the end, even the mother–son relationship is doomed to succumb to the logic of arithmetic. Thus in XVIII Vallejo appeals to his mother, 'lovable keeper of innumerable keys', to help him against the four walls of the cell.

> Contra ellas seríamos contigo, los dos,
> más dos que nunca. Y ni lloraras,
> di, libertadora![39]

The appeal has a defiant hopefulness, but the mother is dead.

Two is set up as an ideal number in *Trilce* and it seems to me to stand for the ideal pairing of mother and son. Yet how can you keep two from becoming three? How can you preserve a 'dicotyledon' intact and stave off its 'propensiones de trinidad'— 'propensities towards trinity'? In a strange poem on the 'grupo dicoteledón (dicotyledon group—V) there is a desperate plea that the dicotyledon should remain unmultiplied ('A ver. Aquello sea sin ser más'), undisturbed ('y crome y no sea visto'), and safe from catastrophe ('Y no glise en el gran colapso'), and that 'the betrothed be betrothed eternally' ('los novios sean novios en eternidad'), unmarried and therefore free of progeny ('trinity').[40]

[37] p. 9. 'The grown-ups / what time will they come back? / Blind Santiago strikes six / and it has got very dark. / Mother said she wouldn't be long.'

[38] p. 101. 'All of them are now for ever asleep / and so very fine, that at last / my horse grows tired and starts to nod off / himself, and half asleep, every time he bows, he says / that it's fine, that it's all just fine.'

[39] p. 31. 'Against them you and I would be, the two of us, / more two than ever. And you wouldn't even cry, / tell me now, deliverer!'

[40] p. 13.

This poem (which one must admit is so potentially obscure that any 'explanation' of it such as my own may be wide of the mark) seems to contain most of the obsessions of *Trilce*, and perhaps suggests ways of tying them up. For is not this hankering after a pure, sexless love that we also found in *Los heraldos negros* really a search for a mother–son relationship? One would be perhaps going too far if one were to suggest that his fear of 'trinity', of a 'third party', signified a fear of an intruding father. The important fact is that Vallejo appears to be seeking in the love affairs of *Trilce* (a neologistic title which ominously suggests three) a blissful, pure, eternal 'togetherness' which he may only have achieved with his mother, an unprecedented ecstasy which he certainly seems to think copulation unable to provide. And certainly the most dearly remembered lovers are often more maternal than sexy, such as the *amada* in XXXV, busily preparing him lunch, sewing a button on his shirt, and sewing his 'flank' ('costado': ribs?) to hers. Alas, no togetherness, no 'dicotyledon', can last; there is no number which will not multiply, roll into the next, and then the next:

> Pues no deis I, que resonará al infinito.
> Y no deis O, que callará tanto,
> hasta despertar y poner de pie al I. (V)[41]

Such is the logic of arithmetic, of unstoppable time, of nature, of all those things Vallejo battles against in *Trilce*, a startling, pent-up, dramatic book which is also relentlessly authentic, free of even a momentary lapse into easy phrase-making, and free too of illusions, despite the vastness of its quests.

In June 1923 Vallejo left Peru for Europe, arriving in Paris a month later. He was never to return.

During his first decade in Paris Vallejo appears to have written very few poems, although the dating of his poetry subsequent to *Trilce* is very difficult indeed. None at all appeared in book form until his death, *Poemas en prosa*, *Poemas humanos*, and *España aparta de mi este cáliz* having all been published posthumously by

[41] p. 13. 'So don't give 1, for it will resound unto infinity. / And don't give o, for it will be silent, / until it awakens and gives rise to 1.' *Dar* could also be translated as 'strike' (as of a clock). The relentlessness of time is thus being incorporated into this poem about the relentlessness of numbers.

his French widow, Georgette. According to her, Vallejo tended to date his poetry when he had finished revising it, often many years after writing, so that certainly many poems in *Poemas humanos* that have often been thought to have been written as late as 1937 were probably first drafted much earlier.

From 1925 to 1930 Vallejo did write frequent articles on literature in two Peruvian publications, *Mundial* and *Variedades*, and in a review which he himself helped to set up in Paris, *Favorables-Paris-Poemas*. A selection was published several decades later under the title *Literatura y arte*.[42] None of these articles is particularly distinguished as such, yet they provide useful insights into Vallejo's attitude to poetry at the time and, I think one can safely say, for the rest of his life. In them he seeks primarily to expose what he sees as the sham nature of contemporary poetry. According to Vallejo, for poetry to be innovatory, its newness must spring from a genuinely original sensibility, not from some arbitrary decision to be original.[43] Instead poets seem to think that by just naming new inventions like the aeroplane and the telegraph they are being original and modern whereas only a genuinely sensitive assimilation of new things will create a new poetry. Ultimately 'most writers who opt for the *avant-garde* do so out of cowardice or indigence', out of self-defence in order to conceal the poverty of their talent.[44] Cocteau, for instance, 'is deep down a conservative, despite his modernist efforts and poses. His postures are all make-up; his acrobatics are those of a clown—false ones.'[45] Similarly lapidary statements are made about contemporary Spanish American poets, such as Neruda and Borges and Gabriel Mistral. The diatribes are often unjust, and never well documented, but they reveal a reluctance to be satisfied which was always to stand him in good stead, because he never failed to apply it to his own work. Other articles can be revealing in a more general way. Thus he says of the colour black that it can symbolize 'according to the hemisphere and the time, sadness or joy, death or epiphany', and that 'each thing potentially contains all the energies and directions of the universe. Not only is man a microcosm. Each thing, each phenomenon is also a microcosm on the march.'[46] Neither of these statements is particularly profound, but they remind one of the extent to which the 'things'

[42] Buenos Aires, 1966.    [43] pp. 11–12.
[44] p. 39.    [45] Ibid.    [46] p. 28.

evoked in Vallejo's poetry are above all things, and never components of a decipherable 'code'. If an object in a poem by Vallejo is symbolical it is symbolical in so many directions that one is forced in the end to contemplate the object itself for its own sake.

The articles also reveal a growing political awareness in Vallejo, the beginning of a process which culminated, in 1928, in the first of three trips to the Soviet Union. Vallejo came to be an extremely militant, indeed rather dogmatic, Communist in the thirties—he is said to have greeted the advent of the Spanish Republic with wary indifference, because he did not believe in the compromises of Popular Front regimes. His militance can best be observed in works like *Rusia en 1931*, a book of observant but often sycophantic reportage, some little-known plays, and *El tungsteno* (1931), a novel that sought to expose the exploitation of Peruvian tungsten miners by an American company. None of these works is particularly distinguished, their purpose being wholly didactic, though none is ineffective as propaganda, because a clearly very genuine passion sustains them. What is remarkable is that Vallejo never let his political faith significantly affect his poetry. Politics are present in many of the poems in *Poemas humanos*, but always as just one new element in Vallejo's consciousness. Unlike Pablo Neruda, who as we shall see in the next chapter was prompted by militance wholly to abandon the hermetic, neurotic vision of *Residencia en la tierra*, Vallejo regards Communism, in *Poemas humanos* and 'España aparta de mí este cáliz', as just one more component of an essentially unchanged vision, just the vague sighting of a way out from a world that nevertheless remains as hermetically frontier-bound as that of *Trilce*. It would seem that Vallejo was too rigorous a man to believe in miracles; or conversely, that political affirmation outside his poetry was mostly just a necessary and convenient way of preserving his sanity. In order to arrive at the self-discovery that he was aiming for in his poems, he had to keep all his options open, however terrible. In his ordinary life he could take time off from so dangerous an enterprise and choose the option that seemed most promising to him. How else can one explain the almost schizophrenic gap that separates the relentless affirmations of the prose from the tortured neurosis of the poetry?

*Poemas humanos* is Vallejo's most remarkable book. Unlike *Trilce*, it develops logically from its predecessor. There is the same struggle against limitations as in *Trilce*, the same neurosis, and in particular the same search for an unprecedented language that rarely allows itself the luxury of facility, yet never indulges in complexity for its own sake. The writing is difficult because what has to be said is difficult, and what has to be said has to be said truthfully, undistracted by literary formulae, unfalsified by too easy a flow of words.

What strikes one most about *Poemas humanos* is the very personal, almost eccentric nature of Vallejo's sensibility. The poems are nearly all about neurosis, about suffering in general, but the specific problems described are always very precise, very subtle. Vallejo seems to be trying to locate the exact shape of a malaise that nevertheless remains elusively intangible despite the precise but enigmatic forms it takes. It is not quite illness, not quite the fear of death, not quite, say, hunger, which Vallejo knew very well in his early days in Paris, not quite the passing of time, yet it is related to all these things. It is an ontological malaise, beyond specific cause. In a prose poem ironically called 'Voy a hablar de la esperanza' ('I am going to speak of hope'), he writes,

I hurt now without explanation. My pain is so deep it had no cause any longer, nor does it lack cause ... My pain is from the north wind and from the south wind, like those neuter eggs some rare birds lay in the wind. If my girlfriend had died, my pain would be the same. If they'd cut out my throat from the root, my pain would be the same. If life were finally of a different order, my pain would be the same. Today I suffer from further up. I just suffer today.[47]

How does this pain manifest itself? In a manner that is at once precise and deviously enigmatic. It is like 'the pencil I lost in my cavity'[48], like an unknown something quivering in one's tonsil's,[49] like 'plastic poisons' in the throat,[50] like a splinter,[51] like something that 'slips from the soul and falls to the soul';[52] it is 'as if they'd put earrings' on him,[53] it is 'below, above, right here, far',[54] and it stands

[47] César Vallejo, *Sus obras poéticas*, Lima, c. 1966. pp. 232–3.
[48] p. 249.    [49] p. 295    [50] p. 310.
[51] p. 269    [52] p. 239.    [53] p. 218.    [54] p. 212.

> ... oblique to the line of the camel,
> fibre of my crown of flesh[55]

—a subtle location and a subtle texture!

Indeed everything in *Poemas humanos* is subtly off centre, or ex-centric, and everything gets intangibly under the skin. Even his hopes are distinctly odd, in poems where stolidly political lines like 'Let the millionaire walk naked, stark naked'[56] are undermined by a flurry of whimsically nonsensical ones like 'let a candle be added to the sun' or 'let the naked strip / let the cloak dress in trousers'[57]. In another poem, he expresses his longing for love, 'a vast political longing for love', yet the love he wishes to manifest turns out to be strikingly personal:

> Ah querer, éste, el mío, éste, el mundial,
> interhumano y parroquial, proyecto!
> Me viene al pelo,
> desde el cimiento, desde la ingle pública,
> y, viniendo de lejos, da ganas de besarle
> la bufanda al cantor,
> y al que sufre, besarle en su sartén,
> al sordo, en su rumor craneano ...[58]

It is as though he wanted deliberately to invalidate its more sensible propositions with a touch of uncompromising madness:

> Quiero, para terminar ...
> cuidar a los enfermos enfadándolos,
> comprarle al vendedor,
> ayudarle a matar al matador—cosa terrible—
> y quisiera yo ser bueno conmigo
> en todo.[59]

[55] Ibid.     [56] p. 276.     [57] Ibid.

[58] p. 293. 'Ah to love, this, my, this, the world's / interhuman and parochial, project! / Just what I wanted,* / from the foundation, from the public groin, / and, coming from afar, I'd like to kiss / the singer on his muffler, / to kiss the sufferer on his frying pan, / the deaf man on his noisy cranium.'

[59] p. 293. 'I'd like, finally / to care for the sick infuriating them, / to buy from the salesman, / to help the killer kill—a terrible thing— / and I'd like to be good with myself / in everything.'

* Literally, the expression *me viene al pelo* means 'it comes to my hair'. Vallejo is here typically visualizing the literal potential of a metaphorical cliché, while incorporating its normal figurative meaning too.

The strangely precise intangibility of *Poemas humanos* manifests itself often in descriptions of Vallejo's own body. Just as
things outside him seem relentlessly to be slipping away from
any recognizable centre, support, or point of reference, so Vallejo's
own body begins to fall apart from itself, in poems that make a
very personal contribution to that venerable literary topic, the
*doppelganger*. Thus in 'Poema para ser leído y cantado' ('Poem
to be read and sung'):

> Sé que hay una persona
> que me busca en su mano, día y noche,
> encontrándome, a cada minuto, en su calzado.[60]

Men flee from their feet, from their 'rough, caustic heels',[61] Vallejo
flies to himself 'in a two-seater plane',[62] the body separates itself
from itself in order merely to end up scurrying enigmatically
around 'a long disc, an elastic disc',[63] and these disengagements
occur precisely at those moments when his normal hold on things
breaks down, and the intangible malaise in the form of a bristle
or a splinter or whatever takes over.

In the end, Vallejo is attempting to describe, in *Poemas
humanos*, that sense of indefinable confusion which he announced
as far back as the title poem of *Los heraldos negros* with the
statement 'Hay golpes en la vida, tan fuertes . . . Yo no sé!' ('There
are blows in life which are so strong, I don't know'). The confusion
is such that nothing seems to belong anywhere in particular,
things just happen without cause, or just *are*, one after another,
without hierarchy, without purpose:

> La paz, la avispa, el taco, las vertientes,
> el muerto, los decílitros, el buho,
> los lugares, la tiña, los sarcófagos, el vaso, las morenas,
> el desconocimiento, la olla, el monaguillo,
> las gotas, el olvido,
> la potestad, los primos, los arcángeles, la aguja,
> los párrocos, el ébano, el desaire,
> la parte, el tipo, el estupor, el alma . . .[64]

---

[60] p. 291. 'I know there's a person / who looks for me day and night in his
hand / and finds me all the time in his shoes.'

[61] p. 215.                [62] p. 295.                [63] p. 311.

[64] p. 319. 'Peace, wasp, heel, watershed, / corpse, decilitres, owl / places,
wringworm, sarcophagi, glass, brunettes, / ignorance, stewpot, choir-boy, /

CÉSAR VALLEJO 33

Abstract qualities are indistinguishable from concrete ones, wholes from parts, people from things, and subtle menaces ('drops', 'the needle') are never absent. I mentioned that it is wrong to expect anything to symbolize anything specific in Vallejo—for him the world is too contingent for it to be possible to extract a definitive sign from it. There are indeed poems that seek to emphasize the point that a thing is, after all, merely a thing, that life is, merely, life, 'Just life, like that: quite a thing' ('Solo la vida, así, cosa bravísima');[65] for a 'house, unfortunately, is a house',[66] nothing more. In the end, the fact that things are merely 'there' is the heart of the problem, for there is nothing that Vallejo can do against their oppressive contingency, or against their ordinariness, for we live in the end 'by the comb and the stains on the handkerchief' ('por el peine y las manchas del pañuelo'),[67] and there is nothing more to it. But their very contingency makes them enigmatically menacing. If we cannot perceive their significance, who knows what terrible ones they might not be concealing? At any rate we are lucky in the end if we can pull ourselves together (quite literally) just enough to face one more day:

> Ya va venir el día: da
> cuerda a tu brazo, búscate debajo
> del colchón, vuelve a pararte
> en tu cabeza, para andar derecho.
> Ya va venir el día, ponte el saco.[68]

One would have thought that the problem of facing another day was one a Bolshevik might have overcome more easily. It is a measure of Vallejo's honesty that he knew it was not that easy, just as he knew, too, that Bolshevism had no answer to death, no way of countering time. It is not surprising that when depicting a Russian Bolshevik in 'Salutación angélica' ('Angelic greeting')[69] he should place him on a forbidding pedestal and then give the impression that *he* could never scale it. Vallejo declares that the Bolshevik has a 'soul perpendicular to' his own, and then tells us

---

drops, oblivion, / jurisdiction, cousins, archangel, needle, / vicars, ebony, insult, / part, type, stupor, soul . . .'

[65] p. 272.      [66] p. 238.      [67] p. 308.

[68] p. 296. 'The day is on its way; wind / up your arm, look for yourself under / the mattress, stand again / on your head, in order to walk straight. / The day's on its way, put on your coat.'

[69] p. 223.

how he would like to share the 'fervour' of the Bolshevik's 'faith'. If one is to judge from his poems, Vallejo's faith was to remain 'bristled' and 'splintered'.

It is a measure of Vallejo's unusual authenticity and rigour that 'España aparta de mí este cáliz' ('Spain, remove this chalice from me'), his poem on the Spanish Civil War, is possibly his finest work, and it is doubtful if a better poem was ever written about the Spanish Civil War, at any rate in Spanish. For Vallejo's account of that episode is wholly his own—it was not written according to any political or aesthetic prescription—and it deploys the same unique idiom of *Poemas humanos*.

It must have been as difficult to write about the Spanish Civil War in 1937 as it is to write about Vietnam now. Most poetry about tragic contemporary wars is marred by the fundamental bad faith of the enterprise, unless the poet happens to have participated as a combatant. For otherwise the poetry often consists of the working out, explicitly or not, of a rather too self-indulgent guilt on the part of the poet that he didn't fight himself. If Vallejo ever felt such guilt, he certainly did not impose it on his readers. He had himself probably suffered too much to need to feel it anyway. Another shortcoming of poetry about contemporary events in general is that it is often too much circumscribed by the episode in question, and there is maybe too much gesturing desire on the part of the poet to record the right emotion at the right time about the right thing. With Vallejo it is different because for him the Spanish Civil War is much more than a political event—it is suffering and death, it is that dismemberment of unity which we have seen him observing even in his own body, and it is in general a manifestation of that very intangible malaise that we noted was central to *Poemas humanos*.

Thus in the section on Málaga, disaster is depicted in much the same terms as when it befalls Vallejo's own body, for the curse of the *doppelganger* afflicts that city too:

> Málaga caminando tras de tus pies, en éxodo,
> bajo el mal, bajo la cobardía, bajo la historia cóncava, indecible
> con la yema en tu mano: ¡tierra orgánica!
> y la clara en la punta del cabello: ¡todo el caos![70]

[70] p. 182. 'Malaga, walking behind your feet, in exodus, / in evil, in cowardice, in concave history, unutterable, / the yolk in your hand: organic land! / And the white on your hair's end: the entire chaos!'

That disrupted egg could easily have messed up Vallejo's own hair, in his own room! Death, in 'Imagen española de la muerte' ('Spanish image of death'), is just death, not merely the death inflicted by a specific enemy in a particular war; and like all things that menace in Vallejo's poetry, it is intangible, yet subtly, elusively precise:

> ¡Ahí pasa! ¡Llamadla! ¡Es su costado!
> Ahí pasa la muerte por Irún;
> sus pasos de acordeón, su palabrota,
> su metro del tejido que te dije,
> su gramo de aquel peso que he callado ... ¡sí son ellos!⁷¹

That is not a foe you can fight with rifles, or with anything, even though Vallejo appeals desperately that we should try, that we should pursue it to the foot of the enemy tanks: 'Hay que seguirla / hasta el pie de los tanques enemigos.'

In the end, 'España, aparta de mí este cáliz' is a work concerned less with specific causes than with an endemic human condition and with *individual* suffering. Although we know where Vallejo's heart is, his hatred of the Nationalist intervention being indeed all the more effective for not being spelt out, a compassion for mankind far wider than the issues involved informs the whole work and contributes to its greatness. His compassion is most moving when it is directed at individual victims: now and then, for instance, he will give us a portrait of a specific dead hero, such as Pedro Rojas,⁷² or he will trace the individual destiny of a soldier on the battlefront, such as Ramón Collar (VIII):

> Ramón Collar, yuntero
> y soldado hasta yerno de su suegro,
> marido, hijo limítrofe del viento Hijo del Hombre!
> Ramón de pena, tú, Collar valiente,
> paladín de Madrid y por cojones. ¡Ramonete,
> aquí,
> los tuyos piensan mucho en tu peinado!⁷³

---

⁷¹ p. 187. 'There she goes! Call her! It's her flank! / There goes death through Irún; / her accordeon step, her four-letter word, / her metre of the fabric I told you about, / her gram of that weight I kept to myself ... Yes it's them!'

⁷² p. 184.

⁷³ p. 193. 'Ramón Collar, plough-boy / and soldier to the son-in-law of his father-in-law, / husband, border son of the wind Son of Man, / Ramón of

At first sight, we seem to be in the presence of an archetypal eulogy. Then characteristically, in brutal contrast to Ramón's heroics, we glimpse the family absurdly reminiscing about his hair-style, or we glimpe the pathos of his absence from home: 'Tu pantalón oscuro, andando el tiempo, / sabe ya andar solísimo, acabarse' ('Your dark trousers, as time goes by / already know how to walk quite alone / how to waste away').[74] Vallejo's personal touch is never absent even when he is dealing with the most notorious events of the war, such as for instance the battle of Guernica:

> ¡Lid a priori, fuera de la cuenta,
> lid en paz, lid de las almas débiles
> contra los cuerpos débiles, lid en que el niño pega,
> sin que le diga nadie que pegara,
> bajo su atroz diptongo
> y bajo su habilísimo panal,
> y en la que la madre pega con su mal, con su grito, con el
>     dorso de una lágrima
> y en que el enfermo pega con su mal, con su pastilla y su
>     hijo
> y en que el anciano pega
> con sus canas, sus siglos y su palo
> y en que pega el prebístero con dios![75]

All this indignation, all this retaliatory violence on the edge of despair, is expressed in a language that never lets up on its ability to deliver surprises which however never distract from the urgency of what is being said.

Neruda, in his poem on the Spanish Civil War, 'España en el corazón' ('Spain in the heart'), often lapses into a pious idiom, a sort of socialist anthem rhetoric. Vallejo always avoids piety—

---

sadness, you, brave Collar / paladin of Madrid and with your balls. Ramonete, / your family are thinking about your hair-style.'

[74] p. 194.

[75] p. 180. 'A priori contest, beyond reckoning, / contest of peace, contest of weak souls / against weak bodies, contest in which a child hits out / without anyone telling him to / with his atrocious diphthong, / and with his most able nappy / and in which a mother hits out with her wrong, with her scream, with the back of a tear / and in which a sick man hits out with his wrong, with his pill and his son / and in which an old man hits out / with his grey hairs, his centuries, and his stick / and in which a priest hits out with God.'

maybe he has too few illusions. There is always a note of sardonic irony even in his most tragic passages, with the consequence that they always remain this side of bathos:

> Herido mortalmente de vida, camarada,
> camarada jinete,
> camarada caballo entre hombre y fiera,
> tus huesecillos de alto y melancólico dibujo
> forman pompa española,
> laureada de finísimos andrajos ...[76]

Vallejo, one can see, is writing in the jestingly ironical and macabre tradition of the war-song, not the piously wide-eyed one of the socialist anthem.

There is no poet in Latin America like Vallejo, no poet who has bequeathed so consistently personal an idiom, and no poet so strictly rigorous with himself. It is a curiously subtle, menacing world that he has left us in his mature works, and he has conveyed it in a language that has been very carefully selected, a language which is perpetually just off centre, which has the appearance often of correctness, yet which it is never quite possible to pin down. Perhaps one would have to analyse Vallejo's syntax in order to grasp the manner in which his language works. One might start with his use of adverbs, prepositions, and conjunctions. In normal syntax these words are supposed to qualify or link given concepts. Yet in Vallejo's poetry we meet adverbs that have lost sight of their verbs, prepositions that have been left stranded by an unknown noun, conjunctions that have found their way to the wrong sentence. His poetry is full of stranded loose words like 'after', 'then', 'now', 'which', 'this', 'that', 'but', 'for', 'beneath', which never quite seem to know what word to latch on to, or if they do latch on to one it is usually a stridently enigmatic neologism, or a word they seem fated to contradict, or one that itself seems stranded out of context. Often the poems simply break up into inane exclamations: 'Oh for so much! Oh for so little! Oh for them',[77] 'No! Never! Never yesterday! Never

---

[76] pp. 189–90. 'Mortally wounded with life, comrade, / comrade horseman, / comrade horse half-man half-beast / your little bones, a lofty sad design, / are a Spanish pageant, / crowned with the finest rags.'

[77] p. 263.

later!',[78] 'So much life and never!', 'So many years and always, always, always',[79] 'No? Yes but no?':[80]

> After, these, here,
> after, above,
> maybe, while, behind, so much, so never,
> under, perhaps, far,
> always, that, tomorrow, how much,
> how much![81]

Such helpless inanities express the ultimate stage of Vallejo's statement of fundamental bewilderment, initiated in the cry of *Los heraldos negros*—'yo no sé.'

Vallejo died on 15 April 1938 at the age of forty-six of an illness that was never diagnosed. Legend has it that half an hour before he died he uttered the words 'Me voy a España'—'I'm off to Spain.' Yet according to his widow Georgette, his last words were more enigmatic and more trivial: 'Palais Royal'.[82] To judge from his poetry, the latter version is the more likely, and he no doubt would have been grateful—and perhaps amused— that his widow has corrected a legend whose banality he would surely never have allowed himself.

---

[78] p. 311.      [79] p. 237.      [80] p. 282.      [81] p. 319.
[82] *Apuntes biográficos sobre 'Poemas en prosa' y 'Poemas humanos'*, Lima, 1968, p. 51.

# 4
## Pablo Neruda (Chile, 1904–   )

PABLO NERUDA is the most prolific of the major Latin American poets. He has published some thirty books of poems, and over the last decade or so it has become not uncommon for him to publish more than one book a year. It has therefore seemed necessary to limit a discussion of his poetry to certain key works, and to treat his last five or six books fairly cursorily, for they are perhaps too recent and too vast to be judged effectively as yet.

Like Vallejo's in *Los heraldos negros*, Pablo Neruda's apprenticeship was heavily influenced by *modernismo*. Thus in *Crepusculario* (1923), Neruda reveals himself in the very title of the book to be a late member of that dusk generation that flourished under Lugones and Herrera y Reissig, and much of *Crepusculario* is written in the same sort of borrowed idiom we discerned in early Vallejo. We encounter a 'fragrant soul',[1] a 'fragrance of lilies',[2] a 'silk sky' at dusk. The poet is 'always sad' ('siempre estoy triste')[3] and, in the midst of a sad, grey dusk:

> ¡No hay oído en la tierra que oiga me queja triste
> abandonada en medio de la tierra infinita![4]

Such *poète maudit* gloom does not carry conviction. It is hard not to take it as the mere literary exercise it surely was anyway. Neruda, whose keen sense of humour is generally supposed to have

[1] *Crepusculario*, Buenos Aires, 1961, p. 10.
[2] Ibid., p. 17.
[3] Ibid., p. 40.
[4] p. 88. 'There is no one on earth to hear my sad plaint / abandoned in the midst of the infinite earth!'

developed only in the 1950s, is able to laugh at his melancholy posturing himself in the very book in which he most deploys it:

> ¡Pero para qué es esto de pensamientos tristes! ...
> Después de todo nada de esto que digo existe.
> ¡No vayas a contárselo a mi madre, por Dios![5]

The first book in which a really personal voice emerges is *20 poemas de amor y una canción desesperada* ('20 love poems and one song of despair', 1924). For one, the poems are statements of Neruda's personal experience as a lover. A specific story emerges from them about a man who tried to fulfil himself through love and failed. The poet expects all from the female—guidance, total absorption:

> En ti los ríos cantan y mi alma en ellos huye
> como tú lo desees y hacia donde tū quieras.
> Márcame mi camino en tu arco de esperanza
> y soltaré en delirio mi bandada de flechas.[6]

No doubt he is expecting too much, and anyway he is too narcissistically conscious of himself to achieve the oblivion he desires: the arrows boomerang, and time relentlessly intrudes—'Entre los labios y la voz, algo se va muriendo' ('Between the lips and the voice, something dies').[7] Many of the poems are nostalgic evocations of an impossible hope that has long been abandoned. In short: 'Es tan corto el amor, y es tan largo el olvido' ('Love is so short, forgetting is so long').[8]

This is not, needless to say, the first time a poet has told such a story. The originality of *20 poemas* lies rather in the manner in which the story is told. For in this book, the first attempt is made by Neruda to sustain a deeply personal pattern of imagery. To understand it fully, we must examine its origins.

In 1921, Neruda left the south of Chile, where he was born and bred, for Santiago, the capital. The experience seems to have been as alienating and disturbing as Vallejo's venture to Lima. He was

---

[5] p. 84. 'But what's all this about sad thoughts! ... / After all none of this that I'm saying exists. / Don't go and tell my mother, for God's sake!'

[6] *20 poemas*, Buenos Aires, 1944, p. 19. 'The rivers sing within you and my soul flees along them / as you desire and wherever you will. / Aim my road on your bow of hope / and in a frenzy I will free my flock of arrows.'

[7] p. 64.          [8] p. 97.

to describe it as such in his *Canto general* (1950) in a poem entitled 'Compañeros de viaje (1921)' ('Fellow travellers, 1921'), for
there he tells us how, after arriving in Santiago, 'vaguely saturated
with mist and rain'—that notorious interminable rain of the
south of Chile that plays so fundamental a role in Neruda's poetry
—he found only 'an atrocious smell of gas, coffee, and bricks, and
miserable alleys / without compassion'. 'Every evening' he was
then to search in his poetry for 'the branches, the drops, and the
moon which had been lost'.[9]

Now in *20 poemas*, an alienated man is battling for fulfilment
in a woman. His alienation has been effected by the hostile environment of the capital city, and by the fact that in venturing
there he has uprooted himself from the land of his birth, from the
'branches' and the 'drops' of the south. It is not surprising therefore that the woman is to become indistinguishable from the very
earth he has abandoned, from the very branches that he cannot
locate in the city's 'miserable alleys'. As he fingers the woman's
body, it is the landscape of the south of Chile he is groping for.
The woman becomes Mother Earth, the possibility of a southern
pine forest germinating from the city's relentlessly paved streets.

In the very first poem, the tellurian obligations of the woman
are made immediately evident:

> Cuerpo de mujer, blancas colinas, muslos blancos,
> te pareces al mundo en tu actitud de entrega.
> Mi cuerpo de labriego salvaje te socava
> y hace saltar el hijo del fondo de la tierra.[10]

Thus a blatant sexual statement (shocking incidentally for its
time) at once associates the woman with the fertility of the soil,
turns her into Mother-Earth. In another poem, the woman is
more explicitly decorated with the actual landscape of the south of
Chile—its pine forests, the stormy Pacific ocean, a lonely church
bell:

> ¡Ah vastedad de pinos, rumor de olas quebrándose,
> lento juego de luces, campana solitaria,

[9] *Canto general*, Buenos Aires, 1955, Vol. 2, p. 179.
[10] *20 poemas*, p. 11. 'Body of woman, white hills, white thighs, / you re-
semble the world in your gesture of submission. / My brutal peasant's body
digs into you / and makes the son leap from the depth of the soil.'

crepúsculo cayendo en tus ojos, muñeca,
caracola terrestre, en ti la tierra canta![11]

From the woman, there issues the very earth song which the new
urban setting has trampled—the song of the Pacific Ocean too
perhaps, or its echo, with her vagina acting as a conch-shell
(another meaning of *caracola*). Every other poem offers similar
associations. There are 'large roots' in the woman's soul,[12] her
hands are like grapes countering a room of oppressively damp
walls,[13] she is a 'sweet blue jasmine entwined upon my soul'.[14]

Perhaps Neruda's love is doomed in the end precisely because
jasmine is doomed in the city: like jasmine, like the pine trees,
like the Pacific Ocean, it is doomed to be a mere nostalgic
memory—the vain cry of the conch-shell—or at best an all too fleeting hopeful presence.

The trajectory of his love from hope to despair is ultimately
summarized in the image of a ship that Neruda conjectures himself to be navigating. At first the ship is at sea, stranded, searching
for a port where its navigator may anchor his kisses.[15] Yet in the
final 'Song of despair', the port has become a 'cueva de náufragos'
('a cave of the shipwrecked').[16] And if there was love, it turns out
that it was experienced not in the comfort of a port but in 'the
black, black loneliness of islands'.[17] We learn now that 'Everything, in the girl, was shipwreck.'[18] Yet once she had been like a
lighthouse beam, alone capable of rescuing his 'loneliness' which
had been 'waving its arms like a shipwrecked man'![19]

In *20 poemas* Neruda journeys across the sea symbolically in
search of an impossible port. In 1927 he embarked on a real
journey, when he sailed from Buenos Aires for Lisbon, ultimately bound for Rangoon where he had been appointed honorary Chilean consul. Neruda travelled extensively in the Far East
over the next few years, and it was during this period that he wrote
his first really splendid book of poems, *Residencia en la tierra*, a
book ultimately published in two parts, in 1933 and 1935.

In *20 poemas* one can discern the burgeoning of a conflict
between nature and the city. In a damp city room the poet

[11] p. 19. 'Ah enormity of pines, murmur of the breaking waves, / measured
play of lights, lonely bell, / dusk falling in your eyes, doll, / snail of the earth,
in you the earth sings!'

[12] p. 16.          [13] pp. 27–8.          [14] p. 33.          [15] p. 20.
[16] p. 101.         [17] p. 103.           [18] p. 102.         [19] p. 37.

searches in a woman for the smell and sound of the earth. Orgasm
is like a rain forest glimpsed in a room bound by four relentless
walls. *Residencia en la tierra* is perhaps the ultimate expression
of the failure of this quest. For it is very much a book of closed,
claustrophobic rooms, of stifling Asian cities made all the more
squalid by the tropical Asian heat that envelops them.

Many poets have felt liberated by the East: the most notable
Latin American example is Octavio Paz, the subject of our next
chapter. Such poets for Neruda are ultimately phoney, pseudo-
mystics, who in the end concoct bad parodies of the real thing.
And what is the real thing? Not the dazzlingly liberating Buddha,
not the wisdom of Confucius, but rapacious poverty, jaded English
colonialists, and as far as mysticism is concerned, the same priestly
treachery and inhumanity that he had witnessed in the West. As
he put it in his autobiographical *Memorial de Isla Negra* (1964)
in a poem called 'Religión en el Este':

> Budhas desnudos y elegantes
> sonriendo en el coktail
> de la vacía eternidad
> como Cristo en su cruz horrible.[20]

Of course this latter poem is the work of a man who was by the
time of writing it a long-established member of the Chilean
Communist party, and he was far from being that when he wrote
*Residencia en la tierra*. But it is a measure of Neruda's authenticity as a poet that he was never tempted to dabble, say, in Taoist
imagery. Never does he fall for that hectic portentousness which
so many poets seem to feel obliged to deploy when they describe
the East. The East, in *Residencia en la tierra*, where it is mentioned at all, is never more than a squalid back-cloth for the expression of a tormented soul—of a soul uprooted more fearfully
than ever from the forests of the south of Chile.

The problems being worked out in *Residencia en la tierra* can
be traced to *20 poemas*, but they are far more intensely tortured
now. There is the same quest for liberation through love, but it
is far more rapidly and violently stifled. Sexual contact yields
occasional pleasure, but it is far more often a double-edged one.
In a prose poem called 'La noche del soldado' ('The night of the

[20] *Memorial*, Buenos Aires, 1964, Vol. II, p. 43. 'Nude elegant buddhas /
smiling at the cocktail party / of void eternity / like Christ on his ghastly
cross.'

soldier') he visits Oriental girls and drinks their 'living medicine with a masculine thirst', but the medicine does not last and 'each successive night leaves something of an abandoned ember that slowly burns out, and falls swathed in ruins, in the midst of funereal objects.'[21]

It is impossible really to convey the full implications of the love poems of *Residencia* without examining an entire poem in detail in order to see how Neruda's ambivalent alternations between hope and despair with regard to women actually manifest themselves in complex patterns of imagery. As good an example as any is the poem 'Alianza'. The poem opens characteristically against a gloomy, disintegrating, time-laden background:

> De miradas polvorientas caídas al suelo
> o de hojas sin sonido y sepultándose.
> De metales sin luz, con el vacío,
> con la ausencia del día muerto de golpe.
> En lo alto de las manos el deslumbrar de mariposas,
> el arrancar de mariposas cuya luz no tiene término.[22]

Glances (possibly hopeful) are instantly dust-laden and they fall flat on the ground. Leaves not only fall, they bury themselves, dig their own graves. The surroundings are opaquely metallic—urban. There is emptiness, and the death of another day once more reminds us of that disintegrating monster, time. The sentences are characteristically inconclusive: *from* ('de'), but to where? The sentences stagnate as savagely as the scene they are evoking.

Then, suddenly, there is a dazzling flight of butterflies—flying creatures (birds in particular) are always a sign in Neruda of liberating hope. But what does that hope lead to?

> Tú guardabas la estela de luz, de seres rotos
> que el sol abandonado, atardeciendo, arroja a las iglesias.
> Teñida con miradas, con objeto de abejas,
> tu material de inesperada llama huyendo
> precede y sigue al día y a su familia de oro.[23]

---

[21] *Residencia*, Buenos Aires, 1958, p. 46.

[22] p. 11 'From dusty glances fallen upon the ground / or from leaves without sound burying themselves. / From metals without light, with emptiness, / with the absence of the day dead at a stroke. / Above the hands the dazzle of butterflies / the flying off of butterflies whose light has no end.'

[23] p. 11. 'You were the guardian of the stele of light, of fragmented beings, / that the abandoned sun flings at the churches at dusk. / Tinted with glances,

The first line is immediately ambivalent. At first glance, we expect the woman to be the guardian of the butterflies' light. But she is a guardian of the light's stele, of the deceased lights's (opaque) gravestone, for however desperately the *estela* may be aiming to become an *estrella* (star) it remains an *estela*. In the end, it is a series of 'fragmented beings' that are opaquely inscribed on it, 'fragmented beings / that the abandoned sun flings at the churches at dusk'. It is a fleeting, feeble light that the woman is ultimately the guardian of.

Who is this woman? We know very little about her. She is almost an abstraction. Her fertile, bee-like glances are not wholly a part of her: they're a sort of mask, a dye (she is *teñida*)—mere make-up perhaps. And the unexpected flame in her *flees* the moment it appears: it may precede the morning sun but it succumbs to the same fate—it too must have its dusk.

In short, the stanza depicts a traditional topic of poetry: that of the woman as the sole repository of light after sundown. But what a light it turns out to be! How back-handed the traditional compliments!

The poem continues:

> Los días acechando cruzan en sigilo
> pero caen dentro de tu voz de luz.
> Oh dueña del amor, en tu descanso
> fundé mi sueño, mi actitud callada.[24]

There is the menace of time again in the form of ambushing days ('días acechando') but suddenly, in a manner typical of these poems where optimism and pessimism alternate quite unpredictably, she seems to be able to cope: her light (no longer a mere stele of light) is now contained in her voice, and it looks as if she's going to absorb the ambushing days quite effortlessly. The poet is now happy to come to port and to ground his dreams there. Nothing, now, appears capable of stirring him:

---

with the aim of bees / your stuff of unforseen flame in flight / precedes and follows the day and its family of gold.'

[24] p. 11. 'The days cross secretly and lie in ambush / but they slip into your voice of light. / Oh mistress of love, upon your repose / I grounded my dream, my silent poise.

> ¡Con tu cuerpo de número tímido, extendido de pronto
> hasta las cantidades que definen la tierra,
> detrás de la pelea de los días blancos de espacio
> y fríos de muertes lentas y estímulos marchitos,
> siento arder tu regazo y transitar tus besos
> haciendo golondrinas frescas en mi sueño![25]

Her modest body (once just one more timid number) has suddenly grown to the size of the earth (even if the earth's size, too,
is *defined* in *quantities*), it lies behind (though perhaps not quite
beyond, for she is being set up more as a *shelter* than an agent
of transcendence) the contingent blankness of everyday life. Her
body is sheltering moreover behind the passing of time (the 'slow
deaths'), behind the everyday mediocrity or 'withered incentives'
(yet one notes how the ambivalence of the poem is subsumed in
this characteristic oxymoron). Finally, he feels her 'lap burning'
and her kisses populate his dreams with swallows. Again, there is
the hope of liberation signified by a flying creature, but of course
swallows are very seasonal birds that come and go, like all good
things in *Residencia*:

> A veces el destino de tus lágrimas asciende
> como la edad hasta mi frente, allí
> están golpeando las olas, destruyéndose de muerte:
> su movimiento es húmedo, decaído, final.[26]

In this last stanza, the whole construct of shelter and of life-
enhancing light is typically demolished. In the first place, the
woman is seen for the first time as a person in her own right.
Generally in *Residencia*, Neruda regards the woman in terms
only of her effect on *him* (the way a son, I suppose, regards his
mother before adulthood). But occasionally he becomes suddenly
aware that it is not only a question of whether she can shelter or
illuminate him but also one of whether she, too, might not be
in need of such services. The effect of such awareness is utterly

---

[25] pp. 11–12. 'With your body a timid number, extended suddenly / to the
quantities that define the earth, / behind the struggle of the white days of
space / cold with slow deaths and withered incentives / I feel the burning of
your lap and the movement of your kisses / conjuring early swallows in my
dreams.'

[26] p. 12. 'At times the destiny of your tears rises / like age to my brow, there
/ the waves batter, destroy themselves with death: / their movement is
humid, faded, final.

deflating. She too, then, has a 'destiny of tears' and this fact destroys the dream. Her tears seep through his forehead, and there,
instead of dreams, there are (shipwrecking) waves again. Waves
for Neruda often have the same function that suspended wheels
have for him: they symbolize the notion that whereas time never
stops, little ever happens. Waves ebb and flow, a suspended wheel
turns, but they get nowhere: except, of course, that everything
ultimately disintegrates, dies, and waves in particular can be
agents of devastation. One notes the *dampness* or *humidity* of the
final decay. Of course, waves can be said to be 'humid' or 'damp'
but it should be noted that humidity makes frequent, independent
appearances in *Residencia*. Its presence may well be a function
of the climate of the countries where the poems were written, but
it has too a poetic function to convey the sense of cloying intangible menace that the poems usually deploy.

'Alianza' is a typical poem in that it portrays the rapid alternating between fruition and disappointment that characterizes
Neruda's contact with woman. It is untypical in that more often
his encounters are more violent, more apocalyptic. Poems like
'Tiranía' ('Tyranny'), 'Tango del viudo' ('Widower's tango'), or
'Barcarola' depict relationships that are in different ways more
cataclysmic. Here something much bigger than the mere shelter
of 'Alianza' is being aimed at, something more, perhaps, in the
nature of transcendence. The risks are consequently greater, his
'desperate head [arousing] itself / in an effort of leaping and of
death'.[27] It is as though Neruda preferred any risk, any 'descent
into hell' (such as that described nostalgically in 'Tango del
viudo' where we learn how he had to hide a knife from his
woman lest she killed him) to the drab mediocrity of the city.

The poems in general shift about from descriptions of the
drabness of urban life ('the walls have a sad crocodile colour'),[28]
its feeble yet menacing softness ('it is soft underfoot, like a dead
monster'),[29] its amorphousness ('I weep in the midst of what is
invaded, amid the uncertain, amid the growing savour')[30] to
euphoric wish-fulfilling assertions of aggressive release from it
all. Of the latter mood, the best example is 'Walking around', the
most exuberantly surrealistic poem in a book in which the influence of surrealism is constant.

[27] p. 32.          [28] p. 29.          [29] p. 29.          [30] p. 15.

In 'Walking around', after a description of his impatience with-
the city's mediocrity ('the smell of barber shops makes me scream
with tears ... / I want only to see no more establishments, no
more gardens, / nor merchandise, nor spectacles, nor elevators'),
he dreams a way of getting his own back on it:

> Sin embargo sería delicioso
> asustar a un notario con un lirio cortado
> o dar muerte a una monja con un golpe de oreja.
> Sería bello
> ir por las calles con un cuchillo verde
> y dando gritos hasta morir de frío.[31]

This fantasy of a sort of self-invigorating surreal therapy against
drabness is very reminiscent of Mayakovsky in 'A cloud in trousers'
(1916)—indeed Neruda's nuns, notaries, tailors, and stamp-
collectors, all of which crop up from time to time in *Residencia*,
are very similar to those old men with violins Mayakovsky detested
so vigorously. The difference between the two poets is that
Neruda admits the risk of dying of cold with his green knife:
self-deflation did not come easily to Mayakovsky. Yet the parallel
is interesting simply because it is usually the later, politically committed Mayakovsky who is supposed to have influenced Neruda
when Neruda too had become politically committed. Their
careers turn out to have close similarities at a much earlier date
too.

Neruda, then, desperately attempts to free himself from an
environment that is feeble, opaque, damp, amorphous, claustrophobic, sweaty, bland, grey, heavy, and putrid. At times, the
settings thus described are almost abstract, or at any rate they
could be anywhere. Just as often they turn out to be specifically
urban, and the alarming adjectives are called upon to qualify
certain landmarks of the city Neruda signals out for special de-
testation: barbershops, miserable cinemas, hospitals, offices,
orthopaedic shops, shoeshops, and always, terrible damp houses,
teeming streets, closed rooms. In this urban world love is sordid:

> El pequeño empleado, después de mucho,
> después del tedio semanal, y las novelas leídas de noche en cama,

[31] p. 85. 'And yet, it would be quite delicious / to frighten a notary with a
cut lily / or to kill off a nun at the stroke of an ear. / It would be lovely / to go
along the streets with a green knife / shouting until I died of cold!'

ha definitivamente seducido a su vecina,
y la lleva a los miserables cinemátografos
donde los héroes son potros o príncipes apasionados,
y acaricia sus piernas llenas de dulce vello
con sus ardientes y húmedas manos que huelen a cigarrillo.[32]

Only adulterers love with 'true love', presumably because they
alone take the *risk* of breaking away from the monotony, the
routine, the ghastly life-destroying legality of urban conventions,
in a world where there is 'too much furniture and too many rooms',
and too many trousers, suits, underpants, and stockings to conceal
the body.[33]

We mentioned that for the Neruda of *Residencia* any cataclysmic hell is preferable to drab mediocrity or to the useless
condition depicted in 'Vals' where:

> No soy, no sirvo, no conozco a nadie,
> no tengo armas de mar ni de madera,
> no vivo en esta casa.[34]

—a condition aggravated by the fact that he is again feeling the
loss of the landscape of his childhood—of the Pacific Ocean (*mar*)
and of the southern pine forests (*madera*). There are two poems
in *Residencia* which describe especially cataclysmic attempts
respectively to recover the sea and the wood, no matter if to be
devoured by them. These poems ('Barcarola' and 'Entrada a
la madera'—'The way into wood') are the anguished cries of a
man desperately endeavouring to recover a lost organic past,
however terrible the consequences. In 'Barcarola',[35] the sea is
unleashed by a woman, just as nature was released by the woman
of *20 poemas*. He pleads that she place her mouth, her teeth, and
her tongue 'like a red arrow' upon his heart, in order to unleash
the sea's terrible but real, organic strength, its 'dark sound', its

---

[32] p. 55–6. 'The little clerk, at last / after the week's boredom and after the
novels read in bed at night, / has quite definitely seduced his neighbour / and
he takes her to miserable cinemas / where the heroes are young stallions or
passionate princes, / and he caresses her sweet hairy legs / with his eager
sweaty hands smelling of cigarettes.'

[33] p. 58.

[34] *Tercera residencia*, Buenos Aires, 1961, p. 12. 'I am not, I am no use,
I know no one, / I have no weapons of sea or wood, / I don't live in this
house.'

[35] *Residencia*, p. 78.

'hesitating waves', its 'blood', its 'sudden bell', its 'pigeon in flames', its 'black wings', its 'vast talons', its 'cowing', and its 'flying'. The result of all this unleashing is terrible, but the force that emerges at least is real, organic, as real, terrible, and organic as blood. At least there is the flight of birds even if they are birds of prey, at least there is a pigeon even if a pigeon in flames, at least there is the euphoric sound of a bell, even if sudden and probably fleeting.

For Neruda, the sea is above all organic and real, unlike the city, which is artificial. Its appeal lies mostly in its rawness, in the necessarily physical nature of one's contact with it, in the way it cuts down the notary to his fundamental, archetypal role of being a man, rids him of his paper. It is this fundamental, physical state which Neruda appears to be looking for in *Residencia*, whether in poems like 'Barcarola' or in such a semi-humorous poem as 'Ritual de mis piernas' ('Ritual of my legs'),[36] where the blatant physical reality of his legs is seen to be more extraordinary and more meaningful than the clothes and the routine that disguise them. It is significant that his descent into wood in 'Entrada a la madera'[37] is conducted 'scarcely . . . with reason', but rather 'with . . . fingers', stressing the fact it is the sensual, the physical that he is searching for in the organic and the tellurian. The journey to wood is, needless to say, as violently risky, and as ambivalent in its consequences, as the unleashing of the sea in 'Barcarola', but again, it is at least real and organic.

*Residencia* is the expression of a desperate struggle—a struggle to avoid mediocrity and a struggle with time and with death.[38] It is the story too of a struggle to glimpse the apocalypse in a damp room. But above all it is a book of *images*, images that attempt to convey the elusive nature of the moods and attitudes we have already described.

Neruda's images are never gratuitous or merely private. The choice of image is dictated by its compatibility with whatever it is being designed to signify. We have already met some: the flying bird or the butterfly that signify dynamic release, the pigeon of hope, the all-embracing sea, the optimistic bell. Others

---

[36] pp. 57–9.          [37] pp. 109–10.
[38] For a description of the damp, elusive, and amorphous death that infests these poems, see 'Solo la muerte' ('Death alone'): one of the most horrifying litanies of dying ever written.

include the *copa*—the cup or goblet, a life-enhancing sign of plenty and well-being; fertile horses, grapes, bees, and bread; the rose suggesting beauty; the sword suggesting virility, heroism, adventure; the poppy suggesting mystery and passion. All these images clearly depict positive qualities. None are abstruse, being the dictates of conventionally collective associations, not private ones. Other images, equally obvious, suggest negative qualities: ashes, dust, the salt that corrodes, the suspended wheel that moves but gets nowhere, dampness, and so on. Others, like the flame, or fire (*llama, fuego*), are double-edged, for they uplift or destroy with equal vigour. The images occur obsessively, but they are not mere keywords: they are always placed dynamically in a context, and the context modifies their significance.

Usually, the optimistic images predominate, but they are often savaged by the adjectives or adjectival phrases that qualify them or by the verbs they are governed by. Thus we have 'useless swords',[39] 'dead bees',[40] or, in 'Estatuto del vino' ('Statue of wine'), 'soaked wings'.[41] The latter is a typical example of Neruda's frequent use of a synecdochic version of a key image, another being the petal for the rose. The synecdochic version of course contributes to the poems' general mood of decomposition. (What use a wing without a bird or a petal without a rose?) so that the sense of a statement like 'soaked wings' is that there is at best a glimpse of flight in the air, a very tenuous, dismembered flight that is not going to get very far. This particular phrase has an added significance in that it is the 'soaked red wings' of wine that are being referred to. The ultimate aim of the image is therefore to pay a very back-handed compliment to wine. It may make us fly, but if it does, it is with soaked wings and without a body!

The result of this adjectival or verbal annihilation of positive noun signs is to suggest an original substantival paradise savaged by the movement of time. For most of the adjectives used (like 'soaked' for instance) suggest the modification of an original state produced by an event. Indeed most of the adjectives are past participles that suggest decomposition: *derretido* (melted), *gastado* (wasted), *podrido* (rotten), and so on.

Very often, in the dynamic context in which they are inserted, Neruda's favourite signs are fused or confused: thus we have a

[39] p. 64.                    [40] p. 10.                    [41] p. 113.

'rose with dry wings'.[42] One comes to expect roses to fly (badly), birds to flower (jadedly), and cups to ring out (opaquely) like a bell. Sometimes the positives images have so little chance from the start that they are nothing more than a fleeting glimpse of what they might have been. Thus a bird makes an appearance in 'Estatuto del vino' but as the mere *bone* of a bird with which drunkards knock on a *coffin*.[43] Other times they are splattered with surrealist horror: thus the 'Estatuto's' goblets are full of 'dead eyes'. Sometimes, they are left stranded in the very syntax of the poem. Nowhere does this happen more effectively than in 'Galope muerto' ('Dead Gallop': note the immediately annihilating adjective). Take the following stanza:

¿Ahora bien, de qué está hecho ese surgir de palomas
que hay entre la noche y el tiempo, como una barranca húmeda?
Ese sonido ya tan largo
que cae listando de piedras los caminos
más bien cuando sólo una hora
crece de improviso, extendiéndose sin tregua.[44]

The stanza's effect is achieved largely through the ambiguity of its syntax. At first, there is a very hopeful 'surging of pigeons' that seems competent to annihilate both time and the night. But what becomes of it? Whether the 'humid gorge' refers to time or to the pigeons is not clear. But one thing is: by the end of the second line the pigeons' chances are pretty slim. And what of that 'sound so long now'—is it anything to do with the pigeons at all? And is it the sound of the pigeons that is causing stones to fall upon the roads? It does not say much for the pigeons if it is. More likely, the stanza is endeavouring, in the manner of Vallejo, to recede into near inarticulateness, to become itself just a sound, like the dull, meaningless sound it is evoking. From the surging of pigeons we have shifted unexpectedly to listless noise, to sheer time and extension.

*Residencia en la tierra* is ultimately a dance of images: images

[42] p. 109.
[43] p. 115.
[44] p. 9. 'So then, what is this surging of pigeons made of / situated between night and day like a damp gorge? / That sound so lengthy now / that falls hurling stones on the roads / or rather when for only one hour / it grows suddenly, expanding without end.'

listed, rejected, and reintroduced, images in conflict with each other, images in dialectical play, images that are fundamentally conventional but which acquire their dynamism through contact with each other, pigeons with ashes, swords with salt, bells with poppies, horses with fire; images that are commonplace nouns erected as signs of hope yet lacerated by vicious adjectives and verbs. Verbal and adjectival time has destroyed innocence (the rose, the pigeon); and it has also destroyed spontaneity: adventure, fertility, passion, and mystery (the galloping horse, the butterfly, the sword, the grape, the bee, the goblet, and the poppy). Time has destroyed these elemental, organic, tellurian qualities by driving them into the city, or into the tragedy of history. The adjective reveals what history, what the city, what time in general have done to them, so does the verb when they are its object. Sometimes, they are the subject of the verb, and then the verb reveals what time has made them do. It has made bells ring for the dreary faithful from a church, horses gallop for the army, birds look for prey, and grapes inebriate drunkards. Later, in *Canto general,* Neruda is to search for a prehistoric paradise, a world unruined by history, a dance of original nouns, and he is to search for a man defined by nothing but the earth that made him.

Between *Residencia en la tierra* and *Canto general* came Neruda's conversion to Communism, a direct result of his living in Spain as Chilean consul in the 1930s and of his witnessing the Spanish Civil War. The first fruit of his new political commitment is the long sequence called 'España en el corazón' ('Spain in the heart') which was eventually included in *Tercera residencia* (1947) but which was first published in Chile in 1937. It is an extraordinary poem, different from anything Neruda had written before. It is the work of a once intensely gloomy man who had desperately sought to be absorbed and shaken by women, by the sea, by the very violence of his poetry, and, who suddenly found an all-absorbing passion on his doorstep in Madrid: Spain, not the woman of 'Barcarola', had reached his heart. It is a poem of stirring political propaganda, a wholly public, declamatory poem from a man who had never before really written about anything but himself. Yet there is no reason to doubt its sincerity, and it is not as inconsistent as it seems at first sight. After all, if Neruda

is gloomy in *Residencia*, it is mostly because he is unwilling to
accept mediocrity. He despairs because he wants something big,
too big. Why should critics grudge his finding it? All too often
they have, and it is the critics who are inconsistent, unless they
do not perceive the extent to which his despair in *Residencia* is
the consequence of a rather splendid ambition that man be excellent and happy, not a drab notary.

There is much consistency too in the way his imagery develops
from *Residencia*. For Neruda sees the Republic, as he is later to
see socialism in general, as the assertion of the tellurian and the
organic. This may seem anomalous politically, since socialism has
normally aimed at rapid industrialization. Yet Neruda might
argue that it was the alienating effects of *capitalist* industrial
society that disturbed him in *Residencia*. Maybe socialist industrialization can be organic. Anyway, it is as much his poetic right
to see the Republic as a force of the earth as it was Esenin's poetic
right, for example, to see the Russian Revolution (however im-
probably) as the reaffirmation of the ethos of the Russian village
and therefore as a pastoral sanctuary from the urban debauchery
in which he, like Neruda, had been gloomily immersed. Certainly,
the fact that Neruda sees the Republic as a tellurian force is
evidence of the extent to which his reaction to it is a personal
one, and not an exercise in bad faith made to order, as his political
poetry is often supposed to be.

In 'España en el corazón', the Republican soldiers are born of
the earth. They were like seeds planted in the soil waiting to
germinate.[45] Brought up among pomegranates (*granadas*, also
hand-grenades), onions, and corn, they have acquired the strength
to fight. The enemy, on the other hand, destroy the earth; thus
in the section significantly entitled 'Tierras ofendidas' (Offended
earth') they exterminate bees and rocks and import blood and
crime where once there was corn and clover.[46] Interestingly, the
positive noun-signs of *Residencia* are savaged here by adjectives
whose agent is the enemy. If bread, flowers, bells, horses, and
doves are in trouble, it is because the enemy trample on them.
And it is the enemy that deploys putrefaction, ashes, and dampness. It is as though Neruda had discovered a simple historical
explanation for a condition that had seemed to him to be endemic,

[45] *Tercera residencia*, p. 65.        [46] p. 57.

and if of course there is suddenly a historical explanation there must also now be a historical solution.

In 'España en el corazón' the historical solution aimed at is fairly tenuous. On the one hand it is recommended that Franco be confined to a hell where among other inconveniences blood will fall upon him like rain and where he will slip eternally on a river composed of the eyes he has gouged out.[47] On the other hand, there is the hope, manifested in the last lines of the poem, that nature will summon its secret forces for the achievement of a 'mineral victory'.[48] It is of course in a way an impotent hope. It is reminiscent of the conclusion to a novel by Miguel Angel Asturias, *Viento fuerte* (1950, 'Strong wind') where, when all efforts to fight an exploiting American company have failed, nature, having been summoned by the local witch-doctor, saves the day: a cyclone destroys the hated plantations. It is as though nature were the *only* weapon of the weak against the strong, or worse, as though it were merely an image of the fulfilment of impossible wishes. As such, however, it is a powerful image, comfortably menacing.

The spectacle of Franco slipping eternally in a river of gouged-out eyes marks the burgeoning of an art in which Neruda was to excel with particular relish in the *Canto general*, the art of savage invective. To begin with this aspect of his vast and diverse epic of the American continent might seem unfair to some, but only because his denunciatory poems have been too readily dismissed, on the grounds that they are not 'real poetry', or on the grounds that they are viciously biased. This seems absurd. We often accept a passionate poem about a woman as 'great poetry', and although we suspect that the woman in question was probably nothing like her description in the poem, we do not object that the poem is biased. And anyway, if the poem is a good one, it will carry the conviction that the *passion* was genuine and the poem will impress us as a true manifestation of passion. In the same way, Neruda's poems about, for example, the Chilean President González Videla (1946–52), who drove Neruda into exile and set up a nasty concentration camp to house the Communists who had helped bring him to power, are manifestations of a real and legitimate passion, of a true and justified hate. And hate has just as much a right to be the subject of poetry as love. Even if Neruda, having latterly become a far more benign man, may now himself

[47] p. 61.                    [48] p. 70.

laugh at these poems, they remain the expressions of a hate he once truly felt. They are good hate poems, and the targets—third-rate rapacious politicians that have always infested the Latin American political scene—deserve what they get. Also one is so conditioned to see poets (and to have seen Neruda) in the doldrums that it is refreshing to encounter a man so sure of himself now that he can stand up to accuse others rather than accuse himself. The *Canto general* is a good antidote say to American confessional poetry and it is a good antidote to *Residencia*, however splendid that book was.

Whether or not Neruda's hate poems are effective as propaganda is another question. Only market research could really answer it. But in judging the propaganda passages of the *Canto general* (and these include hopeful recommendations as well as denunciations), one should bear in mind that the purpose of propaganda is above all to move and to persuade. This may often be the purpose of any poetry, but the difference is that propaganda must hope to move a mass of people, it cannot be élitist. For this reason, stylish propaganda such as that devised in the Soviet Union in the 1920s may be less effective than the cruder variety Neruda goes in for.

Robert Pring-Mill has noted that much Latin American protest poetry draws heavily on conventions that have been part of a tradition of protest and patriotism which can be traced as far back as the Independence movements.[49] Often, these conventions consist of well-worn rhetorical clichés, but they are accessible to a wide audience, they conjure immediate, widely shared associations and serve, therefore, as a short cut to communication. Neruda's denunciatory poetry is full of easy stock abuse ('treacherous soul', 'rotten jackal',[50] 'cruel pig',[51] 'jackal with gloves',[52] 'voracious hyenas', 'New York wolves',[53] 'miserable mixture of monkey and rat'[54]) which though perhaps not hectically inventive may be very successful in achieving quick mass communication. The exaggerated *goriness* of Neruda's insults is itself within a readily recognizable tradition: one can find it as far back as Hilario Ascasubi's *gauchesco* denunciations of Rosas in *Paulino Lucero*, in such a

---

[49] *Cambridge Review*, 20 Feb. 1970, p. 114. This excellent article has been my principle inspiration for the next two paragraphs.
[50] *Canto general*, Vol. 1, p. 51.          [51] p. 52.
[52] p. 141.          [53] p. 146.          [54] p. 181.

poem for instance as 'Isidora la federala', where the dictator Rosas is hyperbolically seen as a drunken oaf hoarding the ears and the hands of his dead enemies. Poems like 'Las oligarquías' in the *Canto general* moreover follow a psychologically effective technique of Ascasubi's of making the enemy speak out so insultingly and arrogantly that the reader is incited to want to strike back. Another psychologically effective propaganda technique firmly established by Ascasubi in his poem 'Isidora la federala' can be found in Neruda's 'Margarita Naranjo': we are treated to the cautionary spectacle of what vicious rewards one can expect if one is meekly loyal to the enemy, in Ascasubi's case to Rosas, in Neruda's to an American company.

Neruda uses many conventional clichés to denote hope, too, which can be found in the rhetoric of Latin American national anthems and military marches, or in the independence poems of, say, Andrés Bello and Jose Joaquín de Olmedo. They are the quickly recognizable clichés that children meet, as Pring-Mill points out, in the 'schoolroom context of conventional patriotism'. If one didn't take into account the communicative usefulness of drawing on such a context, much of the *Canto general* could seem like puerile bathos: 'May your instant splendour be known / Your errant heart, your daily fire',[55] 'I will bear throughout my life / the honour of having shaken / your noble warrior hand'.[56]

Of course, there is much more in the *Canto general* than propaganda, and provided one appreciates the context in which the propaganda was devised, and provided one also recognizes its sincerity and its legitimacy as the expression of deeply felt passion, one can be free to admit that it constitutes the worst poetry in the book. Indeed, the fact that there is so much excellent poetry in the book serves as a guarantee that the frequent bathos of the propaganda passages is intentional, not the result of ineptitude.

The fundamental purpose of the *Canto general*, of which the denunciatory poems mentioned are a symptom, is to write, or re-write, the history of Latin America—to write a poetic version of the continent's historical trajectory and to refute the official version, the one imposed upon schoolchildren in the classroom. Thus for one, Neruda aims to view history from the point of view of people who do not normally figure in the heroic tales of the textbooks, for instance, miners, peasants, or private soldiers. Neruda

[55] p. 95.          [56] Vol. 2, p. 130.

reminds us that it was individual Chilean miners, not Anaconda
Copper, who built Chuquicamata, the world's largest open copper mine. And in a section called 'La tierra se llama Juan' ('The
land is called Juan') he imagines ordinary individuals giving
their account of a series of events of which one generally knows
only a more public, official version: indeed much of this and other
sections of the *Canto general* are written in tribute to what one
might call the Unknown Worker, the man who has made things
(copper bars, gold bullion, manufactured goods) from which he
was not intended to benefit, and for which he has been given no
gratitude. Only by going on strike can the unknown worker ultimately make his indispensibility felt: in 'La huelga' ('the strike'),
Neruda vividly demonstrates how futile machines become when
the workers abandon them to nothing but the 'lonely smell of
grease'.[57]

Neruda's rewriting of history has a deeper significance though,
one which is wholly consistent with the tellurianism we discerned
as far back as *20 poemas de amor y una canción desesperada*.
Working on what we can presume to be the assumption that the
written history of the continent is a lie from the very beginning,
he attempts to return to its origins, not only to its pre-Columbine,
indigenous origins, but also to its primeval ones, before the emergence of man. This is the spirit of the first section of the *Canto
general*, 'La lámpara en la tierra' ('The lamp in the earth'), Poems
on 'vegetation', on 'some beasts', on birds, on rivers, and on
'minerals' remind us that nature existed long before man came to
cloak it with lies and disguises, for 'Before the wig and the frock-
coat / were the rivers, the arterial rivers.'[58] Neruda returns to the
primeval in order to trace the original tellurian nature of man, to
rediscover and resurrect the vital, tellurian energies of a race
originally created, as in the book of Genesis, from earth:

> Man was earth, a vessel, the eyelid
> of the quivering mud, a shape of clay ...[59]

'La lámpara en la tierra' is, indeed, Neruda's Genesis. It is about
the lighting of the earth's first lamp, the opening of the first
quivering eyelid. It is a search for the 'green uterus' of the jungle,[60]
a search therefore for maternal nature in order thence to retread

[57] p. 106.      [58] Vol. 1, p. 9.      [59] p. 9.      [60] p. 12.

the steps of a historical trajectory trampled by the sins of the wreckless father—the Spanish conqueror. It is a return to 'lands without names / and without numbers'[61] in order to get behind the deceitful naming and the spurious numbering of conquerors and historians, in order therefore to be able to name again, to appropriate the right to define, rather than submit to the alien definitions of a foreign, conquering Adam. Neruda certainly redefines politically and, like Whitman, or like such Latin American writers as Alejo Carpentier who have similarly had a basic urge to *name* their virgin continent, he provides vigorous descriptions of landscapes that have been scarcely written about, full of copious vocabulary denoting flora and fauna unknown in Europe.

Yet curiously it is here that Neruda misses a splendid opportunity. He does not sufficiently renew his language. It remains too much tainted with the legacy he would appear to be endeavouring to overthrow. We shall see in the next chapter how the Mexican poet Octavio Paz attempts a comparable exercise in redefinition in a poem like 'Blanco'. But for Paz, to redefine the past and to assert oneself against it involves the liberation of the poem from all that has been mechanically inherited from the *language* of the past, its liberation for instance from the ready-made metaphor. In contrast, when Neruda shows forth his primeval landscapes and returns to the primeval in order to be able to free himself from history, he does so in a language all too heavily loaded with the weight of history. Needless to say language is never not historically conditioned to some degree, but it is surely excessively self-defeating to write of the dawn's 'inaccessible cathedral', of a river's 'cross',[62] of a forest as a 'vault of branches',[63] of the primeval earth as a 'cathedral of pale eyelids'.[64] To be fair, these are extreme examples—descriptions of a nature before history in words that lazily borrow from what is for Neruda one of history's most heinous manifestations, the Church. Of course, Christianity is deeply implanted in the received images of the Spanish language. It is merely that Neruda has not suspected that the implications of those received images should perhaps be questioned as rigorously as the received ideas of the school textbook. The same complaint could be made when Neruda employs anthropomorphic metaphors in descriptions of pre-human land-

[61] p. 11.    [62] Vol. 2, p. 39.    [63] p. 37.    [64] p. 19.

scapes. Thus he refers to the '*monastic* ant-hill'[65] or to the '*alcoholic* eyes of the jungle'.[66] Man encroaches upon a language that is aiming to depict the world before his emergence. Yet here, at least, it could be claimed that the anthropomorphic adjectives were part of Neruda's search for connections between man and his tellurian origins.

The five sections that make up the first half of the *Canto general* constitute an epic attempt to tell the story of the American continent. Crudely, the story runs as follows. In the first place, there is the primeval paradise already discussed ('La lámpara en la tierra'). Next there comes an interlude in which Neruda attempts to trace his own relationship with the pre-Columbine past ('Alturas de Macchu Picchu'). The primeval paradise, where man and nature were one, where men lived by the 'science of pollen', 'the law of the beehive / the secret of the green bird / the language of the stars'[67] is then destroyed by the Conquest ('Los conquistadores'). The conquistador 'rapes the nuptial rose of the tribe',[68] refuses the offering of the dove in his lust for gold,[69] and assaults the earth, just as Franco did in 'España en el corazón'. After centuries of colony, the liberators appear, having been foreshadowed by the few people (Las Casas, Caupolicán, Lautaro, Tupac Amaru) who resisted the colony ('Los libertadores'). They are the 'tree of the people',[70] 'hidden flour',[71] 'once buried bells',[72] 'the insurrection of grain',[73] 'the seed'.[74] In short, they are tellurian man reborn. One notes that the same positive images of Neruda's earlier poetry reappear (the rose, the dove, the bell, the goblet, and so on), whereas others appear that were used perhaps a little less insistently in *Residencia*, though most of them can be found there: *primavera* (spring), *espiga* (ear of corn), *semilla* (seed), *maíz* (maize), *manantial* (source, spring, origin), *vertiente* (watershed), *estambre* (stamen), *germen* (bud, shoot), *aurora* (dawn), *sol* (sun), *cristal* (crystal, a traditional Spanish trope for water), *bandera* (flag). All these images are of easy, obvious access: most of them relate the rebirth of freedom from Spain to the reburgeoning of the forces of nature.

The indigenous man who fights the Spaniards is the son of nature, a construct of earth, and his characteristic form of combat,

[65] Vol. 1, p. 12.          [66] p. 13.                    [67] p. 45.
[68] p. 45.        [69] p. 44.          [70] p. 67.          [71] p. 71.
[72] p. 75.                   [73] p. 85.                   [74] p. 87.

guerrilla warfare, uses nature as its accomplice. Thus, the nomadic Araucanian Indians of the south of Chile, who never submitted to the Spaniards and who conducted a guerrilla campaign against them from the beginning of the colony, are almost indistinguishable from the forest trees.[75] The model Indian chieftain, Lautaro, described in 'Educación del cacique' ('Education of a chieftain') is wholly integrated with nature: 'his youth was an aimed wind',[76] 'he educated his head among thorns / he executed the trials of the *guanaco*', 'he ambushed the prey of eagles / he scratched out the secrets of the rock.'[77] Nature as accomplice, nature as education, nature as the source of powerful secrets denied to those who do not live by her, and liberation as the recovery of those secrets, temporarily lost during the conquest—all these notions are the familiar stamping-ground of much Latin American 'tellurian' writing. They are, for instance, basic to Asturias's novel *Hombres de maiz* (1949, *Men of Maize*). But alas, the first volume closes with a description of how the rebirth of nature during independence was betrayed by all those tyrants whom we have already seen denounced ('La arena traicionada'—'The betrayed sand'). Some are named—Francia, Rosas (rather surprisingly, as he is now often seen by left-wing historians as a hero of Argentinian nationalism), García Moreno, Gómez, or Machado. Others are anonymously archetypal—ivory-tower poets, parvenus, diplomats, or judges.

The second volume merely complements and enriches the first. One section recapitulates its trajectory specifically for Chile ('Canto general de Chile'). Another, 'El gran océano' ('The vast sea'), is fundamentally descriptive: there is nothing more likely than the sea to carry Neruda away from politics. The sea for him is too vastly overpowering to be judged, and it is above history. The sea is neither good nor bad: it just is. This section contains poems which, for their sheer virtuosity, are unsurpassed in the book, poems that evoke the bitter cold of the Antarctic, poems on the flora and fauna of the ocean bed, poems that bring to life a rock, a wave, a passing ship. It is hard to find rhetorical clichés in them.

The central core of the *Canto general* is really the sequence called 'A las alturas de Macchu Picchu'. For here Neruda makes his own personal statement; he establishes the nature of his own place in the *Canto*. In the first part of this sequence, he re-enacts

[75] p. 22.                [76] p. 76.                [77] p. 77.

the tribulations—and even resuscitates or parodies the language—
of *Residencia*. He describes how once he wandered 'from air to
air, like an empty net',[78] blind to the 'jaded spring'.[79] Yet he reminds us that he never abandoned his search for the 'unfathom-
able eternal vein',[80] however persistently time and death seemed
to be defeating him. But it has taken the spectacle of Macchu
Picchu, the spectacular Inca citadel in the Peruvian Andes, finally
to awaken him. In Macchu Picchu, he rediscovers his links with
his indigenous ancestors, and with the liberating secrets of tellurian
man and of nature which the conquest had destroyed:

> A través del confuso esplendor,
> a través de la noche de piedra, déjame hundir la mano
> y deja que en mí palpite, como un ave mil años prisionera,
> el viejo corazón del olvidado.[81]

Neruda rises to the occasion so authentically in this poem that he
even wonders if the aggression of history upon nature did not
start before the conquest. He modifies the idyllically stereotyped
Indianism of 'La lámpara en la tierra' and asks if Macchu Picchu,
too, was not built at the expense of intolerable human sacrifice.
Do its perfect angular stones not presuppose a 'hypotenuse of
hairshirt and acid blood'?[82] He ends the poem with a Whitman-
esque incantation in which he invites his dead Indian ancestors
to speak through him, to bring to 'the goblet of this new life' their
'old buried pains'.[83] Neruda, at last, has found the connections that
always eluded him in *Residencia*.

*Canto general* is Neruda's political testament. One can assume
that in writing it he may have felt that politically, he had done
his best. Certainly, he is never again to concentrate so much
political poetry in one volume, although his concern with social
problems and his faith in Communism were never to be abandoned.

Neruda's next two books, *Los versos del capitán* (1952, 'The
captain's poems') and *Las uvas y el viento* (1954, 'The grapes and
the wind'), were inspired by his European travels in the 1950s.

---

[78] p. 25.          [79] p. 25.          [80] p. 26.
[81] p. 34. 'Through the confused splendour, / through the night of stone let
me plunge my hand / and may the ancient heart of the forgotten man /
throb in me, like a bird held captive for a thousand years.'
[82] p. 34.                              [83] p. 35.

The former, which was published anonymously, was specifically inspired by one Matilde Urrutia, a woman with whom he appears to have had a secret relationship in Italy and who has continued to be Neruda's companion up until now, being also the heroine of Neruda's subsequent *Cien sonetos de amor* (1959, 'One hundred love sonnets'). But his next most important work was his *Odas elementales* (1954).

The *Odas* mark a new departure for Neruda. They are brutally simple poems, strings of lines sometimes only three syllables long, sometimes containing only one word. The effect is to force breath stops on the rhythm where they would not normally occur, sometimes for suspense preceding a surprise image, always in order to maintain a fresh pace. Yet the originality of the poems does not lie in their metre—such strings of short lines had after all been deployed by Apollinaire or Mayakovsky many decades before. The originality of the *Odas* lies in the new vision of the world Neruda manifests in them.

The *Odas'* ancestor in Neruda's work is a poem in *Residencia* we touched on earlier, 'Ritual de mis piernas'. There, amidst the turmoil of a putrid world, Neruda suddenly found himself contemplating his legs. The extraordinary thing about his legs was that they were meticulously, spectacularly *there*. What could be more improbable yet more undeniably real than a knee, separating two halves of a leg as different from each other as two sexes? Similarly, Neruda's *Odas elementales* is a book of wonder at the preciseness and diversity of things, at the meticulousness of the architecture of an onion, a tomato, a bird, or a fish, at the precise diversity of a shopping bag, where an artichoke keeps the company of a pair of shoes, a cabbage that of a bottle of vinegar ('Oda a la alcachofa'—'Ode to an artichoke').[84] It is a book of wonder too at the precise singularity of the most ordinary things' trajectories through the world: that, for example, of an individual onion from soil to salad[85] or of a conger-eel from sea to conger-eel broth.[86] It is a book of wonder that the world exists, that it is full of so many extraordinarily exact shapes, so many fantastically meticulous destinies. Things that before were symbols are now just things: a bird is no longer an abstract sign of liberation but rather just a bird, precise and different. *Odas elementales* is the book of a man who has opened up his eyes (or raised his eyelids, as Neruda

[84] *Odas elementales*, Buenos Aires, 1954, p. 19.     [85] p. 41.     [86] p. 37.

might say) to see, to notice things that up to now he had taken for granted. It is the book of a man who has come to realize that artichokes or onions are as remarkable as the Andes, the Antarctic, or a rain-drenched forest.

Sometimes the optimism these poems deploy becomes a little too automatic, as though he were purging out the last remnants of gloom in him by sheer mechanical insistence. One comes lazily to predict that an ode to winter ('Oda al invierno') will end up with a peroration on the coming of spring,[87] that an ode to the atom ('Oda al átomo') will develop from a description of Hiroshima to an anthem about atoms for peace.[88] Yet the ode to the atom is yet another genuine plea that man be in harmony with nature: a precondition of that harmony is that man use natural resources positively, not destructively.

Anthropomorphic metaphors are certainly justified in the *Odas*: indeed they are the basis of the book's charm and also perhaps of its purpose. They help to charge the very ordinary things described with a sort of human pathos. Thus the tomato, after sitting at rest on a sideboard, alongside 'glasses / butter dishes / blue salt-cellars',[89] meets its ultimate sad fate:

> We must, alas,
> assassinate it:
> a knife
> is sunk
> into its living pulp . . .[90]

Man and nature are linked in mutual compassion: a tomato becomes a human being in order that we may identify with it.

Often the anthropomorphic metaphors are merely humorous: in the *Odas* Neruda begins to strike a consistent note of playful humour which seems to be heralding a definitive maturity, a benign self-assurance that is to characterize his work henceforth. Take this description of a storm:

> Quería dormir
> Y preparó su cama,
> barrió selvas, caminos,
> barrió montes,
> lavó piedras de océano,

[87] p. 99.        [88] pp. 28–32.        [89] p. 198.        [90] p. 199.

y entonces
como si fueran plumas
removío los pinares
para hacerse su cama.[91]

Always in the *Odas* Neruda is looking for connections between whatever he may be depicting, as though he were endeavouring, by force of his poetic will, to subsume a disparate world into an organic whole. He traces the link between the food he eats at dinner and the soil that germinated it, between a building and the tellurian origins of its materials ('Oda al edificio')—('Ode to a building').[92] An ode to energy ('Oda a la energía')[93] wills connections between all those things that produce energy—coal and fire, locomotive and ship, or furnace and grape'; and the anthropomorphic metaphors of course will connections between all such things and man. Ultimately, it is the task of poetry to root out these connections, to *thread* things together ('Oda al hilo'—'Ode to thread'),[94] to thread its way through the world until it envelops it all[95]—until, in short, the disintegrated world of *Residencia* has been pieced together into a single organism.

One begins to detect a hedonistic vein in the *Odas* which is to become increasingly predominant in Neruda's poetry. It is as though Neruda had decided finally to jettison his early gloom with a vengeance and quite blatantly to assert his right to enjoy himself. The very titles of some of the *odas* ('To happiness', 'To love', 'To a happy day', 'To wine', 'To life') indicate the extent to which his neuroses have been finally, euphorically given the sack. Maybe those descents to the 'green uterus' of nature, those returns to the beginning of time, served as a sort of therapeutic recall, whereby not only the history of the continent was retraced in order to stamp out its agonies, but also Neruda's life.

As forecast at the beginning of this chapter, there is no space left to do proper justice to Neruda's poetry of the past fifteen years or so. There have been two more books of *odas* (*Nuevas odas elementales*, 1956, *Tercer libro de las odas*, 1957), his love sonnets to Matilde, and a series of other disparate books of which the most important are *Estravagario* (1958), *Cantos ceremoniales*

[91] p. 201. 'It wanted to sleep / so it prepared its bed / it swept away jungles, roads / it swept away mountains / washed ocean stones / and then / as if they were feathers / it moved the pine trees / to make its bed.'

[92] pp. 57–9.   [93] p. 59–62.   [94] pp. 86–90.   [95] p. 88.

(1961), *Plenos poderes* (1962), and a verse autobiography in five volumes, *Memorial de Isla Negra* (1964). In *Estravagario*, the playful, whimsical humour we discerned in the poem about the storm's bed-making is fully developed. There is a description of 'Furious struggle between sailors and an octopus of colossal dimensions' and above all the magnificent 'Bestiario', where Neruda treats us to a dead-pan declaration of his dislike for such 'smart animals' as wasps or racehorses, and of his love instead for the erotic rabbit, the spider (maligned in 'imbecillic texts / by exasperating simplifiers / who take the fly's point of view'), ruminants, pigs, frogs, and fleas. In *Estravagario*, Neruda's new relaxed hedonism has reached the point where not only can poems be about fun—they can be fun. Humour is present in the other books too, and often it is joyfully self-deprecating: thus in 'El largo día jueves' (*Memorial de Isla Negra*) he pictures himself as an inert Oblomov, taking an entire day to have a bath, shave, and put on his socks. Now and then there is a deeply felt poem of social concern (such as 'El pueblo' in *Plenos poderes*). Occasionally, for instance in 'Pasado' (Past), he goes in for a piece of breath-takingly simple metaphysical speculation. The tone is Tolstoyan: the no-nonsense wisdom of a man who has seen it all.

These books are the work of a poet who has found his faith (the Communist Party), his woman (Matilde), and himself (a benign, uncomplicated, self-possessed, humorous, wise, and compassionate man). They are a far cry from all those damp rooms and drab notaries of *Residencia*. The poetry is now far less tense, far less dramatic, but it is equally valid, and it is written by a man who has never known his trade better.

# 5

## Octavio Paz (Mexico, 1914–   )

IN the work of both Neruda and Vallejo, we discerned a fundamental dissatisfaction with the world and a determination to
change it. The same quest for a better world is basic to the poetry
of Octavio Paz. Yet Paz is never neurotic like Vallejo or like the
Neruda of *Residencia*. No edgy splinters, no humid walls menace
him. His demand that the world be different is the demand of a
healthy man, untroubled by suffering. It is just that nothing can
satisfy him that is not an all-embracing, time-destroying ecstasy. His
poetry, whose central topics have remained more or less constant
throughout his career, constitutes a search for a single moment of
dizzy ecstasy, a splendid *instante* that will annul the world that is,
and germinate instead an altogether new one, where a poplar, a
stone, a mountain, or a river—or, above all, Octavio Paz—will
become transfigured from what they merely are to something immeasurably more vast and magnificent.

An overwhelming proportion of Paz's poetry is erotic. Like
Neruda, Paz searches for the transformation he is aiming at in a
woman. And like Neruda's, Paz's women are conspicuously en-
dowed with the resources of nature. A woman's footprint is the
'visible centre of the earth',[1] her skin is made of bread, her eyes of
sugar, her body includes 'valleys which only my lips know', 'there
are always bees in [her] hair',[2] 'her skirt is made of maize', and she
pierces his chest with 'fingers of water'.[3] She is almost indistinguishable from the landscape she inhabits, for not only is she a con-

[1] *Libertad bajo palabra*, Obra poética (1935–58), Mexico, 1960, p. 22.
[2] p. 82.
[3] p. 295.

struct of nature; nature itself is a woman, triumphantly shedding her clothes:

> ... las piedras dejan caer sus vestiduras
> Y el agua se desnuda y salta de su lecho
> Más desnuda que el agua
> Y la luz se desnuda y se mira en el agua.[4]

The shedding of clothes is an essential prerequisite for the experience of the ecstatic *instante* of transformation. Indeed a joyful hedonism often pervades Paz's poetry, and the poems are often celebrations of what he frequently calls a *festín*, a sheer uninhibited feast, where not only clothes, but anything that might inhibit is shed, even one's name. Paz has praised the hippies for asserting a hedonism of the present against societies that impose upon their citizens the tyranny of the future, sheer enjoyment having always to be postponed until the insurance policy expires or until the mortgage is amortized. Certainly, many of his poems constitute a hippie-like assertion that the present must be grasped and lived to the maximum. But Paz's poetry is a great deal more than a recommendation that we all copulate happily in the open air. Let us therefore examine what exactly it is that he is looking for in his liberating females, and what is the exact nature of their effect upon him.

Now the language of much of Paz's earlier poetry is often strongly reminiscent of the language of the Spanish sixteenth-century mystics. There are for instance frequent variations on that fundamental conceit of the Spanish mystics, that life is death and that death is life, that the crib is the coffin and the coffin the crib. He can write of 'tu voz que me destruye y resucita' ('your voice that destroys me and revives me'),[5] and like St. John of the Cross or St. Teresa, of pleasurable wounds: he is 'herido dulcemente'[6]—'sweetly wounded'—by his woman, and she deploys 'the fire that destroys me without wounding me' ('el fuego que me acaba sin herirme').[7] To fall, moreover, is to rise: 'ascendemos cayendo'.[8]

The paradoxes of course rest on the supposed fundamental

[4] p. 91. 'The stones shed their garments / and the water strips and leaps from its bed / more naked than water / and the light strips and beholds itself in the water.'

[5] p. 20.          [6] p. 55.          [7] p. 23.          [8] p. 36.

duality of the man who is experiencing them. He is two things (body and soul for the Spanish mystics) and for one of them to thrive the other must perish. For one to be reborn, the other must be destroyed, for one to rise the other must fall.

Paz's poetry is not recognizably Christian. If anything, he is endeavouring to shed his soul in order to resuscitate his body, if we perhaps irresponsibly take 'soul' to mean 'inhibiting superego'. But by using the language of the mystics now and then he is acknowledging a similarity between his quest and theirs: they too were involved in a search for something other than what is manifestly given, for a self which though other than the self was yet a part of is, the secret component of a fundamental duality. Paz has frequently equated poetry and religion. He has noted for example that 'in the experience of the supernatural, as in that of love and poetry, man feels torn or separated from himself' and that moreover 'the eucharist, for instance, operates a change in the nature of the believer. The sacred food transmutes us. We become "others" as a result of which we recover our nature or our original condition.'[9] The quest of poetry and the quest of religion are ultimately the same one: to change the world and transmute the self.

The sort of change projected in Christianity is of course well known: the passage posited is one from the world as we know it to God's Paradise. What then does it consist of in Paz's poetry?

Now we note that when we become *others*, 'we recover our *nature* or our *original condition*'. There is indeed in Paz, as there is in Neruda, an urgent search for identity, for a lost *nature*. And for Paz, as for Neruda, the real nature of American man has been disguised beneath the mask of the conquest. This is partly the theme of his famous essay on Mexico, *El laberinto de la soledad* (1950), where Paz sees Mexican history as an attempt to recover the origin and the tradition, and consequently the identity dependent upon them that the conquest has trampled. Like Neruda in the *Canto general*, he attempts to retrace the lost steps to reground his identity and the identity of Mexico at the very spot where it was uprooted, the 'other self' he is looking for turning out therefore to be the secret identity which his current self has masked. Like Neruda, but more insistently and perhaps more rigorously, he asserts his right to be Adam, to become rejoined to

9 *El arco y la lira*, 2nd rev. edn., Mexico, 1967, p. 135.

the man from whom history has separated him.

Adam of course was the first man to speak, and he was also the first man to copulate: Paz converts the writing of a poem and the act of love into Adamic enterprises that are essentially two faces of the same coin. The task of the poet is to rename the world, as Adam named it. He must not accept the definitions of any conquering Adam; his words must erect a wholly new foundation or rediscover the original one. Similarly, to make love is to re-enact the gestures of Adam: the copulating couple is rejoined with the first couple. Their actions destroy the time-gap that separates them and consequently annul the bloody and mendacious trajectory of history.

The link between copulating and writing a poem is fundamental to Paz's poetry. Both acts culminate in the same achievement— the liberation of the poet from all that has moulded him against his will, his liberation from history and from time, and the consequent burgeoning of his real, new, or 'other self'. Both acts constitute a return to the origin, to an 'original nakedness'.[10] The clothes that are shed are those that historical necessity has imposed, historical necessity being nowhere more pervasive than in the received images of language. Shed those clothes, and in the unprecedented words of the poem the poet's true nature will be revealed—and not the nature his *father* willed upon him. For in writing a poem or in making love Paz asserts his right to *father himself*. He conjugates and there issues a text or a progeny which in either case is the incarnation of his new, self-created self. He conjugates the language or with the female and they are consequently the mother of the new self. But it is *his* seed that has moulded it. In 'Blanco', a poem in which these connections are most eloquently established, and where the pun on 'conjugation' is in fact made, we are told that 'thought is a phallus and the word a vulva' ('falo el pensar y vulva la palabra').[11] Paz's imagination thus enters the 'vulva' of language and there issues the real, liberated man, or the poem in which he is embodied. But the issue is the product of an incestuous union. If he has fathered his new self, he must have slept with its mother, who must therefore be *his* mother too. Paz is no doubt very conversant with that contemporary French tradition that asserts that language is like a

---

[10] *Salamandra* (1958–61), Mexico, 2nd rev. edn., 1969, p. 83.
[11] *Ladera este* (1962–8), Mexico, 1969, p. 162.

desired mother where the father is the law that invites transgression.[12] To write a real poem therefore is to betray the father, to shatter the language's proprietor (the Spanish conqueror perhaps, or the inquisitorial colonial priest) in order to *appropriate* it for himself. To write a poem is ultimately to perform an act that is liberating but also illicit: only the iconoclast (and scarcely, therefore, the subserviently orthodox mystic) will achieve the burgeoning of his other, liberated self; only the iconoclast will recover his lost—and forbidden—identity. For any crime is better than to be a 'phantasm with a number / condemned forever to a chain':

> Mejor el crimen,
> los amantes suicidas, el incesto
> de los dos hermanos como dos espejos.[13]

But what exactly are the characteristics of this new or other self? What exactly is it that Paz is achieving in copulation, or in the writing of a poem? We have seen that he is hoping to achieve the recovery of a lost identity. Is there anything more to it?

In the act of love consciousness is like a wave which, having overcome an obstacle, before collapsing swells into a condition of fullness where everything—form and movement, the impulse to rise and the force of gravity—achieves an unpropped, self-sustaining equilibrium. ... Through the body of the beloved we glimpse a life that is more plentiful, more life than life. Similarly, through the poem, we perceive the immobile lightning flash of poetry. That instant contains every instant. Without ceasing to flow, time stands still, overcome with itself.[14]

Apart from heralding the recovery of a lost identity, the achievement therefore consists also of a flash of *equilibrium* and *plenitude* that overcomes time. Like a wave, its moment of glory precedes its collapse only by a fragment of a second, and Paz's poetry is the record of swift alterations between such instant ecstasy and its instant dispersal. One poem, the magnificent 'Piedra de sol' (1957), ends with the same six lines with which it began. The

[12] The concept is central to the thought of Georges Bataille and Jacques Lacan.
[13] 'Crime is better / suicidal lovers, incest / of brother and sister like two mirrors.' *Libertad*, p. 304.
[14] *El arco y la lira*, p. 25.

poem, which is indeed the record of a search for ecstasy and its
inevitable dispersal, has no end therefore. There is no end to the
cycles wherein the contingent world and the ecstatic instant do
battle. There will always be waves swelling into a condition of
fullness, and they will always collapse. But the moment of glory
is so splendid that it is worth seeking. Confronted by

> El hormiguero en pleno sueño
> Cascada negra de la sangre
> Cascada pétrea de la noche
> El peso bruto de la nada
> Zumbido de motores en la ciudad inmensa[15]

—by a vacuous and mechanical urban ant-hill, it is good to be
able to obtain, in any of the city's rooms, an ecstatic release:

> Hoy es cualquier día
> En un cuarto cualquiera
> Festín de dos cuerpos a solas
> Fiesta de ignorancia saber de presencia . . .
> Esculpimos un Dios instantáneo
> Tallamos el vértigo.[16]

Sometimes, when he is feeling the pressure of his urban surroundings, Paz looks in his woman for the *nature* that the city's
paving stones have buried. Nature (whose most attractive component for Paz is flowing water) then reasserts itself in the city
through the woman, her laughter being like the 'sun penetrating
the suburbs'[17] or her body like water flowing into 'a minute room'.[18]
In these instances the woman plays a role comparable to that of
Neruda's women. But nostalgia for the countryside is not so
strong in Paz as it is in Neruda. The woman, when she embodies
the ecstatic instant, can transfigure the city itself, she can make it
altogether more meaningful and more splendid, without having
to cause nature to overthrow it. At these points, 'the city swells

[15] *Salamandra*, p. 16. 'The ant-hill in deep sleep / black waterfall of blood /
stone waterfall of night / the brute weight of void / humming of engines in the
vast city.'

[16] p. 55. 'Today is any day / in any room / feast of two bodies alone / festival
of ignorance knowledge of presence / we sculpture an instantaneous God /
we carve out vertigo.'

[17] p. 63.

[18] p. 87.

like a heart' ('la ciudad se abre como un corazón');[19] it 'navigates in the depth of night' ('navega la ciudad en plena noche');[20] it acquires 'long legs' that are 'the legs of the woman I love'.[21] Even the London underground can become transfigured at the tentative sexual contact of two adolescents, thanks to whom suddenly:

> Todo es puerta
>> Todo es puente
> Ahora marchamos en la otra orilla.[22]

But even they cannot hold the world in suspension for ever, even they cannot avoid the passing of time:

> Pila de años muertos y escupidos
> Estaciones violadas
> Siglo tallado en un aullido
> Pirámide de sangre
> Horas royendo el día el año el siglo el hueso.[23]

A fairly consistent imagery decorates the battleground between ecstasy and contingency in Paz's poetry. We shall now take a closer look at this imagery simply because Paz's poetry *is* its imagery far more than it is any ideas that can be extracted from it, and anyway the ideas are inseparable from the images in which they are embodied. If we as readers ever come near to experiencing the ecstatic *instante* that Paz is aiming for, it is thanks to the exuberant evocativeness of his images. Yet alas whatever can be written about them will not do them justice. The language of Paz's poetry is energetically plurivalent. No word is allowed to settle down, or to attach itself to one single referent. So a description of his imagery will have to content itself with simplificatory generalizations.

Paz's most famous poem is called 'Piedra de sol'—'Sun stone' (1957). Much of his poetry constitutes an enterprise that is summarized in that title: the attempt to turn *stones* into *sun*. The title refers to the famous Aztec Calendar Stone, a vast stone block engraved with signs that embrace astronomy, history, and legend, and which bears the head of the Sun-God at its centre. Yet it is

---

[19] p. 60.     [20] p. 83.     [21] p. 63.
[22] p. 61. 'All is door / all is bridge / we are now striding on the other side.'
[23] p. 62. 'Heap of dead, spat-out years / desecrated seasons / howl-carved century / pyramid of blood / hours gnawing the day the year the century the bone.'

not essential to be expert in Aztec mythology to gauge the significance of sun and stone in Paz's work. The Calendar Stone embodies the infinity of the Aztec universe. But it is nothing without the sun. Stone without sun—or without free-flowing water—
is petrification. The task of poetry is to unpetrify stone, to bring
sun to it and to make it live and breathe like an organism. If not,
it will be a dead symbol of a dead people—as dead as the Aztecs,
who, too, must be resuscitated. So when poetry is flourishing, 'the
stone awakens: / it bears a sun in its belly' ('La piedra se
despierta: / Lleva un sol en el vientre').[24] Stones are used to build
walls, and walls are barriers that screen our view of the liberating
horizon—the *horizonte*. Walls too must come alive therefore, so
that 'the stone may scream / and the wall breathe like a lung' ('Y
la piedra grite / Y el muro respire como un pecho').[25]

Paz's poetry is an endeavour to give life to stones. Stones are
opaque: so Paz's poetry is an endeavour also to turn opacity into
light. Though not quite as frequently as Neruda's, his poetry is
populated with eyelids (*párpados*) whose opening heralds the triumph of light over opacity, the release of the light concealed in
the hitherto dormant, petrified stone:

> Se despeñó el instante en otro y otro,
> dormí sueños de piedra que no sueña
> y al cabo de los años como piedras
> oí cantar mi sangre encarcelada,
> con un rumor de luz el mar cantaba,
> una a una cedían las murallas,
> todas las puertas se desmoronaban
> y el sol entraba a saco por mi frente,
> despegaba mis párpados cerrados,
> desprendía mi ser de su envoltura,
> me arrancaba de mí, me separaba
> de mi bruto dormir siglos de piedra ...[26]

[24] p. 112.
[25] p. 74.
[26] *Libertad*, p. 310. 'This instant fled into another and another / I dreamed
dreams of a stone that does not dream / and at the end of years like stones / I
heard my imprisoned blood singing / the sea sang with a murmur of light /
one by one the walls were falling / every door was crumbling away / and the
sun was plundering its way through my forehead / unsticking my closed eyelids / unfastening my being of its swaddling clothes / rending me from myself
and separating me from brute sleeping centuries of stone. . . .'

Many of the components of Paz's imagery are contained in this passage: the dormant time-laden stone, the imprisoned (seminal?) blood about to be released at last, the incarcerating walls and closed doors waiting to be opened or to crumble to the deafening light of the sea, the liberating sun opening eyelids and, finally, awakening the dormant stones. One can see how hectic an effort there is to release all that is imprisoned, to unburden the landscape, and to will its euphoric triumph.

A quest such as Paz's for an ecstatic *instante* implies a journey, and Paz is always metaphorically travelling in his poetry. His journey is a sort of groping in the dark ('a tientas'):

> sigo mi desvarío, cuartos, calles,
> camino a tientas por los corredores
> del tiempo y subo y bajo sus peldaños
> y sus paredes palpo y no me muevo,
> vuelvo adonde empecé, busco tu rostro,
> camino por las calles de mí mismo[27] ...

His entry into the woman is also often the beginning of a journey, where he is to grope around for something far greater than a clitoris: 'voy por tu cuerpo como por el mundo' ('I go through your body as through the world'), 'voy por tus ojos como por el agua' ('I go through your eyes as through water'), 'voy por tu frente como por la luna' ('I go through your forehead as through the moon').[28] The poem itself is a journey in the dark in search of light. Poems are not 'huellas de lo que fuimos' ('the footprints of what we were') but rather 'caminos / hacia lo que somos' (*paths / towards* what we are').[29] For Paz therefore a poem should never be merely descriptive of what is given but rather it should be a quest, an adventure, a *journey* into the unknown whose outcome moreover the poet can never predict. And consequently he writes in ignorance of the poem's denouement—'Escribo sin conocer el desenlace / de lo que escribo.'[30]

The journey is initiated at the opening of a door. When the door opens, a horizon is glimpsed and that horizon is the goal of

[27] p. 305. 'I follow my delirium, rooms, streets / I walk groping my way through the corridors / of time up and down its steps / and I feel its walls and do not move / I return to where I began, look for your face / walk along the streets of myself. . . .'

[28] p. 294.     [29] *Ladera*, p. 91.     [30] p. 60.

the journey. If it is not a horizon, it is an *orilla*, the other bank of the river, the other unknown 'side'. The aim of the poem, or of the love act, is to build a bridge (*puente*) from one side to the other. The bridge may be 'un puente de latidos' ('a bridge of heart-throbs')[31] or it may be the body of the woman converted into 'an arch of water that turns into air on touching the other shore'—

> Un arco
> De agua que al tocar la otra orilla
> Se vuelve aire.[32]

In contrast, in the monotonous city of 'Repeticiones', where poetry and copulation are not flourishing at all, there is only a 'puente roto y el ahogado' ('a bridge broken and a man drowned').[33]

The idea of an 'other side' that must somehow be attained has always been central to Paz's poetry. In 1955, in answer to a *questionnaire* prepared by André Breton on 'l'art magique', he wrote of the 'saut mortel' that must be made in order to reach 'l'autre rive'.[34] And Paz has found confirmation of this very Bretonian idea in oriental mysticism. In a note to 'Vrindaban', a poem in his eastern collection *Ladera este* of 1968, he mentions the presence of the concept of the Other Side in the Prajnaparamita Sutras: in crossing from one 'side' to the other the Wise Man abandons the phenomenal world and attains wisdom.

Poems then are journeys, bridges of words between one 'side and another' and the poet travels across those words like an errant pilgrim:

> *Pasos de un peregrino son errante*
> Sobre este frágil puente de palabras.[35]

Poetry has perhaps always aimed to be a bridge of words; it has always aimed verbally to fuse and connect the world's disparities: thus the italicized line in the above quotation is borrowed from Góngora's *Soledades*, Góngora being perhaps the most ambitious verbal connector and verbal traveller in the Spanish language. Paz's poetry too aims ambitiously at the achievement of fusion,

---

[31] *Libertad*, p. 31.    [32] *Ladera*, p. 93.    [33] *Salamandra*, p. 16.
[34] Céa, Claude, *Octavio Paz*, Paris, 1965, p. 46.
[35] *Ladera*, p. 16. 'Steps of an errant pilgrim / upon this flimsy bridge of words.'

where life, death, body, water, earth, light, darkness are one,
where

> vida y muerte
> pactan en ti, señora de la noche,
> torre de claridad, reina del alba,
> virgen lunar, madre del agua madre,
> cuerpo del mundo, casa de la muerte ...[36]

The hectic journey often takes the poet to the most vertiginous
heights. The love embrace is then enacted at such terrifying alti-
tude that we cannot be surprised that its ecstatic *instante* should
culminate so frequently in *vértigo*.

> Tus ojos se abren y se cierran
>                 Animales fosforescentes
> Abajo
>         El desfiladero caliente
> La ola que se dilata y rompe
>                 Tus piernas abiertas.[37]

At these high altitudes we often encounter a *cleft in a rock*, a
'*peña* (or *piedra*) *hendida*'. Thus in 'Vrindaban' Paz writes of a
*sadhu* (or ascetic nomad) grasping the form of a woman 'in a cleft
stone' ('una piedra hendida'), its rent becoming a 'formless dizzi-
ness' ('su desgarradura / el vértigo sin forma'),[38] and in 'Blanco'
we are

> girando girando *visión del pensamiento gavilán*
> en torno a la idea negra *cabra en la peña hendida*
> el vellón de la juntura *paraje desnudo*
> en la mujer desnuda *snap-shot de un latido de tiempo*.[39]

What is the significance of this cleft? A tentative clue can be
found in a note to 'Vrindaban'. Here Paz tells us that in Hindu

---

[36] *Libertad*, p. 309. 'Life and death / are reconciled in you, lady of the night
/ tower of clarity, queen of daybreak / lunar virgin, mother of mother water /
flesh of the world, residence of death.'

[37] *Ladera*, p. 105. 'Your eyes open and close / Phosphorescent animals /
Down there / The hot canyon / The wave that swells and breaks / Your legs
apart.'

[38] p. 61.

[39] p. 158. 'Swirling swirling *vision of the sparrow-hawk thought* / around the
black idea *goat on the cleft rock* / the fleece of the juncture *naked place* / in
the naked woman *snapshot of a beat of time*.'

mythology 'certain stones are signs of the Great Goddess, particularly if their form suggests the sexual fissure (la hendidura sexual) or yoni'.[40] Hindu mythology is thus helping to do what Paz always seeks to do in his poetry: to make stones live, to convert them into organisms, for the stone is now triumphantly being furnished with nothing less than the sexual opening of the goddess. But the image has, we shall see, a more complex significance.

In the passage from 'Blanco', quoted above, the left-hand column happens (according to a prefatory note) to be a love poem, whereas the right-hand column is a poem on the imagination. Read together, the two columns therefore correlate the sexual act with the imagination, and consequently with the writing of a *poem*. The poet when writing a poem must, like a goat or sparrow-hawk, reach immense altitudes, and so must the lover, but when he does, he confronts an *hendidura*, a cleft. Now if this cleft is the sexual opening of a woman, it is a gap that it is not hard to fill. But it is also something else. It is the gap that separates *two words*, and it is this very difficult gap that *poetry* must fill:

> La poesía
> Es la *hendidura*[41]
> El espacio
> Entre una palabra y otra.[42]

What characterizes a gap between two words? A blank space of course, a space which is *en blanco*. Yet this very space is the poet's target (or *blanco*) for above all poetry must overcome the limitations of the written word, poetry must do the impossible—fill the space between two words or even two syllables. In 'Blanco' the two syllables that must thus be joined and fused turn out to be the words 'Sí' and 'No'. They are, we are told, 'Dos sílabas enamoradas'—two syllables in love. But it is not enough that they be in love: the gap between them must be closed, they must be one.

In 'Blanco', the nirvana-like vision in which the poem culminates is itself akin to blankness. It is utterly transparent—a nothing in which 'only transparency remains' ('la transparencia es todo lo que queda').[43] It has a dazzling white (*blanco*) clarity,

---

[40] p. 178.
[41] My italics.
[42] p. 92. 'Poetry / is the cleft / the space / between one word and another.'
[43] p. 154.

but the whiteness of that clarity is only the remotest fragment removed from sheer blankness. The illumination that follows coitus is also dazzling and speechless, and it too walks a tightrope between speechless awe and blankness, like the blankness of the page which follows the written text, perhaps, eloquently *pregnant* for an instant flash while the poem is still operating on the reader, but doomed eventually to a definitively blank void. Not only can you not make the nirvana-like transparancy speak (you cannot describe it): it itself is only an instant removed from the blank nothing of the blank page. And that blank void will rapidly be invaded again by the everyday thoughts which the nirvana-like vision had sought to supplant. 'Pensamientos que no pienso'[44]— 'thoughts I do not think'—will uncontrollably return and force the poet to retreat again to 'this' side.

Paz's poetry is a heroic enterprise that attempts therefore to fill blankness—the blankness of an unwritten page but the blankness too that the limiting words available to us leave between each other. His poetry is an endeavour to express the inexpressible. It is also, we have seen, an attempt to achieve the impossible in that there is in it a heroic determination to change the world, to annul what is given in order to create the world anew and to render invisible all that is visible, visible all that is invisible.

A final image of his quest is the mirror. Mirrors of course remind us of what is given. We look at ourselves in them, and we see our relentless body repeated with brutal faithfulness. During a bad moment in his questing journey through the woman in 'Piedra de sol', Paz complains that he is in a 'corridor of mirrors that repeat / the eyes of the thirsty man' ('pasadizo de espejos que repiten / los ojos del sediento').[45] Instead of seeing himself anew in the woman, he is seeing his old, all too familiar *thirsting* self. In 'Discor', there is an

> Espejo llagado y llaga perpetua
> Cuarto lleno de ojos
> Multiplicación de cuerpos
> Cuarto lleno de rostros y labios y nombres
> Fornicación espectral de los espejos.[46]

[44] p. 161.                                [45] *Libertad*, p. 299.
[46] *Salamandra*, p. 96. 'Wounded mirror, perpetual wound / Room full of eyes / Multiplication of bodies / Room full of faces and lips and names / Spectral fornication of mirrors.'

The mirror is not only a brutal, wounding reminder of what is given, worse, it turns the fornicating bodies into spectres: it reminds them that they are all too real while rendering them unreal or insubstantial. It is bad enough that mirrors should remind us that we cannot escape our bodies; it is simply intolerable that they should also make them seem spectral, although even when they do so the bodies *still* remain inescapable. Yet at the end of the poem, the mirrors are triumphantly 'abolished in a fixed present' ('abolidos en un fijo presente').[47]

If he keeps his eyes open, the poet will only witness the given world, he will not escape from it. The visible will remain all too visible, and the invisible will remain invisible. The answer therefore is to close his eyes. Only then will he see not his given familiar self but his renewed, other one. Only then will he escape the brutal reminders of the mirror in order to confront another secret mirror in the woman's body, that 'land of closed eyes' ('país de ojos cerrados')[48] where suddenly it is his newly created other self that is reflected:

| | |
|---|---|
| me miro en lo que miro | *es mi creación esto que veo* |
| como entrar por mis ojos | *la percepción es concepción* |
| en un ojo más limpido | *agua de pensamientos* |
| me mira lo que miro | *soy la creación de lo que veo.*[49] |

He sees himself in what he sees (a mirror) but it is no longer 'the eyes of the thirsty man' that he sees there but rather his newly created self: 'it is my creation I see'. The poet is recreated by the poet, and the poet is both creator and creature. This new creature is reflected in a secret mirror that inhabits the woman's body. What is this secret mirror? It is the *poem*, which Paz has created in order to create himself. The poem is triumphantly a mirror image not of his old self, but of his new one. He has travelled through his ordinary eyes that can see only the given world or that can see only his given body in some ordinary, conventional mirror and he has crossed over to 'another more limpid eye' which in the very act of perceiving *conceives*. This eye, the eye of

[47] p. 98.
[48] *Ladera*, p. 144.
[49] p. 154. 'I see myself in what I see / *It is my creation I see* / like entering through my eyes *perception is conception* / into another more limpid eye *water of thoughts* / what I see sees me *I am the creation of what I see.*'

the creative *poet*, is not there merely to perceive and mirror the given world. The moment it is brought to bear upon the world it transforms it, creates or conceives a new one, and it conceives the new or other self of the poet. What this eye sees is the poet newly conceived, the poet embodied in the poem, which in turn is the creator of the poet ('I am the creation of what I see').

The task of the poet therefore is to turn perception into conception. A poem must be creative, not descriptive. But what it must set out to create is not just some gratuitous fantasy. It is nothing less than the poet himself. To write a poem is to create one's identity, to father oneself, one's real, liberated self—not the one that was fathered by another. If a poem is to be a mirror, it must be a mirror not of the given world but rather the secret mirror of a secret, invisible world which it must render visible. If that secret world can only make its appearance in momentary and passing *instantes*, and if it must vanish into blankness as often as it appears, no matter. The poet must heroically attempt to capture it, to 'fijar vértigos',[50] even if, deep down, he is aware, with Bataille that 'All that is left for us ... is to write commentaries / senselessly / on the senselessness of writing':

> No nos queda dijo Bataille
> Sino escribir comentarios
>     Insensatos
> Sobre la ausencia de sentido del escribir.[51]

And in the end the instant magic of the poem must surrender to the blankness of the space that follows it.

[50] p. 90.                          [51] p. 91.

# 6
# The Regionalist Novel

---

THE poetry that Vallejo, Neruda, and even the as yet youthful Paz were writing in the 1920s and 1930s was wholly comparable in skill and interest to contemporary European poetry. The Latin American novel, however, took longer to mature. The novels of the twenties and thirties are afflicted by certain fundamental limitations. Yet it is worth examining them simply because their failure was an interesting one, and because they constitute the context in which some of the more sophisticated novelists of the past three decades started writing.

It has often been argued that the First World War led Latin American intellectuals to become disenchanted with Europe. The birth of the 'regionalist' novel, which sought to investigate the neglected interiors of its authors' various countries, is often supposed to have resulted directly from this disenchantment: Latin American novelists supposedly began to turn their attention to their own countries when they decided that Europe was too decadent to teach them anything more. But regionalist novels had been written in Latin America long before the First World War. In Peru, for instance, literary nationalism had already begun to flourish in the 1880s, under the inspiration of a man who was also, paradoxically, a *modernista* poet—Manuel González Prada (1848–1918). *Aves sin nido* ('Birds without nest'), a novel by one Clorinda Matto de Turner (1854–1909) which was published in Peru in 1889, contains most of the ingredients of that variety of regionalist fiction that predominated in Peru, Bolivia, and Ecuador—*indigenismo,* a movement that sought specifically to investigate the problem of the Indians of the interior. Moreover, if Latin American intellectuals were affected by disenchantment with Europe in 1918 it was probably because they were influenced by many European intellectuals' own disenchantment with their own traditions. Nativism flourished conspicuously in Europe in the 1920s, and many Latin American 'novels of the earth' seem to have been written at the direct bidding of their authors' European friends. In general it is hard not to suspect that the myth of the vital, tellurian native which is to be deployed so insistently in the novels of say Asturias, Güiraldes, and Ciro Alegría—and indeed in Neruda's *Canto general*—is not more European than Latin American. Its roots are in Rousseau, and its resuscitation was to a large extent encouraged by the visits to Latin America of such European intellectuals as Count Keyserling, who proclaimed the splendour of Latin America's 'mineraloid being'. The myth of indigenous vitality was of course central to D. H. Lawrence's *The Plumed Serpent*.

There are different kinds of regionalist novel. The problems at issue differed from country to country. In the Brazilian regionalist novels of Jose Lins do Rego, Graciliano Ramos, and Jorge Amado, they usually concerned the depressed sugar-plantations of north-east Brazil; in Peru, Bolivia, and Ecuador, the marginalized Indian of the sierra; in Colombia and Venezuela, the virgin jungle, the abuses of rubber exploitation or the vicissitudes of the cattle-raising *llano*. There were ideological differences too, most, of the Brazilians and some of the *indigenistas* being militantly radical whereas the Venezuelan novelist Rómulo Gallegos was a middle-class liberal, and the Argentinian novelist Ricardo Güiraldes was an aristocrat whose principal work, *Don Segundo Sombra* (1926), deployed a conspicuously conservative ideology.

They had one thing in common, however: whatever the nature of the area they were exploring, the point about it was its very marginality, its marginality in particular with respect to the capital cities where the bulk of the literate population lived. The novelists aimed heroically to incorporate the interior regions into the national consciousness—but their endeavour was doomed to failure.

For one the interior was often marginal to the novelists' own experience. Lins do Rego was indeed brought up—and exploited —on a sugar plantation, but he was an exception. The regionalist novel was usually about 'them', not 'us'. An unbridgeable gap separates the authors from their material. As a result, regionalist novels are rarely authentic or convincing, and they rarely get below the surface of the problems they are exploring. All too often they are just superficially exotic, full of standard set-pieces about quaint marriage ceremonies and burial practices and colourful clothes, of lengthy lessons on how to brew *mate*, how to break in horses, or how to stage a cock-fight. For an equivalent one would have to imagine an English novel that lengthily set about explaining the rules of cricket, or one that we could consult if we needed to find out how to make a cup of tea. The distance separating the authors from their material can be discerned too in the language in which the novels were written. When 'they' speak— the Indians or gauchos or rubber-tappers—it is in an outlandish dialect. Yet the author's own narrative is cultured and 'beautiful' —sonorous, poetic, full of long, contrived periods. In short the regionalist novel is all too often a patronizing attempt on the part of a usually urban author to present alien, exotic material to an urban market—the regionalist novels' subjects were after all predominantly illiterate (or worse, *quechua*-speaking), so that the novels could not have been intended for them. The regionalist novel is informative about alien cultures but it does not express them.

Another shortcoming of the regionalist novel was that it did not outgrow the didacticism we discerned in the fiction of the nineteenth century. The regionalist novel deploys rigid dichotomies: rapacious landowners are contrasted to gentle Indians, lascivious politicians to innocent country virgins. The rich are Satanic tramplers of a tellurian Eden. There are exceptions: Jorge Icaza's Ecuadorean Indians in *Huasipungo* (1934) are not idyllic. They are in fact brutal, though it is the system that has made them so. The brutality itself however is exaggerated, as indeed are most things in these novels. The civilization/barbarism dichotomy that was inaugurated nearly a century before by Sarmiento is central to the work of Gallegos. His best novel, *Doña Bárbara* (1929), describes the 'civilized' attempts of one Santos Luzardo to overthrow the 'barbarism' that the tendentiously named eponymous heroine has implanted on the cattle-raising *llano*. 'Civilization' means law and order; barbarism means anarchy and the violence of the strongest. Yet underlying the rigid dichotomy there is a whole range of implications and

assumptions that Gallegos never explores. A novelist more attentive to the complexities of the issue might have acknowledged
that the barbaric Doña Bárbara had many points in her favour.
Gallegos is blissfully innocent of the unedifying fact that when
you come to think of it Santos Luzardo is a Caracas oligarch
attempting to reassert his rights over a property his family has
long not bothered to administer, and which has been overrun by
an impudent mulatta upstart. Civilization comes to be a synonym
of the right to property. It is a synonym of upper-class manners
too, as it was for Sarmiento: a considerable portion of the novel
is concerned with Santos Luzardo's attempts to educate Doña
Bárbara's daughter Marisela, and it is remarkably important for
him that she should drop the plebeian vocabulary she has learnt
on the *llano*, and adopt the speech and manners of 'the exquisite
young ladies of Caracas'.

Oddly enough a genuine artistic impulse often asserts itself in
Gallegos's work. Santos Luzardo for instance is often on the point
of succumbing to 'barbarism' himself, and the novel has an
internal logic that irresistibly suggests that he will only be able
to stamp out 'barbarism' with barbaric methods, that you can
only implant law and order with illegal violence. But alas the
didact then takes over from the novelist, and a complex, interesting dilemma is wilfully shirked. 'Civilization' *must* win, and
it must win in a civilized fashion. So Doña Bárbara is miraculously converted to saintliness. An optimistic solution is thus
artificially superimposed on the internal logic of the narrative.
The trouble is that Gallegos, and the regionalist novelists in
general, were too much concerned to teach, and too frightened
perhaps merely to show their material forth—too frightened
because often the truth of the matter might have undermined
their tendentious distortion of it. The demands of their didacticism led them to stifle their genuine artistic impulses.

Good novels are successful precisely because they show things
as they are, not as their authors would want them to be. And
novels that show things as they are are potentially far more subversive, far more politically effective than didactic ones. Governments after all—and tyrannical ones in particular—always attempt
to impose a simplified, didactic, monolithic version of reality. It is
enough for a novelist to present a genuinely complex one for the
official version to look silly, limited. But if a novelist insists on

presenting yet another simplified version, albeit an alternative one, it will not constitute a lasting threat. For there will always be a more complex reality there to overthrow it, too, in the end. One of the main reasons why Latin American novels have in the past thirty years or so far surpassed their regional predecessors is that they have not shirked the complexities of the issues before them.

# 7

# Latin American Fiction from 1940

MANY confusing assertions have been made about what exactly is 'new' in the so-called Latin American 'new novel'. The most irritating is the claim that the 'new novel' is urban, whereas its predecessor was rural. This is doubly untrue. The first Spanish American novel ever written, *El Periquillo Sarniento* (1816), was, after all, an urban novel, as were most of the best novels written in the nineteenth century. Moreover many of the new novels are in fact rural like their immediate regionalist predecessors. Rural topics predominate in the works of João Guimarães Rosa, José María Arguedas (1911–1970), Juan Rulfo (1918–   ), and Gabriel García Márquez (1928–   ). Other novelists such as Alejo Carpentier (1904–   ) and Mario Vargas Llosa (1936–   ) have written both urban and rural novels. Another claim is that the new novel has abandoned the regionalists' obsession with the struggle between man and a hostile nature. Yet this theme is conspicuously present in García Márquez's *Cien años de soledad*, in Guimarães Rosa's *O grande sertão: veredas*, in Carpentier's *Los pasos perdidos*, in Mario Vargas Llosa's *La Casa Verde*, and in many other novels as it could not fail to be: the terrain of Latin America remains—and may well always remain—hostile. But there are many less fanciful reasons why the new novel is indeed 'new'.

The 'new novel' is above all wholly free of didacticism. It has deliberately overthrown the rigid dichotomies of the regionalists. Thus Guimarães Rosa's *O grande sertão: veredas* (1956) is a description of the violent life of the vast highland desert of Minas Gerais—the Brazilian *sertão*—that is not at all belied by a

88     MODERN LATIN AMERICAN LITERATURE

determination to 'civilize' it at all costs. The *sertão* bandits are presented as they are—in all their amorality. The people of the *sertão* are ultimately like the cassava plant: 'the same construct of leaves and branches ... yields the sweet cassava, the one you eat, and the wild cassava that kills.' Sometimes, the sweet cassava turns sour, poisonous. Other times, the killer cassava turns sweet. There is good and evil in all men—the world is not neatly divided between those that are unremittingly vicious and those that are uncorruptibly gentle.

On the whole, contemporary Latin American novelists do not write about subjects that are alien to them. There is no spectacular gap separating the writer from his material. They have jettisoned the cult of the exotic, although no doubt some of their work will seem exotic to Englishmen, for example, whose immediate surroundings are not tropical. There is moreover no spectacular difference between the language of the author and the language of his characters.

Latin American writers are no longer aiming to *document* an alien environment. This is not only because they have become sensitive to the potential inauthenticity of such an enterprise. There is too a general feeling among them that documentation had best be left to anthropologists, sociologists, historians, and journalists, who are anyway far better qualified to undertake it. Latin American writers have become aware rather that the writing of a novel is a *creative* activity. We shall see how prominent this belief is in the novelists we investigate in detail.

If a novel is a fictive construct, a creation, and not a mirror that meticulously reflects reality, it follows that there is not much point in measuring up the events it depicts against real known facts. Contemporary Latin American novelists have allowed themselves therefore to unleash their imaginations, and sheer fantasy is a prominent ingredient of contemporary Latin American fiction. One can conjecture many explanations for its prominence, and I shall offer some in my chapter on García Márquez, its most masterful exponent.

Fantasy takes many forms in contemporary Latin American novels. Sometimes it constitutes a sheer wish-fulfilling *escape* from a rather grim attendant reality. Fantasy can help a character escape from a Spanish prison for instance (and all that that signifies). Thus in *El mundo alucinante* (1969) by the Cuban novelist Reinaldo Arenas[1] a Mexican friar, Servando Teresa de Mier, is firmly enchained to the floor of a Spanish inquisitorial cell. One day the sheer weight of his chains brings down the entire building. Still clasped to a great 'iron mass' of chains, the friar then rolls over Madrid, which he triumphantly razes to the ground, and past Cadiz harbour into the Atlantic Ocean—all in a flash—in time to witness Nelson's dying words at Trafalgar. Fantasy has served admirably to turn his chains against their makers! For some writers—and often for Arenas—fantasy is merely an excuse to indulge in a comic surrealist romp, the humour and the fantasy serving as therapeutic exercises in liberation from a given environment. Other times fantasy is almost imperceptibly brought to bear upon a perfectly normal situation in order to shake the reader's complacency, to shake our complacent belief that the world necessarily is as we think it is. *What if* we suddenly started vomiting up fluffy, throbbing little rabbits, as a character does in a story by Julio Cortázar? *What if* we suddenly found ourselves in the clutches of omnipotent seals—the dilemma of a character in a story by Adolfo Bioy Casares?

Latin American novelists very often seek to create a reality that is quite deliberately *alternative* to the one they are living in. The lesson is not missed that although the new creation may well be fictive, the society it is aiming to replace is fictive too—it is the mendacious invention of politicians, generals, and oligarchs. Much contemporary Latin American fiction is indeed engaged in an attempt to expose authoritarian lies, to seek out the truth concealed by them. We shall see how the concern to reveal the scandalous truth behind the mask of society is central to the novels of Mario Vargas Llosa.

Most Latin American novelists are in some way dissatisfied with their respective societies. The most extreme case of dissatisfaction is that of Julio Cortázar (1914–    ). His rejection of the *status quo* is indeed ontological, not social. He is quite simply tired of being *homo sapiens*. His somewhat mystical quest is similar to that of Octavio Paz. The language that defines it is even similar. In such novels as *Los premios* (1960), *Rayuela* (1963), and *62, modelo para armar* (1969) Cortázar's characters search for *open doors* which will lead them, if only for an *instant* but preferably for ever, to the *other side*. There is alas an alienating modishness

[1] Translated into English as *Hallucinations*, London, 1971.

in Cortázar's novels, a dogged determination to impress us with the vast range of his reading for instance which does not afflict Octavio Paz. Yet his work is redeemed by the sheer anarchic humour that is often deployed in it. If ever, as readers, we come near to glimpsing the 'other side', it is when Cortázar is content to be just liberatingly funny, when he chooses to forget to spell the nature of his quest portentously out.

Cortázar's quest ends in failure. His characters never reach the 'other side'. At best they glimpse it. Most contemporary Latin American writing is indeed about failure of some kind or another, failure to materialize a glimpsed ideal. Thus the novels of Carlos Fuentes—notably *Las buenas conciencias* (1959) and *La muerte de Artemio Cruz* (1962)—are populated with Mexicans who, having longed to put their youthful ideals into practice, and having hectically rejected the corruption of their elders, end up mimicking it, themselves corrupt and defeated. We shall see how Vargas Llosa's characters too betray their youthful ideals, or simply capitulate to a demanding and immutable *status quo* that ultimately saps their energy.

Failure takes many other forms. Many Latin American novels manifest the feeling that Latin American history in general has failed because there has been no *progress*. Latin American history is full of *events*, but they have led nowhere. The grimmest exposure of this condition can be found in a book that is not specifically about Latin America at all, although it could well have been and some of it is set in Cuba—Alejo Carpentier's *El siglo de las luces* (1962). In this novel we are presented with the full *cycle* of the French Revolution: from monarchy to Jacobinism to Bonapartism back to monarchy. In a crucial scene the hero, Esteban, becomes so disenchanted with the political vicissitudes he has witnessed that he strides off to a forest in order to climb a tree, an activity he despairingly concludes to be more real, because it is archetypal, than the historical ones that he has up to now indulged in. In the end, Carpentier seems to be rejecting history in favour of an anthropological vision of man for only archetypal actions seem to have any lasting meaning for him. In the end, there is no history, for man does not basically change.

A cyclical vision of historical events certainly characterizes a great deal of contemporary Latin American writing. We shall see how basic it is to the works of Borges, Vargas Llosa, and García

Márquez. We saw how a cyclical vision was basic to such a poem of Octavio Paz's as 'Piedra de sol'. And indeed Paz's work constitutes a consistent quest for the sort of a-historical, archetypal experience Esteban has when he climbs the tree.

In contemporary Latin American fiction the characters always fail even to communicate with one another. Thus in the novels of Bioy Casares each character is presented as a wholly separate *island*. Sheer conversation between one character and another is like an adventure across a stormy channel, a risky crossing between islands. Standing on one's own island, one can moreover only perceive a fragment of the other island's coastline. Who knows, maybe it is concealing an entire continent? The *other* is ultimately an inscrutable mystery.

Bioy Casares extracts a great deal of fun out of his characters' failure to communicate. His novels and short stories are fundamentally comic, the comedy being based on the vast gap that separates what a character imagines his interlocutor to be from the fact of what he really is. Thus in stories like 'El don supremo' and 'Confidencias de un lobo'[2] the heroes are convinced they have achieved a spectacular success with the girls they respectively encounter only to discover that their motives were notoriously less flattering than they imagined them to be. Even more hair-raising is the dilemma of the narrator of *La invención de Morel* (1940), who falls in love with a woman without suspecting that she is living on a different plane of reality from him altogether: she turns out to be a sort of holographic image, a three-dimensional, living photograph of her now long-deceased original self.

We shall see that the failure to communicate is most prominent in the novels of Vargas Llosa and Cabrera Infante, and even more so in a novel whose very title proclaims it—García Márquez's *Cien años de soledad*.

Two final distinguishing features of the new novel are its preoccupation with formal presentation and its attention to language. Carlos Fuentes has asserted that a Latin American novelist must at once be a Balzac and a Butor. Latin American novelists have indeed incorporated the technical innovations of European and American fiction with cavalier eclecticism. Unlike the *modernistas*, they rarely indulge in innovatory imitation for its own sake. One always gets the feeling that the form of their novel has been

[2] *El gran serafín*, Buenos Aires, 1967.

urgently dictated by the demands of their subject-matter. But the formal presentation is always an essential ingredient of the undertaking. We shall see for instance how in *Conversación en la Catedral* (1969) by Mario Vargas Llosa the very structure of the novel is so eloquent and so expressive of the novel's themes that it ultimately functions as a sort of non-verbal language.

The structural experiments of contemporary Latin American novels often impose a difficult task upon the reader. Indeed the structural peculiarities of such a novel as Cortázar's *Rayuela* seem to be designed with the express purpose of straining the reader's patience. You can read *Rayuela* in two ways: either conventionally, or in a shuffled order, starting, according to the author's directives, with chapter 73, then going back to chapters 1 and 2, then turning to chapter 116, and so on. The second, alternative method thus undermines all those readers who frequently glance up at the page number to see how swiftly they have progressed, plunging them instead into a labyrinth. The second reading has other purposes of course (it is a deliberate aggression on linearity, and it incorporates hitherto 'expendable' chapters which, in Proustian fashion, open out a new perspective on the events described) but the fact that it wilfully makes difficult demands upon the reader is significant. It is symptomatic of one vast difference between contemporary Latin American fiction and its regionalist predecessors. For gone are the days when the reader was treated like an incompetent simpleton for whom the aim of a novel had to be spelt out on every page. The new novelists rather trust the reader's intelligence and invite his active participation. He must disentangle the novel's complexities as strenuously as the characters have to. Many contemporary Latin American novels are indeed examples of what the French engagingly call *le roman puzzle*. Life is puzzling, so why should not a novel be?

It is a truism that novels are inseparable from the words in which they are written. Like Vallejo and Paz, contemporary Latin American novelists have aimed to find their way to an authentic language in which to write. Like the Brazilian *modernistas*, they have sought to bridge the gap between spoken and written language, and to write a Spanish or a Portuguese that tells the truth, not one that masks it with literary prettiness. Yet language is treacherous—it always masks something, and it can never express even the simplest percept faithfully. Latin American writers are therefore frequently attentive to the treachery of language—none more so than Borges and Cabrera Infante, as we shall see.

Some writers have simply decided to feast on that very treachery. Thus in the novels of the Cuban writer Severo Sarduy the word aggressively takes over: action is dictated by phonetic association, and in general by the internal logic of language.

The following four chapters aim to study in detail four contemporary Latin American writers of fiction. They are very different from each other, and I hope my discussions of them will reveal that ultimately one cannot in fact generalize about the so-called 'new novel'.

# 8
## Jorge Luis Borges (Argentina, 1899–   )

In Latin America, and especially in Argentina, Borges is usually either revered or detested. For the apostles of committed literature he is an irrelevant, reactionary aesthete. For others, he is the stylistic genius who has taught a whole generation of Latin American novelists to write Spanish, and he is above all the man who has restored the imagination to its proper place in Latin American literature, by liberating fiction from the duty to document 'reality'. Yet whether revered or detested, Borges is someone no Latin American writer can easily escape. He is a monumental point of reference for every Latin American novelist, even for those who write in reaction to him, and he fulfils therefore a role in prose fiction similar to that of Vallejo and Neruda in poetry.

How can one account for this formidable position? There is perhaps no writer more difficult to write about than Borges. He has been an amateur philosopher all his life and his work is full of *ideas*. Yet to abstract those ideas from his work is to reduce it to a string of perhaps not very startling propositions about the human condition. All too often when reading books on Borges one begins to wonder what all the fuss is about, and to feel that Borges might have done better to leave, say, time and identity to the experts. Yet if one then returns to his actual writing, the spell is reborn.

Not long ago Borges wrote, with his friend Bioy Casares, a satirical account of a critic who set himself the task of describing the *Divine Comedy*. 'On 23 February 1931, it occurred to him that for it to be perfect, the description of the poem would have to coincide word for word with the poem. ... On mature reflection

he eliminated the preface, the footnotes, the index, and the name
and address of the publisher, and handed Dante's poem to the
printers.'[1] Problems of space and copyright do not permit me to
do the same with Borges's work. Yet there is no writer in Latin
America for whom criticism is a poorer substitute for the text
than it is in his case. Alas, it is necessary to attempt it.

The most recurring concern of Borges's work is to reveal the
gap that separates our intellectual aspirations from our intellectual
limitations. In most of his stories, he presents us with the spectacle
of men who set out to 'decipher the universe', only to discover
that they cannot even decipher an infinitesimal fragment of it,
not even that which constitutes their own person. Sometimes,
maybe they think they have found the answer. If they do, they are
ultimately all the more comically pathetic. The metaphysical
systems they doggely conceive are in the end arbitrary. An irreducible universe intimidatingly reasserts itself.

Borges's work abounds in emotive descriptions of that moment
of reassertion and its consequent defeat of the intellectual quest.
Thus, the Arab scholar Averroes: 'The fear of the crassly infinite,
of mere space, of mere matter touched Averroes for an instant.
He looked at the symmetrical garden; he felt aged, useless, unreal.'[2]
Paradoxically, the role of metaphysics turns out to be the opposite
of what it set out to be. Rather than explain the universe, metaphysics shows it up to be inexplicable, serves in the end rather to
shake our initial complacent belief in a possible solution. The
more we speculate, the more perplexed we become, and we can
only conclude with 'that lucid perplexity which is metaphysics'
only claim to fame, its remuneration and its source'; for metaphysics is the 'art of being puzzled'.[3]

A healthy, lively scepticism has always pervaded Borges's work.
It is a scepticism that was probably originally inherited from his
father, whom Borges has described as a 'philosophical anarchist':
'Once he told me that I should take a good look at soldiers,
uniforms, barracks, flags, churches, priests, and butcher shops,
since all these things were about to disappear, and I could tell

[1] *Crónicas de Bustos Domecq*, with Adolfo Bioy Casares, Buenos Aires, 1967,
p. 61.

[2] *El Aleph*, Buenos Aires, 1957, p. 96.

[3] *Historia de la eternidad*, Buenos Aires, 1953, p. 65.

my children I had actually seen them. The prophecy has not yet come true, unfortunately.'[4] There has always been a sceptical, almost Voltairean streak in Borges with regard, for instance, to Christianity. Take this lapidary assault on the Trinity, from an early essay, 'Historia de la eternidad' (1936):

Imagined at a stroke, its conception of a father, a son, and a phantasm, articulated in on single organism, seems like a case of intellectual teratology, a deformation which only a horrific nightmare could have yielded. Hell is mere physical violence, but the three inextricable persons are a horror of the intellect, an infinity as stifled and specious as that of mutually reflecting mirrors.[5]

He is no less devastating on Platonic archetypes. 'Of those conveniences of the intellect I can no longer offer an opinion: I suspect that no man will be able to intuit them without the assistance of death, fever, or madness.'[6] Ultimately, no hypothesis about the afterlife can be tested without a visit to it. Yet it is paradoxically our very limitations which are the principle source of our yearning to surpass them, while remaining the obstacle that prevents us from doing so. 'The truth is that successive time is an intolerable misery and that men of magnanimous appetite covet every minute of time and the entire variety of space.'[7] It is characteristic of Borges that he should entitle the essay in which he presents these thoughts the '*History* of eternity'—one is reminded of another, later essay called 'A *new* refutation of time'.[8] To posit eternity or to refute time is merely to re-enact the same 'weary hope' that man has always entertained throughout history, in time.

How do these propositions manifest themselves in the stories? One of Borges's favourite expedients to symbolize or re-enact the problem of the limitations of knowledge is to present us with a detective with a limited command over the limited evidence at his disposal. The best example is the story called 'La muerte y la brújula' ('Death and the compass'). A close look at that story will, I hope, reveal many of Borges's concerns and techniques.

The bare outline of the plot is as follows. Two detectives, Lönn-

---

[4] *The Aleph and Other Stories*, New York and London, 1970, p. 206.
[5] *Historia de la eternidad*, p. 25.
[6] p. 20.        [7] p. 35.
[8] In *Otras inquisiciones*, Buenos Aires, 1960. First published separately in 1949.

rot and Treviranus, are called to investigate the murder or Dr. Marcelo Yarmolinsky, the delegate from Podolsk to a Third Talmudic Congress that is to be held in the unnamed city in which the story is set. They find, in the hotel room where Yarmolinsky has been killed, the following inconclusive sentence written on a sheet of paper on his typewriter: 'The first letter of the name has been uttered.'[9] Treviranus suggests that the murderer has mistaken Yarmolinsky's room for that of the Tetrarch of Galilee across the corridor: the Tetrarch owns the most famous sapphires in the world. Lönnrot insists there is a less mundane, more 'rabbinical' explanation, and he gathers up the books on Yarmolinsky's bookshelves, most of them on Jewish mysticism, in order to look for clues.

A further two crimes occur which seem to bear out Lönnrot's conclusion that the murders are connected with a search for the secret name of God, the Tetragrammaton, for again the criminal has left messages to the effect that in turn 'the second' and then 'the last' letter of the name have been uttered. The three crimes have been committed moreover at points equidistant from each other which when joined form a perfect equilateral triangle, and they have been committed on the third of each of three successive months. Everything suggests both a mystical motive and that the series has been completed in the form of a 'mystical' triangle that is equilateral both in time and in space.

Yet Lönnrot encounters an underlined passage in a book (Leusden's *Philologus Hebraeocgraecus*, 1739) found on the scene of the third crime, to the effect that '*the Jewish day begins at sundown and ends the following sundown.*'[10] According to the Jewish calendar the crimes have therefore been perpetrated on the *fourth* of each month. A compass helps him find the point where he surmises that the *fourth* and last crime will take place. The sacred figure drawn by the assassin must be a rhombus, not a triangle. The ineffable Tetragrammaton is, after all, a *four*-letter word. Lönnrot visits the scene of the fourth crime the day before it is to be committed, in order to savour his imminent victory over the simple-minded Treviranus, in order to gloat on the assassin's

[9] *Ficciones*, Buenos Aires, 1956, p. 146. All quotations here are from the translation by N. T. di Giovanni in collaboration with the author in *The Aleph and Other Stories*, New York and London, 1970, pp. 65–78.

[10] *Ficciones*, p. 150.

impending apprehension. The assassin, alas, is there waiting for him: Lönnrot himself is the intended fourth victim. The assassin, Red Scharlach, a notorious bandit from the Southside who has never been able to forgive Lönnrot the imprisonment of his brother, has invented the whole series in order to trap him. The first crime was indeed a mistake as Treviranus had maintained. Scharlach got the idea for the rest of the series when he read that Lönnrot was seeking a 'rabbinical' explanation. In the second crime he killed two birds with one stone: he further stimulated Lönnrot's erudite intellect while usefully disposing of the subordinate who failed to acquire the Tetrarch's jewels. The third crime was a put-up job—the 'corpse' the assassins rushed out from the tavern where the 'crime' took place was alive and well: Red Scharlach himself, in fact. The simple-minded Treviranus, by the way, had guessed this too, much to Lönnrot's indignation at the time.

From this bare outline it can be seen that 'Death and the compass' can be read as a cautionary tale about the vanity of the intellect. The simple-minded detective, Treviranus, was always much nearer a solution because he was free of intellectual pretensions. It took a *clever* man, Lönnrot, to perceive the clue about the Jewish day, and to think therefore in terms of the rhombus figure. A 'clever' reader might have picked up other clues suggesting a rhombus. On the scene of the second crime, the message about the secret name of God is scrawled 'on the wall, on the shop's conventional red and yellow *diamond* shapes';[11] in their third foray, the 'assassins' are dressed as harlequins with 'costumes of red, green, and yellow *lozenges*'.[12] Red Scharlach plants recondite clues in order to trap Lönnrot. Yet it is only because Lönnrot is *clever* that he perceives them. That is his undoing.

Many of Borges's stories seek to demonstrate the extent to which the quality of an argument rests on the quality of its premiss. A flawless argument may be elaborated in blissful innocence of the fact that the premiss that initiated it was faulty. Lönnrot's argument is flawless, but his original premiss, that the first crime was 'rabbinical' in nature, was a mistaken one.

Another problem encountered by Borges's investigators is the problem of the nature and quality of the evidence investigated. A

[11] p. 147. My italics.                    [12] p. 149. My italics.

detective, for instance, in order to solve a crime, must work on the evidence that *happens to come his way*. He may deduce a solution from that evidence, but how can he know that the evidence is complete? How can he be sure that a clue as yet unperceived by him will not come to throw fresh light on the case, and force him to a radical reappraisal of his solution? How, moreover, can he be sure that the clues really signify what they *appear* to signify? How can he be certain that his interpretation of them is correct?

In a story called 'Funes el memorioso' ('Funes the memorious') Borges describes an Uruguayan farm-hand who is incapable of forgetting anything, and who is able to perceive every conceivable detail of his environment:

We, at one glance, can perceive three glasses on a table; Funes, all the leaves and tendrils and fruit that make up a grape vine. He knew by heart the forms of the southern clouds at dawn on 30 April 1882, and could compare them in his memory with the mottled streaks on a book in Spanish binding he had only seen once and with the outlines of the foam raised by an oar in the Rio Negro the night before the Quebracho uprising. ... Two or three times he reconstructed a whole day; he never hesitated but each reconstruction had required a whole day.[13]

In order really to think empirically, in order to make sure that *none* of the evidence on which an argument is based is missing, one must be a Funes. Yet for Funes every detail perceived was so unique that 'Not only was it difficult for him to comprehend that the generic symbol *dog* embraced so many unlike individuals of diverse size and form; it bothered him that the dog at 3.14 (seen from the side) should have the same name as the dog at 3.15 (seen from the front)'.[14] Funes, in short, was not able to think at all. 'To think is to forget differences, generalize, make abstractions. In the teeming world of Funes, there were only details, almost immediate in their presence.'[15]

We are left with an unsurmountable paradox, central to Borges's work and to Lönnrot's dilemma. In order to think proper-

[13] *Ficciones*, p. 123. All quotations are from J. E. Irby's translation in *Labyrinths*, ed. D. A. Yates and J. E. Irby, New York, 1964, and Harmondsworth, 1970 (pp. 87–95 in the Penguin edition).

[14] *Ficciones*, p. 125.

[15] p. 126.

ly, it is necessary to marshal *all* the evidence, for only then will it be certain that a clue is not missing which will throw light on or even contradict the rest. Yet to marshal all the evidence is to become imprisoned by it, to end up by seeing nothing *but* clues. And *what* clues? The tens of thousands of impressions stored in Funes's brain each day are merely the percepts that happen to be available to a man who is confined to an Uruguayan shack, for Funes is, significantly, paralysed and therefore chair-ridden (and very limitingly provincial). His world of innumerable fragments is therefore itself but an infinitesimal fragment of the universe. And even if Lönnrot were a Funes, he would be no better off. For as in the case of any investigator, it is not sufficient that he should merely perceive with competence what is given. There is always something (an invisible criminal for instance) beyond his field of vision, beyond his immediate grasp. The problem is therefore not only one of how much he can afford to 'forget' of what is before him but also one of how much relevant evidence is wholly unsuspected by him and outside his field of vision.

Lönnrot's field of vision is not only limited topographically, but also mentally, because he brings to bear notorious *a priori* assumptions on the evidence. 'Here's a dead rabbi', he declares. 'I'd much prefer a purely rabbinical explanation, not the imagined mistakes of an imagined jewel thief.' Of course, we don't all limit our fields of reference so brutally. We don't all look at evidence through a spectrum of rabbinical assumptions, although no doubt we all have assumptions of our own, albeit less recondite ones. Lönnrot's very spectacular assumptions are merely hyperboles of the fact that it is impossible to look at any evidence without some assumption or other.

Lönnrot's solution of the crime then is based on limited evidence, and on an interpretation of that limited evidence that is limited too in view of the interpreter's limited assumptions. The 'pure reasoning' Lönnrot is said to exercise therefore turns out to be a limited and vain enterprise. Worse still, it is not as pure (what reasoning is?) as he imagines it to be, for although 'Lönnrot thought of himself as a pure logician, a kind of Auguste Dupin ... there was also a streak of the adventurer and even of the gambler in him.'[16] The limited game fails not only because it is

[16] p. 143. Ironically, Dupin is of course a detective of Edgar Alan Poe's. A 'pure logician' can exist only in a work of fiction.

limited but also because it can never be played to perfection. But finally Lönnrot's hypothesis collapses as a consequence of its negligence of specific detail, as a consequence of its abstracted formality and resultant innocence of reality. 'He had practically solved the puzzle; the mere circumstances—reality (names, arrests, faces, legal and criminal proceedings)—barely held his interest now'.[17] Those 'mere circumstances' include the fact that Lönnrot's own murder was the whole aim of nearly every action deployed by the criminal!

Such is the nature of Borges's amused critique of pure reason, and of his playful dramatization of the impossibility and vanity of definitive knowledge. For like Lönnrot we can only piece together infinitesimal fragments which in turn we can only interpret through a spectrum of limiting assumptions. Indeed the joke is not only on Lönnrot, it is on all intellectual enterprises, and not least on the reader's attempt to decipher the story. Some readers, unlike Lönnrot, may spot those diamonds and lozenges before Scharlach explains them at the end, and they might imagine themselves at their peril to be cleverer even than Lönnrot. The story is in fact full of traps for the reader in the form of clues that point to the significance of the figure three and the figure four alternately. Yarmolinsky is attending the *Third* Talmudic Congress, and he possesses 'the ageless resignation that had made it possible for him to survive *three* years of war in the Carpathians and *three* thousand years of oppression in the pogroms'.[18] Lönnrot comes upon the passage about the Jewish day in the *thirty-third* dissertation of the *Philologus* (although that passage points to the fourth, not the third day of the month). The supposedly dead Red Scharlach emerges in *trio* with two harlequins from the tavern where the third, spoof crime is committed. At the tavern he had moreover given three false names. Unforgettably, when Lönnrot begins to elaborate his rabbinical hypothesis, *Tre*viranus says 'No hay que buscarle tres pies al gato'[19]—literally 'there's no point in looking for *three* legs on the cat', an eccentric version of a Spanish expression that means something like 'Let's not complicate matters' and which normally states that 'there's no point in looking for *five* legs on a cat' ('No hay que buscarle cinco pies al gato'). Yet cats of course have *four* legs, and four is at present as three in the story: in the lozenges, in the discovery about the Hebrew

[17] p. 152.　　[18] p. 144. My italics.　　[19] p. 144.

day, in the Tetragrammaton, in the Tetrarch of Galilee. It is characteristic of Borges that several of the numerical clues (such as the *Tetr*arch of Galilee) are gratuitously irrelevant to the plot. They are aimed at the reader, not at Lönnrot, forcing the reader to emulate Lönnrot's dangerous intelligence at his peril, turning the reader, too, into a detective.

There is no end to the game of recondite exegesis that Borges invites the reader to play. Like Red Scharlach with Lönnrot, Borges delights in allowing the reader the illusory gratification of his intellectual vanity. Let us then fall headlong into the trap, and investigate two possibilities, one that Red Scharlach is God, and the other that Red Scharlach and Lönnrot are the same person.

The first clue to the possibility that Red Scharlach is intended to stand for God is presented, characteristically, in the form of a joke. The editor of the *Judische Zeitung* comes to interview Lönnrot about the first crime. Yet instead of talking about the crime, Lönnrot, obsessed with the Tetragrammaton, talks to him about the various names of God. 'The following day, in three columns, the journalist stated that Chief Detective Erik Lönnrot had taken up the study of the names of God in order to find out the name of the murderer.'[20] This devastating irony of the journalist at Lönnrot's expense is also an irony of Borges's, for the game that equates Scharlach to God is played throughout the story. For instance, in his final exposition to the captured Lönnrot, Red Scharlach reveals himself to be ominiscient. For how else could he know that Yarmolinsky was suffering from 'insomnia' on the night of his death, and even more remarkably how else could he quote back at Lönnrot remarks made in private by Treviranus, such as that the third crime was no doubt a hoax? More frivolously, at the tavern he gives three *false* names: is his triple identity not a parody of the Trinity?

In Borges's work, God steps in where the intellect breaks down. Where explanations no longer hold water, where man's intellectual quest for them collapses, there is God. Yet 'God' in Borges's stories is often something more active than a mere symbol of intellectual confusion. Let us turn momentarily to Borges's favourite image, the labyrinth. In nearly every story, there are allusions to

[20] p. 144.

labyrinths, and many of the stories describe specific labyrinths. Yet the labyrinth need not be a specifically concrete one—for Borges the universe itself is a labyrinth, as is any intellectual puzzle (such as an enigmatic crime) that a man may attempt to solve. Now Borges has said that he uses the labyrinth rather than any other image to express the bewilderment of man because labyrinths are places that have been constructed artificially and *deliberately* to confuse. The confusion of those that enter it is the labyrinth's sole purpose. Now a good criminal is like a labyrinth-maker. If he plants false clues for the detective it is so as to lead him down false trails—the planting of false clues is a skill that all Borges's criminals possess. Suppose the criminal is God, and there emerges the image of a God who deliberately plants false clues, who deliberately goads man's intellectual vanity into the belief that he is arriving at a solution only to laugh in his face in the end by killing him. For the death that God provides for all men is, like the death that Red Scharlach provides for Lönnrot, the ultimate mockery of all those vain attempts at rational explanation they may have indulged in.

We have seen how fundamentally sceptical Borges is, how grimly he endeavours to demonstrate that nothing is knowable. Yet if nothing is knowable, nothing can be affirmed to be impossible. Borges revels in the description of weird exotic sects, ridiculously limited theologies, arbitrary rituals all in conflict with each other. But he does this not only to show how absurd it is to attempt to reduce the irreducible to any kind of system but also to incite the suspicion that anything is possible. Borges is as superstitious as he is sceptical, and not inconsistently. For if you cannot *know* even that the world exists, or who Borges is, neither can you *know* that, say, the markings on a jaguar's hide are not a secret message from God,[21] or that four simpletons do not unconsciously control the universe in each generation.[22]

A labyrinth-maker constructs his artifice deliberately in order to confuse, yet *he* knows its secret order. Red Scharlach plants his clues deliberately in order to confuse Lönnrot, but *he* knows what he is doing. Similarly, the ultimate labyrinth, the universe, may have been constructed with an aim to confuse its inhabitants by Someone cognizant of its arcane design.

[21] *El Aleph*, 'La escritura del Dios' ('The writing of the God'), p. 117.
[22] 'El hombre en el umbral' ('The man on the threshold'), p. 147.

Among the books found by Lönnrot in Yarmolinsky's room there is one *Vindication of the Cabbala*. It is a typically mischievous joke of Borges's that this is the title of an essay by Borges himself. Yet Borges's interest in cabbalism is not a joke. For if the universe has an arcane design, and if everything is possible because nothing is knowable, it may well be that all things, let alone the Bible, mean something very different from what they appear to mean. Borges can sympathize with Leon Bloy's belief that 'Every man is on earth in order to symbolize something he is ignorant of and to realize a particle of a mountain of the invisible materials that will serve to build the city of God.'[23] He can sympathize, like Bloy, with the words of St. Paul (1 Corinthians 13 : 12): 'Videmus nunc per speculum in aenigmate: tunc autem facie ad faciem.'[24] The visible ingredients of the world are signs pointing to something else, and what they will ultimately signify may be very different from what they appear to signify now. Who knows? Maybe 'the steps a man takes from the day of his birth until that of his death trace in time an inconceivable figure. The Divine Mind intuitively grasps that form immediately, as men do a triangle. This figure (perhaps) has its given function in the economy of the universe.'[25] If everything in the world perhaps signifies something arcanely different from what it appears to signify, then the evidence from which we infer our explanations of the universe might well signify something very different from what we have imagined it to signify. We return therefore to the point that such explanations are impossible not only because the evidence they draw upon is by definition fragmentary but also because the evidence may be of deceptive appearance; thus the deceptive nature of the evidence Red Scharlach plants. There are several other stories by Borges (such as 'Emma Zunz', 'El muerto', or 'Tema del traidor y del heroe') which explore situations where elaborately contrived evidence has been erected from which plausible conclusions can be inferred that turn out however to be wildly off the mark simply because the evidence was deliberately designed to deceive.

It is possible to read 'Death and the compass' therefore as a fable about a man (Lönnrot) who attempts to explain God's (Red

[23] *Otras inquisiciones*, p. 174.
[24] p. 172.
[25] p. 175 (translation by J. E. Irby from *Labyrinths*, p. 247).

Scharlach's) deeds not suspecting that his apparent success is an illusory gratification God (Red Scharlach) has condescended to allow him before invalidating it by killing him, not suspecting that the evidence he has worked from is the make-believe of an elusive conjuror.

Now let us start again and explore another possibility, that Lönnrot and Red Scharlach are the same person. To quote a typically devious commentary by Borges on the story:

> The killer and the slain, whose minds work in the same way, *may* be the same man. Lönnrot is not an unbelievable fool walking into his own death trap but, in a symbolic way, a man committing suicide. This is hinted at by the similarity of their names. The end syllable [*rot*] means red in German, and Red Scharlach is also translatable, in German, as Red Scarlet.[26]

There are of course other clues too. Red Scharlach's 'omniscience' with regard to the remark made by Treviranus to Lönnrot could be explained by the fact that he 'is' Lönnrot. Their intricate minds do certainly work in the same way. Indeed their ideas sometimes coincide even in the detail of their expression.

Now the victim and the killer are the same person in the first place because for Borges all men are somehow the same person. For Borges the history of the world is potentially contained in one day in the life of any one man. A man who hates is all men who have hated; a man who loves is all men who have loved; a man who kills or dies is all men who have killed or died. Nowhere is this sense that nothing fundamental changes, that everything repeats itself, better expressed than in a short prose-poem' 'La trama' ('The plot'), collected in Borges's book *El hacedor* ('The maker') and in his *Personal Anthology*:

> To make his horror complete, Caesar, pursued to the base of a statue by the relentless daggers of his friends, discovers among the faces and blades the face of Marcus Junius Brutus, his favourite, his son perhaps, and he ceases to defend himself to exclaim; '*You too, my son!*' Shakespeare and Quevedo echo the pathetic cry.
>
> Fate takes pleasure in repetitions, variants, symmetries. Nineteen centuries later, in the south of Buenos Aires province, a gaucho is assaulted by other gauchos, and, as he falls, recognizes a godson and with gentle reproach and gradual surprise exclaims (these words must

[26] *The Aleph and Other Stories*, p. 269.

be heard, not read): 'But *che*!' He is killed and never knows he dies so that a scene may be re-enacted.[27]

Although Borges does not deny that every infinitesimal instant is unique, and that every incident, however archetypal in its essence, is different—the overtones for instance of the remark 'Pero *che*!' are inexorably if subtly different from those of the remark 'Et tu, Brute!'—the sense that *fundamentally* everything repeats itself has always pervaded his work. It is for instance a central concern of the essays in *Historia de la eternidad*. Thus after rejecting with an ironical display of mind-boggling mathematics Nietzsche's belief in the return of atoms,[28] he approvingly turns to Marcus Aurelius, who

asserts the analogy, not the identity, of the many individual destinies. He asserts that any period of time—a century, a year, a single night, perhaps the ungraspable present—contains the whole of history. In its extreme form, this conjecture is easy to refute: one taste differs from another taste, ten minutes of physical pain are not the equivalent of ten minutes of algebra. Applied to long periods, to the three score and ten years that the Book of Psalms adjudges us, the conjecture is plausible or tolerable. It merely affirms that perceptions, emotions, thoughts, and human vicissitudes are limited in number, and that before dying we shall exhaust them.[29]

That we live only to re-enact the fundamental emotions and perceptions of those that have lived before is both true and horrifying. For one, our freedom of choice is annulled, or narrowed down to a choice of mere trivial detail. Each man's life is moreover a vain repetition of others' lives. For Borges copulation is abominable as mirrors are abominable: both multiply the species and therefore vainly repeat what was already there. Now if one feeling emerges from Lönnrot's final journey to the villa in which he is to be murdered it is that he is doomed, that he is being driven by an irrepressible destiny. This is of course particularly true if we consider the sequence retrospectively (i.e. after we know what was in store for him), but then it is always in the present that our sense of free will exists, whereas events seen in the past

---

[27] *El hacedor*, Buenos Aires, 1960, p. 28. The translation by Elaine Kerrigan, is taken from *A Personal Anthology*, ed. A. Keerigan, London, 1968, p. 15.

[28] *Historia de la eternidad*, pp. 75–6.

[29] pp. 96–7.

generally look altogether more inevitable. He is doomed because he is a man, because the intellectual enterprise of man is doomed and because man is doomed to death. He is all the men who have conducted an intellectual enterprise before, and he is all the men who have failed. Red Scharlach is doomed too, for Lönnrot's death merely prefigures his own. That I think is partly why for Borges murder is somehow suicide, and the killer is his victim. It is Red Scharlach as much as Lönnrot (in so far as they are not the same person and one can distinguish between them) who is committing suicide, for by killing a man he is killing Man, he is killing himself, his mirror image. Lönnrot, incurably intellectual to the end, suggests to Scharlach that in *another incarnation* he employ a simpler labyrinth to hunt him down, that ancient maze of Zeno, the straight line, for 'in your maze there are three lines too many.'[30] The point is not only that Lönnrot is doomed to be incurably intellectual down to the most desperately unpropitious moment but also that Scharlach (man) will be hunting Lönnrot (man) down to the end of time (it is noteworthy that he speaks to Lönnrot with a 'hatred the size of the universe')[31] and that to the end of time Lönnrot's irrepressible intellectual quest will wither down the same labyrinthine path.

Roger Caillois has pointed out that Borges's labyrinths are primarily spatial projections of cyclical time.[32] It is interesting that the angular labyrinth, the rhombus, that Scharlach weaves for Lönnrot culminates in a villa where *circularity* is a prominent feature. Identical 'dusty stairways' lead to identical 'circular ante-rooms'; most important, the staircase leading to the mirador where Scharlach is writing is a spiral one. In the circular ante-rooms he is 'multiplied to infinity in facing mirrors'. This is because he is multiplied by all those men of which he is a mere repetition, who reflect him, and whom he in turn reflects.

Now if there is a temporal reason why Scharlach and Lönnrot may be read as the same man, namely that all men through the ages are because all men through the ages re-enact the same intellectual failure, there is another possible reason. Given that Scharlach may also be read as God, it can be argued that this 'God', this arch-deceiver, this planter of false trails, this frustrater

[30] *Ficciones*, p. 158.
[31] p. 154.
[32] *Cahiers de l'Herne*, Paris, First Quarter, 1964, pp. 211–17.

of the intellect, is merely a sector of the deceived and frustrated intellect itself. Man is his own labyrinth-maker, man is his own labyrinth. The obstacle that impedes the intellect's progress is nothing other than the very intellect itself. And that evidence that Scharlach plants in order that Lönnrot's hypothesis may be substantiated is simply the evidence any thinking mind might plant for itself, in order to substantiate its own *a priori* assumptions. Borges's stories continually attempt to demonstrate the fact that it is possible to marshal evidence to prove or justify anything—thus in 'Deutsches Requiem' he shows how easy it is to justify Nazism, or in the memorable 'Three versions of Judas' how it is possible to substantiate the hypothesis that Judas, not Jesus, was the Saviour. Unwittingly, all men tend to justify their assumptions by finding means to substantiate them, whether they be philosophers, detectives, or ordinary men making everyday decisions. The intellect, in the end, is the intellect's principal deceiver. The God that entices man's vanity into believing he has achieved a solution is merely man's own instinct to wish-fulfilment. The labyrinth in the end is to a large extent the labyrinth of its victim's own mind, a fact that gives further richness to Borges's propensity to describe *mirror*-mazes which dramatize the extent to which man is ultimately incapacitated largely by *himself*.

It is interesting that when Lönnrot reaches his final destination, the villa of Triste-le-Roy,[33] his confidence begins to flag for the first time at the sight of the villa's labyrinthine structure. Yet the labyrinth is to a large extent very much of his own making. In many respects it is a fantasy of his own condition: *'The house is not so large,* he thought. *It is made large by the dim light, the symmetry, the mirrors, the many years, my ignorance, the loneliness.'*[34] It is not only that the labyrinth itself is formidable but also that it is made so by the nature of its victim's perception of it and by the nature of his state of mind: by his ignorance and loneliness and possibly by his age—it is not clear if 'the many years' ('los muchos años') refers to the house or to Lönnrot or, more abstractly, to

---

[33] Note the name, implying failure at the height of power. It is noteworthy too that Lönnrot *climbs* to his death in the *mirador*, and also that it is a *compass* that has led him to his doom. Compasses normally guide men! All these images corroborate the view that for Borges, the higher you climb the harder you fall, intellectually speaking.

[34] *Ficciones*, p. 154. The italics are, significantly, the author's.

that intimidating demon, time. Thus in the same way that it is
Lönnrot's own predispositions as much as Scharlach's deceit that
have led him to the house, so it is his own predispositions as much
as the architect's design that frighten him at the house. Lönnrot,
Scharlach, the architect, and 'God' are all in a way one and the
same, for Lönnrot is in a way his own deceiver and his own labyrinth-maker. In a way of course it is because—who knows?—
there may always be a God who, like Scharlach, quite extraneously
plants clues that mean something different from what they seem
to mean, and who entices the intellect, conceals himself, and keeps
one infinite step ahead.

'Death and the compass' has many supplementary richnesses
that have not yet been explored. Not to forget the obvious it is
of course a good detective story, but it is also a parody of the genre
and a meditation on its implications. Many of the clichés of the
genre are deliberately included: a mysterious telephone call cut
off at the most interesting moment,[35] the lone detective entering
through a creaking gate into a large house which may or may not
be deserted,[36] the genius detective in conflict with a simple-minded
colleague, the revelatory denouement, and so on. Yet one notes
that ultimately the clichés are stood on their head. The 'genius'
detective is wrong, the simple-minded policeman is right: it is as
though Sherlock Holmes or Father Brown, not Scotland Yard, had
made spectacular blunders. I mention Father Brown because
Borges has always been an avid reader of Chesterton, and it is in
particular the Father Brown pattern that is being meditated upon
in this story. In the Father Brown stories, as Borges has pointed
out in his essay 'On Chesterton',[37] an apparently supernatural
crime is always solved by the sober commonsense of the eponymous hero. What appeared to be a fantastic event turns out to
have been a very ordinary one. The same, of course, occurs in
'Death and the compass', but with a very significant difference,
for it is the criminal alone, not the detective, who is aware of the
commonplace truth. In the Father Brown stories, moreover, the
world is presented as an apparent fantasy which however becomes
easily explainable when subjected to the scrutiny of reason. In
'Death and the compass' it is the reasoning mind that turns a

[35] p. 148.
[36] p. 153.
[37] *Otras inquisiciones*, pp. 119–23.

perfectly commonplace event into a recondite fantasy. By presenting the Father Brown pattern in inverted form, Borges is therefore implying a criticism of Chesterton's faith in reason, although one should say that there is another fundamental difference between Father Brown and Lönnrot. Father Brown brings to bear an eclectic commonsense on the fantasy, whereas Lönnrot does not question the fantasy as a premiss from which to argue in a logical vacuum which excludes all other possible premisses.

'Death and the compass' is one of Borges's earlier short stories (it was first published in 1942), yet it is as good an example as any of Borges's methods and ideas. Certainly, there are many others which could have been discussed at similar length for the same purposes of showing how Borges's stories work and what they aim to demonstrate. Borges's ideas do not indeed differ greatly from story to story. The stories differ rather in emphasis, with the result that they fertilize each other. Memories of one story often help to elucidate the more recondite points of another. The fact, for instance, that Scharlach speaks to Lönnrot with a 'hatred the size of the universe' would probably pass unnoticed if we were not aware, from stories like 'El inmortal' ('The immortal'), 'Los teólogos' (The theologians'), or 'Historia del guerrero y de la cautiva' ('Story of the warrior and the captive'), of Borges's interest in archetypes.

Some stories emphasize the *moral* implications of arguing from questionable premisses. Take the Histriones, for instance, a sect described in 'The theologians'. Their main premiss is St. Paul's dictum 'for now we see through a glass darkly', from which they conclude that 'everything we see is false.' The line from Matthew 11 : 12 'the kingdom of heaven suffereth violence' leads them to believe, moreover, that 'the earth influences heaven', and from the *Zohar* they learn that 'the higher world is a reflection of the lower.'[38] Thence:

Perhaps contaminated by the Monotones, they imagined that all men are two men and that the real one is the other, the one in heaven. They also imagined that our acts project an inverted reflection, in such a way that if we are awake, the other sleeps, if we fornicate, the other is chaste, if we steal, the other is generous. When we die, we shall join the other, and be him. ... Other Histriones reasoned that the world

[38] *El Aleph*, pp. 40–1.

would end when the number of its possibilities was exhausted; since there can be no repetitions, the righteous should eliminate (commit) the most infamous acts, so that these will not soil the future and will hasten the coming of the kingdom of Jesus.[39]

Of course not all thinkers argue from premisses as questionable as these and not all are driven to crime as a result of their consequently faulty reasoning. Yet it is not only the Histriones who have committed crimes in the name of some more or less spurious reasoning. Not so long ago priests found it easy to rationalize the burning of their fellow men. In 'Tlön, Uqbar, Orbis Tertius' Borges describes how the existence of an imaginary planet with a rigidly ordered metaphysical system came to be believed in by everyone on earth. Is this surprising, he asks? 'Ten years ago any symmetry with a semblance of order—dialectical materialism, anti-Semitism, Nazism—was sufficient to entrance the minds of men.'[40] So Borges's distrust of the intellect plainly has a moral dimension. One can discern it in many other stories, but nowhere more than in 'Deutsches Requiem', a story which some critics have absurdly thought to show Borges in unwitting sympathy with Nazism. On the contrary, its aim is to demonstrate the ease with which one can justify the most repugnant actions on the most rational grounds. One should be sceptical about the intellect's powers not only because it is vain but also because it is morally dangerous not to be.

Other stories emphasize the extent to which our knowledge and our values—in general, our interpretation of the evidence, as it were—depend on the assumptions of our cultural environment. Here Borges's most frequent technique is to present a first-person narrator (such as the Cretan Minotaur, or a citizen of a 'Babylon' where everyone's life is governed by an arcane lottery system) who makes statements that are alien to us but which the narrator takes for granted. Thus the narrator who turns out to be the Cretan Minotaur in 'La casa de Asterión' makes odd statements like 'Even my detractors admit there is not *one single piece of furniture* in the house.'[41] His assumptions about furniture are clearly different from ours. But the effect is to make us question our own assump-

[39] p. 41 (translation by J. E. Irby from *Labyrinths*, p. 154).
[40] *Ficciones*, p. 33.
[41] *El Aleph*, p. 67.

tions too, and to make them seem just a little bit more gratuitous and relative. Thus the Mlch, a Swiftian tribe described by the Scottish missionary Brodie (who calls them the Yahoos), are exotic indeed in their customs and beliefs. But might we not seem just as exotic to them?

After a fashion, they profess the doctrine of Heaven and Hell. Both are subterranean. In Hell, where it is light and dry, the sick, the old, the abused, the monkey-men, the Arabs, and the leopards are to reside; in Heaven, which they imagine to be swampy and dark, the king, the queen, the wizards, and those who on earth have been happy, hard, and cruel. They likewise worship a god, whose name is Dung, and whom they have probably conceived in the image and likeness of the king; he is mutilated, blind, feeble, and all-powerful.[42]

And then there is their leisure culture: is ours that much less exotic?

The people's entertainment consists in staging cat fights and executions. Someone is accused of having affronted the queen's modesty or of having eaten before the eyes of another; there is no testimony of witnesses and no confession and the king pronounces his sentence. The prisoner suffers torments which I endeavour not to remember and then they stone him. The queen has the right to throw the first stone and the last stone, but the latter is unnecessary. The multitude ponders her skill and the beauty of her parts, and applauds her frantically, showering her with roses and foul things. The queen, without a word, smiles.[43]

From the above passages it will be discerned that Borges is not lacking in sense of humour. Indeed, his stories are usually very funny indeed. Sometimes they are funny on the surface. Stories like 'The Aleph' and 'The Zahir', while being concerned with vaster issues, find time to furnish often hilarious satires of society ladies, second-rate poets, academicians, critics, nationalists, and so on. With Bioy Casares, Borges has indeed produced several books whose principal aim it has been to satirize the more pompous aspects of Argentinian life. The most notable is their *Seis problemas para don Isidro Parodi* (1942), a book in which social satires are woven into the plots of six Chestertonian detective stories.[44] Yet there is a much more fundamental humour in Borges's

---

[42] *El informe de Brodie*, Buenos Aires, 1970, pp. 146–7.

[43] *Brodie*, p. 143.

[44] Much of the humour of these stories resides in the characters' use of language. Modulations in the use of language according to the social class and

own stories which underlies its incidental manifestations. For Borges's stories are comedies of the intellect, of an intellect doomed to trip over a banana skin. As comedies they are particularly effective because, as we have seen, the joke falls heavily on the reader too. But the generally light-hearted tone of the stories at the incidental level makes the reader's reaction to his own tripping up one not of anguish but rather of grateful self-mockery. We can laugh at ourselves reading Borges moreover because Borges laughs so readily at his own self. And we can feel gratitude because the stories continually help to jolt our complacent belief in the order and sense of our environment. Such dispersal of complacency leads not only to confusion, but also to a joy in the fact that the world is a more fabulously mysterious place than we had perceived it to be. Moreover the more metaphysical stories may well attempt to spell the vanity of metaphysics, but in that very vanity there is a kind of splendour. For Borges there is something splendid in the spectacle of men striding out to explain the universe. That they do so is a measure of their spirit, indomitable against overwhelming odds. There may be a contradiction here, in view of what has been said about the moral danger that underlies man's attempt to explain the world. But Borges would not want to deny himself the right to self-contradiction. For, after all, part of the mystery of the world for Borges is that it is sustained on paradox. And the perception of paradox has its own cerebral rewards, its own beauty. Borges's stories entertain one, absorb one as puzzles do, thrill and amaze one, and, one hopes, make one wiser; but they do not make one despair.

Just as metaphysics for Borges is ultimately an absorbing game, a willed suspension of time and place which has little relation to anything but itself, so is literature ultimately a game too, self-regulating and autarchic. Every story by Borges has built into it more or less recondition a reminder of its fictive status. With great subtlety we are reminded that what we are reading is a mere story, a fiction. In the satirical book I mentioned at the start of this chapter which describes how a critic concluded that the

---

emotional disposition of the characters are more visible in the work of Bioy Casares than in Borges's. Indeed it would appear that Bioy Casares, not Borges, was predominantly responsible for this aspect of the work they do together.

*Divine Comedy* was the only possible accurate description of the *Divine Comedy*, there is an account also of a poetry competition for which competitors are invited to submit a poem about a rose. The prize is awarded to one Urbas, a young poet who 'candid and triumphant submitted . . . a rose. There was not a single dissenting vote; words, those artificial daughters of man, could not compete with the spontaneous rose, daughter of God.'[45]

The problem investigated in 'Funes the memorious' is as much a problem of literature as it is one of philosophy, as much a problem of realism as it is one of empiricism. A realist novel aims to describe real things, and to describe them realistically. The aim is a vain one. In the first place, all writers must brutally select their material. No description of a room, for example, in any novel, however realistic, can be real, for if it were the room would have to be described as Funes would see it, and the description would cover many hundreds of pages. The writer would have to emulate another friend of Borges's and Bioy Casares's, Ramón Bonavena, who writes an entire novel about a small section of his desk. Of course, not even Bonavena's novel—not even the novel Funes might write—could ever be truly 'realistic'. For a description of a desk, however meticulous, is not the same thing as a desk. As the narrator of 'The Aleph' discovered a decade or so before Marshall Macluhan, language changes what it describes, for our perception of things is simultaneous, whereas language describes them in succession. Ramón Bonavena can see on his table a copper ash-tray and a pencil in one flash. In order to describe them he must laboriously take them one by one, he must confer upon them a false temporal sequence. And his description of each will anyway be merely a distant approximation, from which each reader will subjectively infer very different objects. Indeed every word in our language, as Funes discovered, is a brutal simplification. How many millions of different kinds of percept are summarized in the word 'dog'? How indeed can a dog seen at '3.14 (. . . from the side)' have the same name as the same dog seen at '3.15 (. . . from the front)', not to mention having the same name as another dog?[46]

One of Borges's favourite ways of undermining the status of his stories is by discrediting the competence of his narrator as a

[45] *Crónicas de Bustos Domecq*, p. 42.
[46] *Ficciones*, p. 125.

witness to the events he is describing. On one occasion it is hinted
that the narrator was drunk when the story he is telling occurred
('La forma de la espada', 'The shape of the sword').[47] Usually the
narrator's problem is one of faulty memory. It is for instance
a characteristic irony of Borges's that the narrator who evokes
the impeccably memorious Funes uses the words 'I remember'
almost obsessively throughout the story. Thus on the first page
alone of the story we have 'I remember him (I have no right
to utter that sacred verb)', 'I remember (I think) his angular,
leather braiding hands', 'I clearly remember his voice',[48] and so on.

A large proportion of Borges's stories are tales of fantasy; they
describe such things as imaginary plants, imaginary books, a city
inhabited by immortals, situations in general in which it is not
clear where the line can be drawn between fantasy and reality.
Yet Borges has always written realistic stories too, and the realistic
mode is predominant in his most recent book, *El informe de
Brodie* (1970), in the preface of which he asserts that the stories
'observe ... all the conventions of a genre [realism] which is no
less conventional than any other'.[49] Now it is significant that it is
in this very 'realistic' book that his discrediting of the narrator's
memory is most insistently exercised. Often the narrators of these
stories were *children* when the events they are describing occurred.
In the intervening years, how many other experiences have got
tangled with what they witnessed at the time? Or to what extent
has their perspective of what happened so long ago significantly
changed? In 'Pierre Menard, autor del Quijote' ('Pierre Menard,
author of the Quixote'), Borges demonstrated how our reading
of a given book is affected by what books we have read before, or
conversely how our memory of a book is affected by what we then
read afterwards.[50] *Don Quixote* is something of a different book

[47] p. 130.
[48] p. 117.
[49] *Brodie*, p. 9.
[50] Borges's point is, I think, marginally different from that of T. S. Eliot in
his essay 'Tradition and Individual Talent' (*The Sacred Wood*, 1920). Eliot
asserts that a new work of literature modifies those that have been written
before. But his emphasis is on a modification that takes place in an 'ideal
order'. For Borges it is the chronological order in which an individual reads
books that dictates the nature of the modification. For Borges, all books are
contemporary to us, in the sense that we can draw on them all, without
temporal discrimination, from a bookshelf.

according to whether or not we approach it after reading, say, Nietzsche. Similarly, the books we read after *Don Quixote* will affect our memory of it. The same is true of memory in general: the shape and import of any event in the past changes constantly in the light of subsequent experience. And it is as a result of this fundamental creativeness of memory that every remembered fact is a fiction. Since, moreover, a writer draws on memory in order to compose a story, a story must, by definition, be fictive, a *creation*, not an expression of what really happened.

Let us take some typical comments the narrators of *El informe de Brodie* make on their own memory:

I do not know whether there were two or three emptied bottles on the floor or whether an excess of movies suggests this false memory to me.[51]

The intervening years of course have exaggerated or blurred what I saw.[52]

Anyway, here is the story, with the inevitable variations brought about by time and good writing.[53]

I see in advance I shall give in to the writer's temptation of emphasizing or adding certain details.[54]

[The old lady] related historical events, but always with the same words and in the same order, as though they were the Lord's prayer, and I suspected that the words no longer corresponded to images.[55]

The last example is the most important, for it stresses the gap that separates words from the images in the past they purport to describe. An old lady who has told the same anecdote over several decades is left only with the almost memorized words of the anecdote, not with the real images that prompted them. Similarly a man who has written something many years earlier and who one day reads it over, will find there nothing but words, as though they had been written by another—'Words, displaced and mutilated words, words of others'.[56] So the past exists only in our creative memory of it, or in the fictive words we wrote when we were living it.

In a story called 'La busca de Averroes' ('Averroes's search'), Borges evokes one Averroes, a Moorish scholar in medieval Spain. At the end of the story we learn that Averroes disappears 'as if fulminated by an invisible fire',[57] and with him his entire sur-

[51] p. 180.        [52] p. 181.        [53] p. 177.        [54] p. 161.
[55] p. 81.              [56] *El Aleph*, p. 26.                [57] p. 100.

roundings disappear, including 'the houses and the unseen fountain and the books and the manuscript ... and perhaps even the
Guadalquivir'.[58] For the Averroes of this story is merely a creature
of words, alive only so long as the words are there to describe him.
There may have been a real Averroes, but like any real person,
even the most famous historical personage, he is doomed to become a fiction the moment he dies, for he can only survive after
death either in the words that were written about him, and all
words are simplificatory fictions, or in the creative memories of
others. In the end, the 'realistic' stories of *El informe de Brodie*
read as though they had been written in order to demonstrate that
realistic stories are as fictive as fantastic ones, because language
and memory, the stuff of which they are made, are fictive by
definition.

Another devious game that Borges plays in order to question
the status of his stories is to inject fragments of his personal life
into some of their most unlikely characters. Thus Otto Dietrich
zur Linde, the unrepentant Nazi of 'Deutsches Requiem', shares
with Borges a cavalry-charging ancestor, an interest in Schopenhauer, a love of Bràhms (the only classical composer Borges en-
joys), a preoccupation with tigers, an opinion about Whitman,
and a notion about the destiny of the precursors of great literature.
All this despite the well-known fact that Borges has always detested Nazism. In 'El duelo' ('The dual') an absurd society lady
shares Borges's much publicized opinions about the Spanish
language, and in 'Guayaquil', the two leading characters, though
they loathe each other, both share with Borges a great many
traits. In the first place one of them, the narrator, shares with
Borges a notoriously bookish disposition, and also an ancestor
called Suárez who led a cavalry charge at the battle of Junín. And
yet he is, unlike Borges, a professor of history and blatantly anti-
Semitic (Borges, who wrote a euphoric poem about the Six Day
War, is devoted to the Jewish cause). The narrator's rival, Zimerman, though unlike Borges a Jew, shares with Borges the view
that Government should be as invisible as possible (cf. Borges's
remark in the preface of *El informe de Brodie*, the book in which
the story appears: 'I believe that in good time we will deserve to
have no governments')[59] and an almost insulting modesty, which
Borges characteristically mocks. Both characters share with Borges

[58] pp. 100–1.     [59] *Brodie*, p. 8.

an interest in Schopenhauer and, more reconditely, an interest in Gustav Meyrink's *Der Golem*.

'Guayaquil' is therefore an exercise in self-mockery, in that for instance a character who sounds so much like Borges is made to utter lapidary remarks against the Jews whereas the Borgesian modesty of the other character turns out to be an aggressive sham. The story is moreover self-mocking in another, more subtle manner. It depicts the rivalry of two historians. Which of the two will be chosen to investigate some newly discovered letters of Simón Bolívar? These letters are said to throw light on the *rivalry* between Bolívar and San Martín at their famous meeting in Guayaquil in 1822. The story therefore is a characteristically Borgesian meditation on the eternal return of archetypal situations. The archetypal situation that repeats itself in this case is a Schopenhaurean one: the triumph of one will over another. For Zimerman talks the narrator by sheer force of will into not pressing his claim just as Bolívar is supposed to have talked San Martín into resigning his command. Yet it is the mischievous spirit of the story that Schopenhauer and eternal return turn out to be mere fantasy consolations for the narrator in that they endow his sheer feeble-mindedness with a grandly archetypal dimension and better, with a *distinguished* precedent. Characteristically, Borges has erected a grandly metaphysical design in this story only self-mockingly to demolish it. At the very point that the narrator and Zimerman appear to have magically 'become' San Martín and Bolívar respectively, we realize that they have become so only in the narrator's self-consoling fantasy.

The autobiographical ingredients of 'Guayaquil' and other stories constitute a final, deliberately ironical comment on the nature of writing. Whatever you set out to describe, 'realistically' or otherwise, you are in the end writing, however obliquely, about yourself as much as about what you set out to describe. And writing is therefore fictive not only because the limitations of language and memory make it so, but also because it is subjective. Inexorably the subject transforms (creates) the object it perceives, and converts it into a projection of itself.

In an Epilogue to *El hacedor* ('The maker') Borges tells the following short tale: 'A man undertakes the task of sketching the world. Over the years he populates a space with images of provinces, kingdoms, mountains, bays, ships, islands, fishes, rooms,

tools, stars, horses, and people. Shortly before he dies, he discovers that this patient maze of lines traces the image of his own
face.'[60] It is the image, of course, not the face itself, for the face,
like the rose, is contained only in itself. But Borges's work is indeed an image of himself. If one man is all men, it is an image of
man too, but there are certain characteristics in it which are
peculiar to Borges's personality. His very style is perhaps his most
revealing image. Borges writes, on the *surface* at any rate, an
English-sounding Spanish, full of understatements, of affirmations
by negation, of phrases like 'not without a certain ostentation',
'not without a tremble', 'the memory of which the years have
not erased'. There is an elegant delicacy about Borges's writing
that signifies a very particular kind of man, a rather Edwardian
gentleman, perhaps.[61] Yet behind his elegant stylistic mask, assum-
ing that it is a mask, there is a similar tension in Borges to the
one he intuited in Chesterton, of whom Borges once wrote that the
Catholic faith was a disguise for the Poe or Kafka buried within
him: 'Something in the mire of his self tended to nightmare,
something secret, blind, and central.'[62] Borges's own work, despite
its apparent cerebral coolness, is furnished with oblique images
of the intimate dreams and nightmares that reside in 'the mire of
his self'. To take an example, his stories are full of brave rough
men expert at handling a knife—these would seem to be inverted
images of what he has often described as his own fear of physical
violence, or images of his longing to overcome it, or of his longing
to have been a man of action, not a librarian and a writer. Of
course he may well be not all that unhappy that he is a librarian.
For action is seen in his stories as ultimately both gratuitous and
destructive. His men of action always die, and they die compulsively, as though they could not stop themselves. Yet Borges cannot stop himself from admiring them, as he admires the fierce

[60] *El hacedor*, p. 111.
[61] Borges learnt English from a no doubt very Edwardian governess, and had
an English grandmother. The literature he most frequently returns to is the
literature of late Victorian and Edwardian England.
[62] Indeed, there is something more to Borges's style than understated elegance. There is no room here to discuss the extent to which Borges subverts
the very elegance he creates in his writing, for instance by the masterly and
disturbing use of oxymoronic adjectives. A great deal of tension is created in
Borges's writing by the contrast between its Edwardian elegance and its very
subtle subversion of that elegance.

tigers that pace his fiction, emblems of the real tigers in the jungle who hunt down their own quarry and live in the open, and which no writer can pin down in a poem.[63] In contrast, the mirror, Borges's most pressing image, reveals the 'detested face' from which he cannot escape. It will never be the face of a knife-fighter or of a tiger. It is the fated face of Borges, the sign of his destiny. Mirrors for Borges are horrifying because they remind him of all that is inescapable but also because they help to confirm his suspicion that though he cannot escape them, neither Borges nor the world may exist at all, that Borges too for instance may be an insubstantial reflection of something else, just as his mirror-image is an insubstantial reflection of him. Mirrors intolerably underline a central paradox of Borges's work: that not only is the world inescapable; it may also be unreal.

Borges has always been interested in Idealist philosophy. He wrote an essay on Berkeley as far back as 1923 which appeared in his first book of essays, *Inquisiciones* (1925), and an early Berkleyan poem, 'Amanacer',[64] in which he speculated on the peril that befell Buenos Aires every day just before dawn, when most people are asleep, not watching it. Idealism for Borges has always served as an image—more poetic perhaps than philosophical—of the fragility of things, as an image in particular of how little we can know for certain. For if we cannot be certain that the things we see exist outside our perception of them, we are truly absurd and hopeless creatures. We have seen that Borges takes pains to stress that his stories are fictions. Yet he wonders, too, if we may not also be fictions. If, in *Hamlet*, the characters on stage are watching another play, may not we, watching *Hamlet*, be characters in yet another play and so on to infinity? If I dream a man, may I not too be the dream of another? May not he be the dream of yet another, and so on? If I play chess, may I not too be a pawn on yet *another* board? What, anyway, is real? If life is a mere spectacle of insubstantial percepts, are not the percepts of a dream as real as those of waking life? The fictiveness of his stories is therefore a reflection of the possible fictiveness of a world whose status is as dubious as that of the stories. The stories often look real. Borges indeed always deploys illusionists' tricks to make them look so, before demolishing them as fictions. The stories are

---

[63] 'El otro tigre', *Obra poética*, Buenos Aires, 1967, p. 191.
[64] p. 45.

full of scholarly footnotes, references to real people, precise dates, all sorts of devices designed to give an appearance of reality to extraordinary things. Yet these illusionists' tricks are reflections of the tricks life itself plays to persuade us that our extraordinary world is real.

Borges's stories, in the end, are not only coolly lucid cerebral games but often highly affective, poetic expressions of the fragility of the world and of man. Again, that fragility is not a desperate one. It has a certain splendour. It is a measure of the odds against man and a measure therefore of his spirit. That spirit, which always reasserts itself in Borges's work, is perhaps best reflected in his poetry, particularly in those deeply personal, later poems such as the 'Poema de los dones' or 'Elogio de la sombra', where against all *personal* odds, in the face of ageing and of mounting blindness, in the face therefore of all that has dramatized the fragility of man for Borges personally, a love of life, and a dogged, sensitive hope remain undestroyed. They remain undestroyed in particular because they are relentlessly sustained by Borges's irrepressible sense of humour.

# 9
# Mario Vargas Llosa (Peru, 1936–   )

---

THE Peruvian novelist Mario Vargas Llosa (1936–   ) is, despite his comparative youthfulness, the author of five works of fiction: a book of youthful but skilful short stories called *Los jefes* (1958), a novella, *Los cachorros*, published in 1967, and three long novels, *La ciudad y los perros* (1962), *La Casa Verde* (1966), and *Conversación en la Catedral* (1970).

All these works have one thing in common: they are profoundly discontented visions of Peru, attempts to expose the indecencies of his country by a man who has thus summarized his ideas of what a novelist's task should be:

Novelists who speak well of their country should be distrusted: patriotism, which is a fruitful virtue in soldiers and in bureaucrats, is usually a poor one in literature. Literature in general and the novel in particular are expressions of discontent. Their social usefulness lies principally in the fact that they remind people that the world is *always* wrong, that life should *always* change.[1]

His works attempt to unravel the exact form this sort of original sin has taken in Peru, its exact texture. The entire strategy of his art is directed at the fulfilment of this aim, so that Vargas Llosa's fiction not only attempts to tell the truth about Peru, but attempts also to find its way to the proper formal structure and the proper language to tell it.

The complex stories Vargas Llosa tells have their own eloquence outside the complex forms in which they are expressed, and it is

[1] *Marcha*, Montevideo, No. -1553, 23 July 1971, p. 31.

best to begin by attempting, at risk of savage simplification, to summarize at any rate his three novels.

*La ciudad y los perros* is set in the Leoncio Prado Academy in Lima, a secondary school run by the military. A number of boys have formed a group within the school known as as El Círculo. They plan to steal the year's chemistry exam paper, and they draw lots to decide who is to do it. The task falls on Cava, a boy from the sierra. Alas, like all *serranos*, Cava is clumsy, and he breaks a window on the scene of the crime. The crime is discovered, and the whole school is punished. No one may go out at weekends until the culprit has owned up. One boy, known as the Slave because of his puniness and susceptibility to bullying, despairs. He must see his girl-friend. He denounces Cava to the authorities in exchange for a day's leave. A few weeks later, the Slave is shot in the back during a military exercise and killed. His only friend in the school, Alberto, suspects the Jaguar of the murder. The Jaguar is the leader of the Círculo, and his motive would be to avenge Cava against the informer. The school authorities, however, will not hear of Alberto's suspicion. What would the Minister's reaction be to such a crime? What of the school's good name? Eventually Alberto capitulates and revokes his accusation. Coronel Garrido, the headmaster, discovers that Alberto writes pornographic stories for his friends, and he is able to use them to blackmail Alberto into silence. The official version of self-inflicted, accidental death is sustained. But in the book's epilogue we learn that Alberto was right: the Jaguar did kill the Slave.

In general the novel is a tale of lost innocence, a story of young boys who have been driven by their environment to jettison their most sensitive instincts and assert their most brutal ones. That repressed innocence is symbolized in the novel in the school's pet *vicuña*, a beautiful animal from the sierra which is tied pathetically to a post, and which the boys ritualistically stone as though to punish their own better selves, or which is occasionally evoked as a fleeting, innocent counterpoint to some of the novel's countless scenes of gratuitous brutality.

*La Casa Verde* ('The Green House') is a far more difficult novel to summarize, for it contains several interlocking stories of equal importance. The novel is set half in Piura in the north-west of Peru, and half in the *selva* or jungle in the province of Amazonas —more precisely in Santa María de Nieva and along the Marañón river—north-east of Piura across the Andes. Here we learn of a young girl called Bonifacia who has been brought up by the missionary nuns of Santa María de Nieva, having been picked up among a group of *aguaruna* Indians from the jungle. One day she allows the mission's younger *aguaruna* pupils, who have been put in her charge, to escape. Dismissed from the mission, she eventually marries a police sergeant, Lituma, from Piura, where he takes her and where she settles down. One day, the Sergeant is arrested after winning a Russian roulette duel and killing a man. He is taken to Lima. In his absence, Bonifacia is corrupted by Lituma's best friend, Josefino Rojas, and she ends up in the employment of Piura's most notorious brothel, the Casa Verde or Green House of the title.

Meanwhile, we have been treated to parallel descriptions of the buildings of the Casa Verde, and its forerunner too, a previous Casa Verde built by a mysterious harpist called Anselmo that was burnt down in wrath by the local priest and by Piura's pious ladies, or *beatas*. The second Casa Verde stands in the Mangachería, the place where Sergeant Lituma and his friends were brought up, a fiercely proud shanty town devoted to wine, women, and song, and lovingly described by Vargas Llosa. Two other main stories are told, both of them set in the jungle: the exotic story of Fushía, a Japanese renegade from a Brazilian prison who enlists the aid of *huambisa* warriors in order to steal rubber from other tribes and then sell it, and whose hazardous career is curtailed by leprosy; and the story of Adrián Nieves, a river pilot who escapes from the army, works for a while for Fushía, then abducts Fushía's wife when Fushía is down, and settles in Santa María de Nieva. His story interlocks with Bonifacia's because Bonifacia goes to live with his family after her dismissal from the mission, and indeed meets her husband, Sergeant Lituma, through him.

All this is a bare outline. There are many minor sub-plots too.

*Conversación en la Catedral* is a novel that both in complexity and in excellence—so skilfully is the complexity administered— makes the two previous novels seem like the exercises of a beginner. Essentially a political novel, it is set mostly under the dictatorship of Manuel Odría (1948–56). Its protagonist is Don Cayo Bermúdez, Odría's Home Secretary or Ministro de Gobierno. We see him simultaneously, in parallel, alternating sections (*a*) as an adolescent and married man in the provincial town of Chincha,

(b) in his office in Lima deploying terror through the whole of Peru, (c) as a lavishly spending, impotent voyeur: two beautiful lesbians perform costly exhibitions for him. Meanwhile, the story is being told of one Santiago Zavala, a young man who shocks his oligarchic family by insisting on entering the University of San Marcos, a place fit only for *cholos*, or half-breeds, becomes a starry-eyed Communist there, only to end up a bored bourgeois husband, working as a hack journalist on a newspaper owned by the oligarchic Prados, where one of his many menial tasks is to report on the lottery. The love–hate relationship of Don Cayo and the oligarchy is also explored, as is the life of the oligarchic family which Santiago has chosen to reject. We discover that Don Fermín, Santiago's father, is not only a respectable industrialist but also a notorious homosexual, known in brothel circles as Bola de Oro (Golden Ball). Finally, parallel to the stories mentioned, we are treated to descriptions of the lives and adventures of maids, chauffeurs, prostitutes, and secret policemen.

There is very little in any of these stories that is edifying, and the novels are, on one level, novels of scandalous disclosure. They are sometimes deliberately unfair. Thus for instance although Vargas Llosa was himself at the Leoncio Prado and although, on the evidence of other pupils, his depiction of the atmosphere of the school is meticulously exact, there never did occur there such an 'accident' or murder as is described in *La ciudad y los perros*. The scandalous event is thrown in so as to test the institution's reactions, so as to coax the school into a sort of disreputable self-revelation.

The Peru Vargas Llosa describes is not only unseemly but also chaotic. One of the most eloquent and conspicuous features of Vargas Llosa's work has been his endeavour to evolve the right structure to express this chaos, and he therefore places his reader in a structural labyrinth in his novels that functions as the equivalent of the political, social, and emotional labyrinths his characters inhabit.

Thus even *La ciudad y los perros*, Vargas Llosa's most accessible novel, is narrated in anything but a linear fashion. To take an example, let us examine the composition of chapter one. It is divided into five sections, each one between two and ten pages long. Section One consists of action-packed omniscient narration: Cava is chosen to steal the chemistry exam paper. He breaks the window as he does it and returns to the dormitory where the Círculo await him. Action, drama, and suspense, quick plot development—what one might expect from a man who admires novels of chivalry as much as Vargas Llosa does. In Section Two, however, the action is broken up, as is the linear sequence, for we are told in flashback of a period in the Slave's childhood—his arrival in Lima from Chiclayo, a town in the north where he was born. Section Three features Alberto as protagonist. On duty as *imaginaria*, he is wondering how to acquire twenty *soles*, the price he must pay Pies Dorados (Golden Feet), his form's favourite prostitute, next Saturday. He wittily negotiates an officer who accuses him of loitering on duty, then meets up with his friend the Slave, on whose behalf he steals a uniform from the Negro Vallano. Section Four furnishes a flashback again, this time to Alberto's life several years back in Miraflores, a wealthy suburb. Section Five is a stream of consciousness scene in which the author focuses into the mind of the (as yet anonymous) Boa, a member of the Círculo. The subject of the stream of consciousness is the rape of a hen by the Boa and his friends. We have only reached page 36. But in each of the five sections we have been taken into the mind of a different character, or to a different place (Miraflores, Chiclayo, the school), or to a different period of time.

Each chapter is thus subdivided into sections, and each section develops one of the stories treated in a preceding chapter. This technique of parallel, juxtaposed narrations is common to all three novels. In *La ciudad y los perros* all the stories told concern the inmates of the school. In *La Casa Verde* the stories cover different regions of Peru and appear at first remote from each other. But in the end they interlock. The same is true of *Conversación en la Catedral*, although we shall see how the technique is further complicated there.

It was mentioned that in a given chapter of *La ciudad y los perros* one section of a chapter can tell a story considerably distant in space and time from that of say the next section, though both may refer to the same character. Similarly, in *La Casa Verde*, there is for instance one series of sections describing Bonifacia's admission to the convent as a child, another her life as an adolescent there, her dismissal from the convent and subsequent marriage, and a third her degeneration in Piura during her husband's absence and her admission to the Casa Verde, the brothel. Eventually, the sections dealing with earlier periods catch up with those dealing with later periods, and in the end it is possible to *extract* from the novel a chronologically sequential chain of events about Bonifacia. Indeed it would be possible to reshuffle all these novels and reorder them into a series of perfectly conventional stories told in conventional sequence. Instead the author chooses to disrupt the sequence of events, with the result that the characters are immersed in a spatial and temporal labyrinth.

In *Conversación en la Catedral* the technique is intensified further because the interlocking parallel stories are told not only in alternating sections of a given chapter but sometimes simultaneously on a given page by means of parallel dialogues. Thus in a given chapter or on a given page several dialogues between different people at different periods of time and in different places can take place simultaneously:

A. 'These subversive little sheets are to disappear at once,' said Bermudez. 'Understand, Lozano?'

B. 'Are you ready Nigger?' said Don Melquíades. 'Your feet must be smarting, eh Trifulcio?'

C. 'You don't know who or where?' said Ludovico. 'How was it then that you had a *Tribuna* in your pocket when they arrested you in Vitarte? How was it then, Daddy?'

BB. 'Am I ready?' laughed Trifulcio, worried. 'Ready, Don Melquíades?'

D. 'When I first arrived in Lima I would send money to the old black woman and now and then I'd go and visit her,' said Ambrosio. 'After that, nothing. She died without news of me. It's one of the things that bother me.'

In this randomly chosen extract, four distinct conversations (each of which I have signalled for convenience with letters) are being sustained at once on the same page. Dialogue A refers obliquely to dialogue C, in that in dialogue C the order issued by Bermúdez in dialogue A is being enacted: a man who has been found in possession of the *Tribuna*, one of the 'subversive little sheets' that 'are to disappear at once', is being tortured. BB is the direct answer to the question put in B. And finally we are introduced to a fourth dialogue, D, which is however connected to B in that

Ambrosio, the chauffeur (here seen talking to his boss and lover Don Fermín), is the son of Trifulcio. The 'black woman' is Ambrosio's mother.

What then is the purpose of these structural gymnastics in Vargas Llosa's work, these shufflings of sequence and juxtapositions of disparate but ultimately connected material that have culminated, in *Conversación en la Catedral,* in passages that are quite cacophonous? Is he merely imposing gratuitous difficulties on the reader? Or is he simply attempting, just as gratuitously, further to refine the structural conventions of post-Faulknerian fiction?

Certainly Vargas Llosa's structures make for difficult reading, and there are many who claim—lazily I think—to have found the reading of *Conversación en la Catedral* an impossible task. Yet the structures (which indeed owe a great deal—but not everything—to Faulkner) are fundamental to the novels, and they serve many purposes.

In the first place, the complex shapes of Vargas Llosa's novels re-enact the complexity of the situations described in them. To write a novel in which a story is told in conventional linear sequence is to imply that you have an ordered vision of the world, that you believe in the possibility of an ordered sequence of cause and effect. Vargas Llosa has attempted to evolve forms which are more suited to evoke, or to re-enact, the perplexities of real life as he sees it. To take an example from *La Casa Verde*: Peru is a geographically disconnected country: a vast chain of mountains, the Andes, separates Piura from Santa María de Nieva. So, in *La Casa Verde*, violent breaks in the narration re-enact this geographical condition. The remoteness of one part of the narration from another re-enacts the remoteness of one part of Peru from another, and the complexity of the novel's structure thus serves to reflect the complexity of Peruvian geography.

Another aim of the novel's juxtapositions of disparate material is to force the reader to *share* the dilemmas of the characters, the dilemma of difficult reading becoming an equivalent of the dilemma of difficult living. As I said earlier, it is possible mentally to reshuffle the novels in order to extract from them the trajectory of a given character's life and see it in conventional linear sequence. But this one can do only when one has *finished* the novels, when one can adopt the privilege of hindsight. Now it is one of Vargas Llosa's most eloquent points that hindsight is not often relevantly available to us. It is not to the characters, so why should it be to the reader? Instead of allowing the reader to be, like the author, complacently omniscient, he therefore puts him in the same boat as the characters, and makes him share with the characters the perplexities of the present moment. The privilege of hindsight, that of seeing those perplexities fall into an ordered pattern, into a neat sequence of cause and effect, is thus removed. It is of course removed only until the end of the novels, when everything falls into place. But by then the characters are in a position to draw on hindsight themselves. Ultimately, the difference between the clear perspective we acquire when finishing these novels and the puzzled one we had when reading them symbolizes the gap that separates the baffled view one has in general of any situation when one is living it from the more lucid one that one may acquire subsequently.

Even more than the other two novels it is *Conversación en la Catedral* that most uncompromisingly forces both character and reader to live in the contingent present. This is because it is fundamentally a novel made up of *conversations*, and conversation is an activity well suited to dramatize the unpredictable and labyrinthine nature of present time. In conversation, one is spectacularly confined to what one is saying *now*. One cannot anticipate what one is going to say *next* because one does not know what the other man is going to say, and one therefore does not know what one is going to have to react to. Conversation, moreover, very rarely does not involve deliberate concealment. One is by definition in the dark as to what the other is really thinking, and as to what he really knows and *could* reveal. Vargas Llosa's technique in *Conversación en la Catedral* of cutting off conversations at crucial moments, of offering snippets of revelation in them and then moving elsewhere, helps I think to re-enact the very nature of conversation and of communication in general, particularly in a society devoted to the concealment of truth and to the flaunting of deceptive images. And whatever is concealed by one character from another in the novels' conversations is concealed from the reader too.

In short, the reader in Vargas Llosa's novels, and in particular in *Conversación en la Catedral*, has no advantages over the characters. and as a result he is forced to *appreciate* their per-

plexities simply because he has had to share them. The effect is
that he is well enabled in the end really to feel what it is like to
live in Peru, to feel the very texture of a society as it is actually
being lived.

The habit of concealment mentioned, which results in there
being a gap separating the image one flaunts in conversation, say,
from one's real self, is a central concern of Vargas Llosa's novels.
It has obvious Sartrean overtones, and Vargas Llosa acknowledges
them by employing a quotation from Sartre as the epigraph of *La
ciudad y los perros*: 'On joue les héros parce qu'on est lâche et
les saints parce qu'on est méchant, on joue les assassins parce
qu'on meurt d'envie de tuer son prochain, on joue parce qu'on est
menteur de naissance.' And it is, again, the novel's structural
juxtapositions which serve to reveal the gap that there exists
between ourselves and the images we project for others. Thus in
*La ciudad y los perros* we do not discover until the end of the
novel that a young boy who has been offering us an *anonymous*
first-person description of his timidly introspective love for an unnamed young girl is none other than the Jaguar, who has been
depicted simultaneously by his friends as the most feared bully in
the school. Flashback, by being kept *anonymous*, helps to dramatize two points: first, that we can be two unrecognizably different people at two different periods of our lives, and secondly, that
we can be unrecognizably different people according to whom we
are with.[2]

In Vargas Llosa's novels two stories are often thus told in
parallel that turn out to be about the same person, the identity of
the person having been disguised or witheld in one of them. In
*La Casa Verde* for instance, Lituma, the fun-loving, mischievous
young inhabitant of La Mangachería, turns out to be the same
person as an unrecognizably different 'Sergeant' in Santa María
de Nieva. Such is the difference between the image a man projects at leisure and the one he projects when fulfilling a public
function. Similarly, in *Conversación en la Catedral* the randy

---

[2] Novelists have borrowed flashback techniques from the cinema. Yet it is
interesting to note that the cinema cannot emulate Vargas Llosa's *anonymous*
flashbacks, at any rate into the recent past. In a film, we cannot but recognize
the face of the actor. (Of course the cinema can do an anonymous flashback
into the distant past where, say, a boy plays the childhood of a given character.)

Bola de Oro of brothel circles turns out to be the same man as the impeccably mannered industrialist called Don Fermín.

Unlike Sartre, Vargas Llosa is not concerned to investigate the philosophical nuances of the gap that separates our real selves from the images we project for others. He takes the fact that there is such a gap for granted. His concern is, rather, a sociological one: what *kind* of images do people find it necessary to project in a given society or, more specifically, in Peru? What is it that Peruvians conceal, what on the other hand do they flaunt, and why?

The images Vargas Llosa's characters flaunt do indeed have very specific characteristics, and their explanation may well be found in the society they inhabit. In *La ciudad y los perros*, for instance, the characters' public images are motivated by a very Latin American condition, that of *machismo* or the assertion of masculinity. The main reason why the characters turn out to be so different when introspectively on their own from what they are when seen by others is that when in company they must, in order to sustain the respect of their friends, be uncompromisingly *macho*, callously tough and ostentatiously 'manly'. They must above all suppress or conceal the very sensitive instincts they all seem to share. *La ciudad y los perros* is never better than when it is showing how for young Peruvians social intercourse presupposes the jettisoning of one's best instincts. Thus in another anonymous first-person narration, we are treated to the spectacle of a young boy, Boa, lavishing his most sensitive thoughts on a mongrel bitch, La Malpapeada (Skimpy). He can only communicate the kindest side of his nature to an animal: in the presence of his friends, he must sustain an image that is based on his principal claim to fame, that he has the largest sexual organ in the school.

*Machismo* is the young boys' passport to mutual acceptance. It is present in their elders too, but above all the images projected by their elders must contain the appearance of unimpeachable *respectability*, whatever the truth that they conceal. The officers' treatment of the Slave's death reveals the extent to which they will go to preserve an image of respectability at all costs and against the most pressing ethical considerations.

Nowhere are images of respectability more ruthlessly scrutinized than in *Conversación en la Catedral*. As in *La ciudad y los perros* respectability is deceptively flaunted in that novel not only by individuals but also by institutions. And the respectable facades of both are mercilessly contrasted, eventually, with the truth. Take the Odría regime itself. At first, we are presented with its brazen image: it is the regime that has brought law and order and material progress to Peru. Then, little by little, we are given the truth: law and order equals gratuitous terror, and material progress is a disguise for corruption. A presidential address is applauded by happy crowds: the crowds have been blackmailed and terrorized into attending; the granting of an imaginative public works contract is announced: we discover that it has been granted as a result of blackmail and bribery. The same contrast between public image and reality is deployed in the case of some of the establishment's individual pillars: Don Cayo Bermúdez, the respected minister, turns out to be a lecherous murderer; Don Fermín, the urbane industrialist, is discovered to be a fawning homosexual.

Again we find that the very structure of the novel is helping to reinforce its meaning. For in the first half of the novel, the scandalous truths, though frequently hinted at, are usually buried in cacophonous dialogues or in elusive snippets of introspection that are bafflingly injected into the characters' public utterances. All the time the reader feels that something is being concealed or that something is about to be revealed, but like most of the characters he never knows quite what. Eventually, when there is no hiding the truth any longer, when whoever was concealing it is caught *in flagrantis,* it is depicted in conventional, explicit language. In short, the novel's formal presentation has its own eloquence. It is, itself, a sort of language.

That the novel's formal presentation is communicating a message of its own becomes most evident if one compares the tortuous elusiveness of the passages that describe the secrets of Bermúdez, say, with the direct simplicity of those that describe the political activities of the students of San Marcos University. The students are not desperately attempting to conceal the truth about themselves. There is no gap separating their public image from their real selves. Consequently, their activities are described quite explicitly. So are the romantic love affairs of Amalia, Fermín Zavala's maid. Again, she has no perversions to be ashamed of, she has nothing at all to hide. So there is no need for the narrative, when it deals with her, to be tortuously fragmented.

Vargas Llosa's structures have another function: to reinforce the feeling which all the novels deploy that there is no diachronic progress in Peru, that events on the contrary at best develop cyclically—when they are not stagnating altogether. There is no way out of what turns out to be a cyclical labyrinth: nothing really *changes*. Take the students' attempts, in *Conversación en la Catedral*, to force the country out of stagnation. Despite their hectic efforts, they get nowhere. How does the structure reinforce the expression of this fact? By dispersing the descriptions of their activities through the whole jungle of the book, by allowing them a few pages and then turning gloomily to Cayo Bermúdez's office, by burying them in short in a vast labyrinth which they must share with the disparate and conflicting activities of others. The students are dispersed in the labyrinthine structure of the novel just as they are dispersed in the labyrinth that constitutes Peruvian politics in general. Moreover we often read about regressive actions *before* reading about progressive ones that in fact preceded them, so that by the time we come to read of a progressive action, we know already that it was doomed. In the end we are left with the impression that past, present, and future are almost inter-changeable. They are, of course, in the book's structure: but are they not too in Peru as Vargas Llosa sees it? And is it not the structure's role to re-enact this fact?

Vargas Llosa is an admirer of medieval novels of chivalry, and indeed all his novels are packed with action, with movement towards a goal. Yet the actions the novels describe are the actions of men charging at windmills. Though often purposeful, they achieve no purpose. *Events* take place but they change nothing. And although in *Conversación en la Catedral* Odría and his henchmen are finally replaced by a legally elected regime under President Manuel Prado, nothing fundamental has changed. Much of the novel indeed takes place under Prado, and given the book's temporal shufflings we often learn about events under Prado before learning about events under Odría: it doesn't seem to make much difference.

Many of the formal techniques Vargas Llosa uses are of course merely echoes of similar techniques employed by any amount of novelists all over the world during the past few decades. What is remarkable in Vargas Llosa is that the complex formal presenta-tion of his material never seems gratuitous, so conscientiously has he evolved it to express his vision of Peru. The sheer professionalism with which it is manipulated is moreover unusual. He is able to give the appearance of chaos and yet maintain rigorous control. There is no elusive detail or incidental phrase that does not prove ultimately to be relevant: as in a well-constructed symphony, every passing note has its purpose. To take an example: every time we are treated in *La ciudad y los perros* to a flashback about the Slave's childhood it is introduced by the phrase 'he has forgotten' ('ha olvidado'). We eventually discover why: he has forgotten because he is lying unconscious in the school infirmary. By shuffling time about, and also by introducing such a note of future discord in often idyllic flashbacks, Vargas Llosa achieves a great deal of dramatic tension. The past dramatizes the simultaneously narrated present, and the future, also depicted simultaneously, dramatizes the past. By bringing the future constantly to bear on the present Vargas Llosa moreover envelops his novels in an atmosphere of determinism. For we are conscious, in the description of an event in the present, of the doom that is to follow, even if we do not know exactly what form that doom will take (the structure indeed contributes a great deal of suspense too).[3] We noted moreover that in Vargas Llosa's novels a character's past eventually catches up, chronologically, with his simultaneously depicted present, and that his present eventually catches up with his simultaneously depicted future. It is then that we see that what seemed two wholly different characters are not only the same one, but also that the one was developing *inevitably* into the other. If a character has appeared to be two different people at two different periods of his life, there turn out to be some fairly deterministic causes for the transition. In the end, though the young boy that timidly courted Teresa can scarcely be recognized in the pugnacious bully and killer who is known as the Jaguar, the path from the former to the latter has been an inevitable one. If, with the privilege of hindsight which we are granted only when we finish the novel, we mentally

---

[3] This is particularly true of the very important second reading of Vargas Llosa's novels, at any rate of the conjectural second reading that one can most fruitfully indulge in on finishing them. For it is then that the fragments fall into place, in consequence of which we are forced to judge each one afresh. Again, the structure has contributed to remind us how differently we perceive evidence when we have a limited knowledge from when we have a more complete knowledge of its context.

rearrange the information we have been given about the Jaguar and put it in chronological order, we shall see how dismally inevitable his fall was. The pattern that emerges is indeed worthy of Natural:st fiction, so determined is it by circumstance: the timid young lover is forced to steal out of dire poverty in order to buy presents for his girl-friend; he must then live by his wits in order to escape the law, and as a consequence he learns of the advantage of violence. In a curious way, his very love for Teresa triggered off a process that led him to become almost the antithesis of what he was when he first entertained it.

In the first paragraph of *Conversación en la Catedral* Santiago Zavala asks the question: 'En qué momento se había jodido el Perú?' (politely: 'at what point was Peru ruined?') The vision presented in Vargas Llosa's novels is, by and large, one of a 'país jodido', one of a country in which every man is compromised or corrupted, and it is the texture of that condition that the novels are most anxious to explore. They are novels that attempt to answer the question 'What exactly is wrong?' and 'When and why did it go wrong?'

The problem is often seen as one of the failure of adults with respect to their children. Every single father mentioned in *La ciudad y los perros*, Teresa's, the Slave's, the Jaguar's, the Boa's, and Alberto's, either abandons his family or beats up his son. *In loco parentis*, the officers in the school do no better, as their performance after the Slave's death reveals. Yet however much the sons instinctively reject their fathers, society demands that eventually they step into their fathers' shoes. When for instance Alberto finally leaves the school, blackmailed and compromised, it is clear that he is going to become much the same sort of callously charming, unprincipled oligarch his father has been. Such is the force of the rules of the game, to which the fathers themselves no doubt had to succumb once also. Such are the demands of *machismo*, the force that obliges the boys to suppress all of their most sensitive instincts and to which they all capitulate.

*Conversación en la Catedral* is even more forcefully a study of capitulations to the given rules of a given adult world. The most notable capitulation described is that of young Santiago Zavala whose passage from idealistic young Communist to hack journalist on an oligarchic paper is eloquent enough. Impressive too are the capitulations extracted through blackmail and the manipulation of material interest by Cayo Bermúdez. When a plot by an embittered ex-minister, General Espina, to overthrow Odría is quashed, the conspirators are not crudely punished. They are merely asked to reaffirm their loyalty to the regime under threat of losing lucrative Government contracts. Rumours of the conspiracy in foreign newspapers are made to look ridiculous by the fact that General Espina himself is not able to *resist* the temptation of his appointment as Ambassador to Madrid. No one indeed can resist compromising himself with an establishment that controls the purse strings, that can tempt one's weaker inclinations as assuredly as it can stir one into panic through the careful deployment of terror.

This sense of inevitable fall, of irresistible capitulation, is one of the most forceful aspects of Vargas Llosa's work. Of course, it is not necessarily a Peruvian phenomenon. Adults may well be corrupt everywhere, and it is certainly not only in Peru that adolescents are confronted with a world they did not shape, but with which in the end they are obliged to compromise. Yet Vargas Llosa's work is particularly valuable in that his observations not only have an obviously universal relevance but are also very deeply rooted in Peruvian society. His novels are perhaps primarily novels about the loss of innocence and the capitulation of ideals, but they are about a specific loss of innocence and specific capitulation in specific conditions. Let us therefore look more now at the specific nature of those conditions, as Vargas Llosa sees them.

Vargas Llosa is extremely alert to the minutiae of class distinctions in Peru, and very clever in that he knows just where the novel can best record them. Novels are nothing if not expressions of *private* life, and it is precisely in relation to their effect on private life that Vargas Llosa examines class and race. How for instance do people of various classes and races spend their leisure time in Peru? How do the various pupils of the Leoncio Prado spend their day off, the school being in effect a microcosm of Peruvian society, since boys of all classes are admitted there? Vargas Llosa is particularly good at describing the leisure culture of upper-class adolescents like Alberto who live in places like Miraflores or San Isidro, the smartest suburbs of Lima. Thus we learn all about the art of telling one's girl-friend in Miraflores that one loves her—what is known as *declararse*, to declare one-self. Girls usually accept a *declaración* if it is expressed with proper aplomb, with the right *mambo* or *bolero* playing in the back-ground. Then the girl and boy 'go steady'—'están juntos'. Another crucial stage in the escalation of a relationship is 'bajar la mano', to lower a girl's hand down to her thigh while dancing, a sign that you are keen on her, which, if not rejected, presupposes reciprocation. The subtleties of this action are described in loving detail when, in *La ciudad y los perros*, Alberto's Miraflores friends teach him to dance.[4] Their comfortable carefree world, by the way, is the subject of Vargas Llosa's excellent novella, *Los cachorros*.

Another group depicted with great love and exactitude by Vargas Llosa are the *huachafos*, the self-respecting, aspiring middle classes. This group features Ana, the girl whom Santiago marries in *Conversación en la Catedral* and whom his family despise, despite her desperate efforts to dress herself impeccably in order to confront them; and Doña Rosa, Santiago's landlady, terrified of what the Apristas, the social democrats, might do to 'respect-able' people like her should they attain power, yet blissfully ignorant of the fact that Santiago's family would scarcely con-sider her respectable at all. A little further down the line are people like Teresa, the Jaguar's girl-friend. Here leisure becomes a problem, not an art. In order to go out Teresa must borrow clothes from her friends. In the case of the Jaguar, who is even poorer, leisure leads, as we have seen, to crime. Lower still, for Boa's father, leisure is merely a brutal escape into perpetual alcoholism.

Critics have complained of one somewhat melodramatic cir-cumstance in *La ciudad y los perros*: Teresa turns out, by sheer coincidence, to have been at different times the girl-friend not only of the Jaguar but also of the Slave and of Alberto. The co-incidence is indeed melodramatic, but as mentioned before Vargas Llosa's novels are fictions, not life, and fictions are fundamentally artificial constructs. In this case the artifice has a very important function, for Teresa becomes a sort of barometer of the very differ-ent reactions three boys of three different social classes can have to one girl. Thus while Alberto dreams of patronizingly impressing her with his father's car, she is the Slave's equal, and the Jaguar in

4 *La ciudad y los perros*. Barcelona, 1968, p. 134.

turn is in awe of her. Here class differences are being expressed through the description of three very different kinds of sexual response to one person.

Vargas Llosa is skilful too in describing the leisure culture of chauffeurs, servants, prostitutes, thieves, and journalists, and in general of a wide variety of the *lumpenproletariat*. The categories that do not greatly figure in his work are categories that have not perhaps fallen within his experience—industrial workers and sierra peasants. The latter anyway have been done to death by the *indigenista* novelists.

What is impressive finally about *Conversación en la Catedral* in its depiction of various Peruvian leisure cultures is that it does for Lima what we shall see Guillermo Cabrera Infante's *Tres tristes tigres* does for Havana: it captures the spirit of the city's night-life, with attention, again, to its class connotations. Thus we have meticulous descriptions of La Catedral, a low café that furnishes cheap rooms for prostitutes and their clients, of Yvonne's sumptuous brothel, frequented by ministers, senators, and generals, the scene of refined perversions, of El Embassy, the smart night-club where La Musa (The Muse!), Bermúdez's Lesbian mistress, used to sing, and of El Monmatre (*sic*), a seedy joint where La Musa lives out her decline, waging a losing battle against drugs, drink, and a faltering voice, of El Negro-Negro, the rendezvous of the city's Bohemians, and so on. The description of the Casa Verde and other assorted bars and cafés does a similar service to Piura in *La Casa Verde*.

Another thing that might be noted about the vision of Peru deployed in Vargas Llosa's novels is that they stand in what has been called the revisionist tradition of Sebastián Salazar Bondy's essay *Lima la horrible*, wherein the capital of Peru is seen no longer as the grand, colonial city of Baroque architecture, the 'city of kings' it was held to be, but rather as the hideous monster surrounded by bare hills and spectacular shanty towns that it is. The meticulous descriptions of Lima in Vargas Llosa's work (the first edition of *La ciudad y los perros* contained a map of the city) are moreover sensitively aware of the rigid class delineations of its various sectors. And the ugliness of Lima (a city where mediocre modern buildings have replaced many of its original colonial ones), the persistence of its mist and drizzle (or *garúa*), the monotony of its colouration—'color moco' (colour of mucus) or 'color caca' (colour of shit) for Santiago Zavala—become a symbol of the 'país jodido'.

Lima of course has long been the Mecca of landless peasants who converge there in the often vain hope of finding work and shelter; and disillusionment following a pilgrimage to Lima has long been a central topic of Peruvian literature. The story told about Lima in Vargas Llosa's novels is indeed in many respects the same story Vallejo told in his poems long before Salazar Bondy. The same drab greyness and the same hostility that crushed Vallejo when he ventured to Lima from Santiago del Chuco crushes another un- suspecting outsider from the sierra, Cava, the serrano of *La ciudad y los perros* whose venture to Lima ends in his expulsion from the Leoncio Prado because it has been his lot—it had to be a poor *serrano*'s lot—to steal the exam paper. Another *serrana* savaged by Lima is of course the poor *vicuña*, forced to live tied to a rope outside its normal habitat, in unaccustomed stifling heat: the *vicuña* symbolizes the 'exile' of the *serrano* in Lima as forcefully as it symbolizes the repression of innocence and sensibility that society has imposed upon the boys.

There are many other things that Vargas Llosa's novels tell us about Peru although most of them have, too, a great deal of universal relevance. Not to forget the obvious, *La ciudad y los perros* is a novel about a Peruvian school which Vargas Llosa happened to attend, although it can be appreciated too as a novel about *any* boarding school. Anyone who has been to a boarding school will appreciate its descriptions of the agonies of getting up in the morning, the sordid chaos of the dining hall, the vicissi- tudes of sports day, the problem of finding one's bootlaces on time and keeping one's uniform clean against terrible odds, the schoolmaster that one discovers can be teased, the tactics employed to gain admission to the infirmary in order to miss classes, and in general the cycles of arbitrary reward and punishment that arbi- trary discipline imposes. Finally the claustrophobia that is com- mon to most boarding schools and which is intensified in the Leoncio Prado when leave is abolished is forcefully dramatized in *La ciudad y los perros* by being set in obsessive contrast to the sea, intolerably audible from the school, a symbol of the freedom the boys are denied.

What *La ciudad y los perros* does for a Peruvian school—and for any school—*Conversación en la Catedral* does for the university, for as we have seen a substantial section of that novel depicts the activities of the students of San Marcos. Vargas Llosa's descriptions of Peruvian university life in a way are perhaps the least professionally controlled in the book, but they are none the less effective. It is as though his days at San Marcos were still too nostalgically close to him for him to have been able to impose upon their depiction the rigorous detachment that pervades other parts of the narrative. Yet the rawness with which these passages come across is admirably suited to express the raw earnestness of the students, the dead-pan seriousness of their discussions about life.

Finally, amidst all the social groups analysed, there stands out the military, most obviously in *La ciudad y los perros* but in *Conversación en la Catedral* too. The Peruvian military have changed a great deal since the periods in which these novels are set. They have jettisoned their alliance with the landowning élite, and in 1968 they took power in order to initiate the most far-reaching social reforms in Peruvian history. Yet readers of Vargas Llosa's novels could not be surprised at these developments.

As is evident from *La ciudad y los perros*, recruitment into the army in Peru is not restricted to any class. In fact the upper classes have always despised a military career in Latin America, and officers have normally been recruited from the middle or lower middle classes. The logical result of the military's heterogeneous class recruitment is that in the end they should not be anxious to serve any class, but rather serve their own interests. The death of the Slave in *La ciudad y los perros* indeed reveals how it is above all the interests of the military, their good name and prestige, that Coronel Garrido is most anxious to preserve at all costs. In the 1940s and 1950s those interests were obviously best satisfied through an alliance with the upper classes and with the United States, who supplied the arms. The army now have simply found that the masses are a more reliable and lasting ally. The upper classes anyway are unlikely to move against them, because it was precisely the army they relied on as their only solution in an emergency. As for arms, other countries, particularly Western European ones, are only too anxious to provide them. Why therefore depend on the United States?

As a political study of Peru *Conversación en la Catedral* is all the more effective in that it is perceptively aware that even in the

1950s the seeds of these developments had already been sown. Until he gets too haughty the military dictator Odría is an ideal president for a man like Don Fermín, and yet the like of Don Fermín despise Odría, see him as a *cholo*. The military, and their stooge Bermúdez, similarly loathe people like Don Fermín, whom they refer to contemptuously as *señorones*. The scarcely disguised tension that is seen to exist between Odría's circle and the upper classes in *Conversación en la Catedral* is a measure of Vargas Llosa's authenticity and perceptiveness. A more dogmatically left-wing analysis would no doubt have far less subtly and far less truthfully presented them as idyllically united.

All Vargas Llosa's novels are of course in that tradition of contemporary Latin American fiction that has sought to overthrow the stereotyped vision that characterized Latin American novels in the 1920s and 1930s. Rather than populate his books with characters that are unremittingly good or bad, he has, like most contemporary Latin American novelists, attempted to show that the conflict between good and evil can exist within a person and not necessarily just between persons, and that all people and all actions are intrinsically complex.

Take the Jaguar's killing of the Slave for instance. There is little doubt—although ultimately nothing is *certain* in Vargas Llosa's novels—that he has perpetrated a murder, on the face of it a cowardly one at that, for he shoots from behind.[5] And yet we can never doubt that the Jaguar is a better person than his alleged superiors, the officers. For the Jaguar has at least acted out of conviction—out of the conviction that the Slave's treachery was a monstrous crime that had to be punished—for he transgressed the group's code of loyalty. The officers on the other hand have no conviction other than that they must preserve their good name. Moreover, loyalty is the only standard to which the Jaguar can be *expected* to adhere, for it alone qualifies as a 'manly' virtue in a society that represses all 'unmanly' ones. The Jaguar's code of behaviour is a restricted one when viewed from a wider ethical context, and if one is to judge his conduct from such a wider context one must pronounce it reprehensible. Yet he has been taught to respect no other standard of behaviour. In the

[5] Some critics have pointed out that in the end we only have Jaguar's word for it that he killed the Slave. If there is any doubt, it does not affect the ethical considerations that follow.

end it is clear that society is as responsible as the Jaguar is for a crime from whose atrocity the novel nevertheless does not shirk. In short one can arrive at no easy judgement with regard to an action which at first sight might have looked like a clear-cut case of murder.

The somewhat stereotyped novels of the 1920s and 1930s were of course primarily responses to a rural environment. Most of the novels of Gallegos, Rivera, Icaza, Ciro Alegría, or Güiraldes were set in the countryside, often in the jungle. *La Casa Verde* is partly a jungle novel too, and it does a great deal to overthrow the rigid division of the world into polar opposites that the 'regionalist' novel insisted on. For instance the *indigenistas'* vision of idyllically innocent Indians being terrorized by sadistic landlords is overthrown, and replaced by an altogether more complex picture. For one, Vargas Llosa's Indians are not at all idyllic. Admittedly they are not the sedentary Indians of the sierra described in the *indigenista* novel but the more nomadic warriors of the Peruvian jungle. Yet there is no attempt to set them up as noble savages. And the man who exploits them most treacherously, Fushía, though wholly lacking in principle, is more pathetic than evil. He makes very little money out of the rubber he acquires at such brutal cost. His life is indeed always at risk, and in the end he becomes a leper. Like the Jaguar's, his actions have been determined by society more than by personal choice. If he had not been unjustly imprisoned in Brazil who knows what he might have done? For he is doomed to live outside the law as a consequence of his escape.

'Civilization' and 'barbarism' too are less rigidly polarized in *La Casa Verde* than, say, in Gallegos's fiction. What is one to say for instance of the 'civilization' the nuns at the mission attempt to implant on the young *aguaruna* girls? They are Christianized, taught to read and write, and they are freed from lice—to what purpose? In order that they might make good maids.

Vargas Llosa has impressively furnished us with a rich, dense fictional world in his novels. That it is a *fictional* world, a dream expressed, moreover through complex technical *artifice*, has been stressed. Yet it is a fictional world which is maybe more 'true', or which signifies things that are more true than the society that inspired it. For Vargas Llosa's novels above all seek to expose lies, if anything to exaggerate the truth, in order to jolt the reader into perceiving the truthlessness of the world he lives in. His novels seek to tear down all the decorous masks that society wears in order to conceal the truth about itself.

Nowhere are such masks worn with more false decorum than in its language, and it has been one of Vargas Llosa's achievements that he has avoided the sort of language that was so common in Latin American fiction before—a language notable more for what it concealed than for what it revealed. He has created instead a language that executes with brutal efficiency his task of scandalous revelation. He does not greatly experiment with language, and he does not question the nature of language itself as we shall see Cabrera Infante does. He rather writes a prose that is simply merciless, brutally ironical, and which relentlessly probes and unmasks. Never do we find Vargas Llosa engaged in writing for its own sake, never do we see him for instance indulging in a 'beautiful' landscape. For him words must above all be efficient, and never be allowed to distract from their purpose of revelation. His prose has been designed above all to desacralize language, to pare down its hypocrisies—if necessary with the therapeutic injection of four-letter words. It is not that his prose is not full of artifices and personal trademarks—there is not a line by Vargas Llosa that is not implanted with a very personal note. All these artifices have rather been designed and mobilized for a purpose, for the proper expression of Vargas Llosa's vision of Peru and of man: a vision that is brutal and bitter, the product of a savagely jettisoned innocence, yet which is pervaded by a yearning for tenderness, for kindness, for what is perhaps not quite irrevocably lost. Vargas Llosa's language is full of the bullying kicks of the Jaguar, the clammy torturing hands of Bermúdez; yet the *vicuña* is there too, tied to a post maybe, but still alive.

# 10
# Gabriel García Márquez (Colombia, 1928–    )[1]

GABRIEL GARCÍA MÁRQUEZ is a man who has so far dedicated his entire literary career to the writing of one novel. That is not to say that he has written only one book. It is rather that such short works as *La hojarasca* ('Chaff', 1955), *El coronel no tiene quien le escriba* ('No one writes to the Colonel', 1961), and *La mala hora* ('The evil hour', 1962), and the short stories collected in *Los funerales de la Mamá Grande* ('Mamá Grande's funeral', 1962), though promising enough, can be seen now as warming up exercises for his masterpiece, *Cien años de soledad* ('One hundred years of solitude', 1967). Nearly all his works explore a remote, swampy, imaginary town called Macondo, a backwater in the Colombian *ciénaga*, the region where García Márquez was brought up. The richly charted town of Macondo is García Márquez's fictional 'world', his contribution to Latin American literature. Yet the Macondo whose hundred years of solitary history is recorded triumphantly in *Cien años de soledad* had to be built, brick by brick, in its creator's imagination. The earlier works serve this purpose of meticulous construction. For this reason I shall concentrate on the definitive novel. Indeed there is nothing of importance that can be said of it that cannot be applied to the previous works.

Of all contemporary Latin American novels, none has captured the public imagination more than *Cien años de soledad*.

[1] The quotations in this chapter have been taken from Gregory Rabassa's translation of *Cien años de soledad*, *One Hundred Years of Solitude*. New York and London, 1970. The page references refer to the passages' original location.

It has sold hundreds of thousands of copies in Latin America and
Spain, and many more in numerous translations. In Latin
America it appears, remarkably, to appeal to most people who can
read. Enthusiasm for it comes readily from university professors,
but also, for example, from ladies who normally read Spanish
translations of Agatha Christie. The enthusiasm, moreover,
appears to be genuine. Why?

The main reason for the book's success may be that it can be
read on many levels, and there is a superficial level on which it
can be read of very obvious appeal. For this town of Macondo
that García Márquez has been inventing for so many years is an
extraordinarily dotty place, populated by endearingly eccentric
people whose antics are, above all, *funny*. The novel is full of
comic caricatures. Thus young Remedios, la bella, a member of
the Buendía family whose trajectory over one hundred years is
the principle topic of the novel:

Until she was well along in puberty Santa Sofía de la Piedad had to
bathe and dress her, and even when she could take care of herself it
was necessary to keep an eye on her so that she would not paint little
animals on the walls with a stick daubed in her own excrement. She
reached twenty without knowing how to read or write, unable to use
the silver at the table, wandering naked through the house because her
nature rejected all manner of convention. When the young commander
of the guard declared his love for her, she rejected him simply because
his frivolity startled her. 'See how simple he is,' she told Amaranta. 'He
says that he is dying because of me, as if I were a bad case of colic.'[2]

The dead-pan depiction of extraordinary people and extraordinary events is indeed one of the principle stratagems the
book employs to achieve its comic effects. Events and personal
characteristics are spectacularly *exaggerated*, made quite absurdly
larger than life, yet in a style that takes the hyperbole for granted,
as though it were a meticulous fact. Thus a young Buendía, Meme,
brings sixty-eight friends back home from school for the holidays:

The night of their arrival the students carried on in such a way, trying
to go to the bathroom before they went to bed, that at one o'clock in
the morning the last ones were still going in. Fernada then bought
seventy-two chamberpots but she only managed to change the nocturnal
problem into a morning one, because from dawn on there was a long

[2] *Cien años de soledad*, Buenos Aires, 1967, p. 172.

line of girls, each with her pot in her hand, waiting for her turn to wash it.[3]

In the same vein, as though they were the most natural of facts, we are told of how a man (the itinerant gipsy sage Melquíades), returns to life after dying because he could not stand the loneliness of death, or of how Remedios, la bella, is lifted up to Heaven like the Virgin Mary. When José Arcadio, a senior Buendía, dies, a rain of tiny yellow flowers carpets the streets. And his mother, Ursula, learns of his death thanks to a thread of his blood that exits from his house into the street and, meticulously turning corners, travels relentlessly to Ursula's house, reaching the kitchen where Ursula 'was getting ready to crack thirty-six eggs to make bread'.[4]

These straightforward descriptions of the extraordinary are the hallmark of García Márquez's art. There is plenty of satisfaction to be derived from this book simply in the savouring of his joy in whimsy and much of the novel's appeal lies in the sense of liberation it inspires in one: liberation from a humdrum real world into a magical one that also happens to be funny. It also happens to be exotically tropical, of course, and part of the novel's success in France or Argentina, for example, may be due also to its differentness.

Yet the novel functions at far deeper levels. Like several other contemporary Latin American novelists García Márquez has discovered that it is possible to tell a compelling story in a novel yet also convey complex thoughts in it which do not disturb the story's rhythm.

A clue to one of the novel's more complex aims can be found in its occasional references to other Latin American novels. Thus one character claims to have witnessed the heroism of Artemio Cruz during the Mexican revolution:[5] Artemio Cruz is the eponymous hero of a novel by Carlos Fuentes. Another character stays in Paris in the same hotel room where 'Rocamadour was to die':[6] Rocamadour is a baby who dies in a hotel room in Julio Cortázar's *Rayuela*. The main implications of these and several other instances where the characters have similar contact with characters in other novels will be discussed later. For the moment it should be merely stressed that these references show that García

[3] pp. 223–4.          [4] p. 118.          [5] p. 254.          [6] p. 342.

Márquez is assiduously *aware* of other Latin American writers. We shall see that *Cien años de soledad* is almost as much a reading of them as an exercise in original creativeness.

Sometimes García Márquez seems deliberately to be invading the 'territory' of other writers. There are scenes which could almost have been written by Alejo Carpentier, others which could almost have been written by Borges or by Juan Rulfo. Take this description of a dream that José Arcadio Buendía[7] recurringly has:

When he was alone, José Arcadio Buendía consoled himself with the dream of the infinite rooms. He dreamed that he was getting out of bed, opening the door and going into an identical room with the same bed with a wrought-iron head, the same wicker chair, and the same small picture of the Virgin of Help on the back wall. From that room he would go into another that was just the same, the door of which would open into another that was just the same ... and so on to infinity. He liked to go from room to room, as in a gallery of parallel mirrors.[8] ...

Borges has created labyrinths of a very similar kind  And who but Borges and the final Aureliano would read an English encyclopedia not for reference, but from beginning to end 'as if it were a novel'?[9]

Messages to Borges are numerous in *Cien años de soledad*, and there are many others directed at Alejo Carpentier. What, then, is their purpose? Is García Márquez merely engaged in some Nabokovian game to be deciphered by some Latin American Mary Macarthy? I don't think so. I believe that he is attempting to suggest to his readers that one of the novel's fundamental aims is to tell us something about the nature of contemporary Latin American writing on which we shall see that it acts as a kind of interpretative meditation. For the novel places many of the obsessions of contemporary Latin American writing in an illuminating context.

This it does in particular with regard to fantasy, which we have noted is one of the central ingredients of contemporary Latin American fiction. In the works of Borges, Bioy Casares,

[7] The father of the José Arcadio whose death was heralded by a rain of yellow flowers. All Buendía males are called José Arcadio or Aureliano, a confusing fact whose significance will be discussed later.

[8] p. 124.          [9] p. 316.

Sábato, Cortázar, Rulfo, Jose María Arguedas, Asturias, and Juan Carlos Onetti, to name but a few, fantasy is spectacularly evident. Why? It would seem to be one of the roles of *Cien años de soledad* to suggest several plausible reasons.

In the first place, the novel shows how there can be no continental agreement on what is real and what is fantastic in a continent where it is possible for a palaeolithic community to reside at an hour or two's flight from a vast, modern city. Backwardness of course need not be palaeolithic. A wholly isolated village in a Colombian swamp with religious beliefs almost unchanged from those imparted by the Spanish medieval Church is sure to have an appreciation of reality somewhat different from the one entertained by the inhabitants say of Bogotá. The Assumption of a local girl, the ability of a local priest effortlessly to levitate, a rain of yellow flowers—all these things are less astonishing for the people of Macondo than the 'modern inventions' that reach the town from time to time, such as ice, magnets, magnifying glasses, false teeth, the cinema, and the railway. One's distinctions between fantasy and reality therefore depend a great deal on one's cultural assumptions. And in an isolated community, such distinctions are likely to be perceived from a particularly *ex-centric* perspective, should one wish, arbitrarily perhaps, to take modern Western civilization as a centre of reference.

Now modern Western civilization is represented in the novel by Bogotá and by an American Company that sets up a banana plantation in Macondo. But neither Bogotá nor the American company turns out to be a very reliable guide as to what is real and what is fantastic. Take the American banana plantation where José Arcadio Segundo initiates a strike. As a result of it some three thousand workers are massacred and their bodies are secretly whisked away one night on a vast train. José Arcadio Segundo witnesses the massacre, but the authorities deny it. The official version predominates, and years later it is possible to read in school textbooks in Colombia that there never even was a banana plantation in Macondo at all.[10]

For the Government and for the Americans reality is something then that you can cavalierly fabricate at your own convenience. So who can blame a mere citizen of Macondo for believing in the Assumption of a local beauty? And who can blame García

[10] p. 329.

Márquez for choosing to liberate himself from official lies by telling his own lies, or otherwise for choosing to exaggerate the Government's lies *ad absurdum*? Many of the fantasies of *Cien años de soledad* are indeed absurd but logical exaggerations of real situations. Thus if the Americans, backed by their lawyers —'those illusionists of the bar'[11]—can change reality (the lawyers had declared during the strike that there *were* no workers employed by the company), it follows that they are all powerful. So, in order to punish Macondo, they order a flood and as a result it rains in Macondo for 'four years, eleven months, and two days'.[12]

The exuberant use of hyperbole in the languge of the novel can be seen, too, as a reaction to officialdom. *Cien años de soledad* is written in a style that reads very much like a travesty of historical narrative. The novel is full of precise yet inflated dates and numbers, of meticulous yet incredible descriptions. The resultant atmosphere is one of a parody of the cruder forms of traditional Latin American historical writing, in particular of the sort intended for schools, in which events are comically inflated as a result of nationalist or political bias. This kind of parody is evident in the title story of *Los funerales de Mamá Grande*, where we are told quite seriously, as though it were a historical fact, that the Pope once came to Macondo for a funeral.[13]

García Márquez's hostility to the 'official version' is similar to Vargas Llosa's. But he expresses it in a very different manner. For whereas Vargas Llosa seeks to subvert the misleading linear sequence of historical narrative and to probe savagely for the truth behind the fantastic facades of authority. García Márquez emulates both and then exaggerates them to a point of absurdity.

So fantasy can function in García Márquez's work both as a parody of the bent for fantasy of official historians, and as a reaction to the authorities' assumption that they can decree what is real and what is not. Yet García Márquez's fantasies are also a parody of Colombian reality itself. For Colombian history is nearly as fantastic as anything that occurs in *Cien años de soledad*. Take the spectacular violence of the endless civil wars between liberals and conservatives that have characterized so significant a portion of Colombian history:

[11] p. 256.  [12] p. 267.
[13] *Las funerales*, Buenos Aires, 1967, pp. 141–2.

Coronel Aureliano Buendía organized thirty-two armed uprisings and he lost them all. He had seventeen male children by seventeen different women and they were exterminated one after the other on a single night before the oldest one had reached the age of thirty-five.[14] He survived fourteen attempts on his life, seventy-three ambushes and a firing squad. He lived through a dose of strychnine in his coffee that was enough to kill a horse. He refused the Order of Merit, which the President of the Republic awarded him. He rose to be Commander in Chief of the revolutionary forces, with jurisdiction and command from one border to the other, and the man most feared by the government, but he never let himself be photographed.[15]

García Márquez's version is hyperbolic, but not all that much so. The Colombian civil wars were very much larger than life. Colombian history is fantastic enough on its own, let alone once exaggerated or distorted by Colombian historians or (more genially) by García Márquez.

It may be objected that all this is very local. The novel successfully places both its own and other Latin American novels' fantasies into a political and cultural context. But is that context not one of merely local relevance, and is the whole exercise therefore not a very limited one? Has the novel, in short, any universal interest at all? I think it has, in the first place for the simple reason that Latin America has no monopoly of biased historians and mendacious politicians. Similarly, with regard to the dependence of our perception of reality upon cultural assumptions, it may be conjectured that an inhabitant of a Cotswold village has a view of what is real that is different from that of, say, the Queen. The differences may be greater in Latin America than in Europe. But in the end García Márquez may be writing a hyperbolic parody of a continent that looks itself from Europe like a hyperbolic parody—of things that are nevertheless all too familiar. García Márquez is, moreover, aware that the problem 'What is real?' is not only a cultural one. He is always alert, for instance, to the extent to which our percepts are coloured by the state of our perceiving faculties at any given moment. Many of the fantasies de-

[14] This is not exactly so: one survives until much later (cf. p. 317). There are many clearly deliberate anomalies of this kind in the book which, we shall see later, questions the reliability of its own written words as relentlessly as it questions the reliability of the written words of, say, official historians.

[15] *Cien años*, p. 74.

scribed in *Cien años de soledad* are therefore the result of its characters' distorted or declining faculties of perception. Drunkenness, blindness, madness, and old age all play a part in the creation of fantasy. Thus old age and blindness impair the old matriarch Ursula's sense of time: ' "Fire!" she shouted once in a temper, and for an instant panic spread through the house, but what she was talking about was the burning of a barn that she had witnessed when she was four years old.' [16]

There is yet another fundamental reason why García Márquez can feel free to deploy fantasy in his writing: it is that his books are indeed books, and there is nothing to stop anything happening in a book that its author is capable of imagining. We saw how Borges demonstrated that even the most realistic writing is fictive because all writing is. He showed, in his poem 'El otro tigre',[17] that a tiger evoked in a poem is a very different thing from the beast that paces the jungles of Bengal. So if you cannot reproduce a real tiger in a book why not write about a tiger with three legs, say, that reads Sanskrit and plays hockey? Both are fictive, but is one necessarily more fictive than the other, or less real within the fictive reality of a book? We may know that yellow flowers do not suddenly pour from the sky to carpet the streets in normal life but we cannot deny that they do in *Cien años de soledad* and, because they do, we have to recognize that they are a legitimate part of that book, of the world that book seeks to create and which is signified in its language. It follows, of course, too, that that world, the world of Macondo, is neither bigger nor smaller, lasts neither longer nor shorter than the sum of the book's pages. Macondo *is* the book, and when the book ends, so does Macondo.

This point is made on the last page of *Cien años de soledad*. For the past hundred years the Buendía family has been befriended by Melquíades, that itinerant gipsy sage who so expertly rose from the dead. Now Melquíades had once presented the Buendía family with a manuscript written in an apparently incomprehensible jargon. It is left to Aureliano Babilonia, the last adult Buendía, to discover that the manuscript is in Sanskrit. Yet even when Aureliano learns Sanskrit and translates the manuscript he discovers it to be written in an apparently undecipherable code. He finally cracks the code in the closing pages of the novel, and dis-

[16] p. 290.                    [17] *Obra poética*, 1967, pp. 191-3.

covers that the manuscript is a savagely prophetic one, for it meticulously records the entire history of the Buendía family as it has been lived over the hundred years since the manuscript was written. On the last page, he reads of the cyclone that finally destroys Macondo, and as he reads, the cyclone itself begins to rage around him:

Macondo was already a fearful whirlwind of dust and rubble being spun about by the wrath of the biblical hurricane when Aureliano skipped eleven pages so as not to lose time with facts he knew only too well, and he began to decipher the instant he was living, deciphering it as he lived it, prophesying himself in the act of deciphering the last page of the parchments, as if he were looking into a sleeping mirror. Then he skipped again to anticipate the predictions and ascertain the date and circumstance of his death. Before reaching the final line, however, he had already understood that he would never leave that room, for it was foreseen that the city of mirrors (or mirages) would be wiped out by the wind and exiled from the memory of men at the precise moment when Aureliano Babilona would finish deciphering the parchments, and that everything written on them was unrepeatable since time immemorial and for ever more, because races condemned to one hundred years of solitude did not have a second opportunity on earth.[18]

In short, the manuscript written by Melquíades is *Cien años de soledad*, the novel we have been reading. That novel describes events, a place, people, but they only exist in so far as the novel exists: they are condemned to live according to the relentless passage of the novel's pages. They do not have 'a second opportunity on earth' because they are 'condemned to *One Hundred Years of Solitude*'. When the writer, or the reader, reaches the last page, they themselves reach the threshold of their extermination. The blank space that follows the last word of the book signifies the void to which they are henceforth consigned. Rather than postulate an existence for them beyond the last word García Márquez underlines their total coexistence with the book by making the book itself signify their disappearance on its last page. Again, we are reminded of Borges, in particular of the memorable end to his story 'La busca de Averroes' ('The search for Averroes', or 'Averroes's search'). After 'describing' (or creating) the medieval Arab scholar, Averroes, Borges concludes that:

[18] *Cien años*, pp. 350–1.

... Averroes disappeared suddenly, as if fulminated by an invisible
fire, and with him disappeared the houses and the unseen fountain
and the books and the manuscript and the doves and the many dark-
haired slave girls and the tremulous red-haired slave girl and Farach
and Albucasim and the rose bushes and perhaps even the Guadalquivir.
... (The moment I cease to believe in him, 'Averroes' disappears.)[19]

Averroes, and every one of the story's props, are annulled by the
blankness that follows the story's last sentence.

Borges's way of making his point is much simpler than García
Márquez's. Why? Why does García Márquez go to such lengths as
to conjure up a Sanskrit text written by a mysterious supernatural
being which translated turns out to be in *code*, and then has to
be deciphered? Let us attempt some guesses.

In the first place, Melquíades's supernatural aura, his apparent
resistance to time, his magical powers (on one visit to Macondo
he is a decrepit old man, next visit he is triumphantly rejuven-
ated)[20] confer upon him a mythical status in the novel. He is as
timeless and mysterious as the gypsies themselves. Now what is
significant is not only that he is a magical, mythical being but also
that supposedly he, not García Márquez, has written the novel.
The point being made therefore would seem to be that to write
a novel is to mobilize powers outside of oneself that are moreover
both timeless and magical. Melquíades in short is García
Márquez's Muse, or perhaps his unconscious. He is the expression
of the fatal fact that writing is not an autonomous exercise, of the
fact that what is written *emerges* in a manner that the writer can
neither fully control nor fully understand.

For many reasons *Cien años de soledad* was not written by
García Márquez alone, despite the fact that his manipulation of
a typewriter was a necessary condition for its emergence. For one,
García Márquez has *drawn* on the folklore of the *ciénaga*: his
novel could not exist if he had not been brought up in Aracataca,
if he had not been able to imbibe its legends and experiences
from childhood. Aracataca, moreover, did not emerge from nowhere. The complex history of the world before its foundation was
a necessary precondition for its existence. Of this fact the book provides some suggestive reminders.

[19] *El Aleph*, Buenos Aires, 1971, pp. 100–1. Translation quoted from *Labyrinths*, Penguin, 1970, pp. 187–8.
[20] *Cien años*, p. 14.

After giving birth, as predicted by Melquíades, to a monster, the final Buendía, Aureliano Babilonia, discovers that 'Sir Francis Drake had attacked Riohacha only so that they could seek each other through the most intricate labyrinths of blood until they would engender the mythological animal that was to bring the line to an end.'[21] Francis Drake's assault of Riohacha as it happens caused a somewhat distant ancestress of Aureliano Babilonia to be wounded in a manner that for reasons that are too complicated to enumerate set in motion the whole complex story of the book.[22] There could therefore have been no Macondo without Drake. One could add that there could have been no Macondo without Spain, and no Spain for that matter without Rome, no Rome without Greece, and so on to the beginning of time. Hence the immemorial nature of García Márquez's Muse, Melquíades. A book is not the mere invention of a particular man at a particular time. Its writing (like its sources of inspiration) is preconditioned by the collective experiences of mankind, indeed by the history of the universe. The Muse is immemorial therefore because immemorial experiences condition and inspire the writing of books. It is, finally, magical because novels are the product of the imagination, not merely of conscious observation. Not only can we imagine the most magical things; the imagination itself works in a magical way, for like magic, it is an 'inexplicable or remarkable influence producing surprising results'.[23]

But why is the novel purported to be a *Sanskrit* text that translates into *coded* Spanish? I think that the Sanskrit is a metaphor for language in general. One of those preconditions for the writing of *Cien años de soledad* that lie outside its author is the Spanish language. Yet the Spanish language itself, like Aracataca, did not emerge from nowhere. Like Sanskrit, it is an Indo-European language and its existence presupposes millennia of linguistic transformations. Just as the collective experiences of mankind and more specifically the discovery and history of America are a necessary condition for the existence of Aracataca and finally of Macondo, so the existence of language, and more specifically the Spanish language, is a necessary condition for the existence of the Caribbean Spanish spoken in Aracataca and finally of that text in which Macondo is signified.

It is not accidental that the Sanskrit text translates into a *code*

[21] p. 350.          [22] p. 24.          [23] *C.O.D.*

that has to be deciphered. That code, I think, stands in the first place for the given language, what Saussure calls the *langue*, the system of word conventions and usages that is given to a writer and which is outside him. He did not create it and he must draw on it in order to formulate his particular text, his sentences, his speech or *parole*, the words he mobilizes from the whole gamut of given words in order to signify something. Where the *langue*, the given language, is the *code*, the *parole* is the *message*, the choice of sounds the writer makes in order to signify Macondo. In short *Cien años de soledad* was originally buried in mere language (Melquíades's 'Sanskrit'); next it passed through the *Spanish* language (the translated *code*); finally it emerges as a text, a piece of writing that draws on the Spanish language in order to signify something—it is a message.

The final pages of *Cien años de soledad* are so suggestive that I have certainly not exhausted their implications. They are, for instance, suggestive not only of the preconditions and implications of writing but also of the nature of reading. For what better expression of the subjectivity of reading could there be than when Aureliano Babilonia finds that the sheets of the parchment he is deciphering are like mirrors? And there is moreover at any rate one other fundamental purpose that these final pages serve.

Let us go back to an earlier section of the book, when the citizens of Macondo are ravaged by a mysterious plague of insomnia. The most serious consequence of their malady is that they begin to lose their memory. Their difficulty in remembering things is ultimately such that they have to label objects in order not to forget what they are:

With an inked brush he marked everything with its name: *table, chair, clock, door, wall, bed, pan.*[24] He went into the corral and marked the animals and plants: *cow, goat, pig, hen, cassava, banana.* Little by little, studying the infinite possibilities of a loss of memory, he realized that the day might come when things would be recognized by their inscriptions but that no one would remember their use. Then he was more explicit. The sign that he hung on the neck of the cow was an exemplary proof of the way in which the inhabitants of Macondo were prepared to fight against loss of memory: *This is the cow. She must be milked every morning so that she will produce milk, and the milk must be boiled in order to be mixed with coffee and milk.* Thus they

[24] This joke is by courtesy of the English language. It is not in the original.

went on living in a reality that was slipping away, momentarily captured by words, but which would escape irremediably when they forgot the values of the written letters.[25]

This crisis of memory would seem to be a parable of a fundamental theme of the novel: the problem of preserving the past, the problem of the extent to which the preservation of the past depends on words. Now writing (like memory) is, as Borges's Funes knew, selective and simplificatory. A word is a mere sign in the place of what it is designed to designate. At the time of writing, a written text about a real event can of course always be compared with what it is aiming to describe. As a result of such comparison, the written sign will evoke rich contemporary associations. But generations later, when those associations have dispersed, there will be nothing left but the text. The *real* 'values of the written letters' will have been forgotten, for a piece of historical writing cannot be compared to any real thing contemporary to it: it can only be compared to another piece of historical writing. History, in the end, is words; events in the past are confined to the words written about them. Since we cannot 'remember' events that took place centuries ago, we must rely entirely on what is written about them. Those events *are* what is written about them. Similarly in the novel, when the plague of insomnia leads people to forget that a given object is a table, they must rely wholly on the label *table* to tell them what it is, and the object is subsumed in the word *table*. The oblivion suffered by the citizens of Macondo symbolizes the oblivion we all necessarily suffer with respect to previous generations; in both cases, an elusive reality (like the one that was 'slipping away') is subsumed in the words that designate it, and should 'the values of the written letters' be altogether forgotten there will be no more such reality.

Yet if the past is a series of texts it is, by definition, a series of fictions, because all writing is fictional in the sense that it never tells the whole truth, but rather another truth: the tiger on the page is not the tiger of the jungle. Colombia's past is as much a fiction as *Cien años de soledad*, all the more so of course because it is contained in words that were written, like the textbook that denies that Macondo ever had a banana plantation, with the

[25] p. 47.

deliberate aim to deceive. So the final pages of *Cien años de solidad*, by showing us how Macondo can exist only within the pages of the book that depicts it, also symbolizes the fact that Colombia's past only exists within the books that have been written about it. Like the history of Macondo, the history of Colombia is a verbal fiction. The 'city of mirrors (or mirages)' is in the end a symbol of a 'country of mirrors (or mirages)'.

It should be noted that this 'city of mirrors' was *dreamt* by José Arcadio Buendía the night before he founded it: 'José Arcadio Buendía dreamt that night that right there a noisy city, with houses having mirror walls rose up.'[26] So *Cien años de soledad* is a novel about a *dream* of a city—or of a country—that proved to be an illusion: as insubstantial as an image in a mirror, as unreal as a fiction. What was that dream all about? It was the dream that perhaps all founding fathers have—a dream of greatness, of progress, of excellence, the Utopian dream that accompanies all acts of foundation. In this sense, the history of Macondo again symbolizes the history of Colombia, or of Latin America: the foundation of Macondo re-enacts the foundation of Bogotá or Lima or Santiago by the first *conquistadores*. What did the dreams of foundation come to? In Macondo, as in Colombia and elsewhere, to nothing much. In the words of Carlos Fuentes, 'the Utopia of foundation [was] exploited, degraded, and finally assassinated by the epic of history, activity, commerce, and crime.'[27]

There was much degrading 'activity', but it led nowhere. It got trapped in a labyrinth of temporal cycles. As in *Conversación en la Catedral* and so many other Latin American novels the view of history offered by *Cien años de soledad* is ultimately a cyclical one. Everything in the end repeats itself and nothing really progresses: Macondo is sometimes on the up, sometimes in the doldrums, but never is there any consistent *development*. The Buendías themselves, all of them called Aureliano, José Arcadio, Amaranta, or Ursula are almost interchangeable. There are different types of Buendía, but there is little to choose between two of the same type even if separated by half a century. The longest-lived Buendía, the family matriarch Ursula, is best qualified to observe the extent to which the family is trapped in a cyclical labyrinth: 'once again she shuddered with the evidence

[26] p. 28.
[27] Carlos Fuentes, *La nueva novela hispanoamericana*, Mexico, 1969, p. 61.

that time was not passing, as she had just admitted, but that it was turning in a circle.'[28]

Once again, García Márquez provides a *context* for a characteristic phenomenon of Latin American literature: in this case for the sense that things repeat themselves cyclically that is so typical of contemporary Latin American writing. For it is possible to discern from the history of Macondo why such a vision is so frequently entertained.

There are political reasons, similar to those depicted in Vargas Llosa's *Conversación en la Catedral*, where a great deal of teeming political activity seemed to lead nowhere, where even revolutions came and went but made no lasting change. Similarly political activity leads nowhere very much in *Cien años de soledad*, however hectic it may be. This is most notoriously the case in the generations of civil wars between liberals and conservatives. They fight relentlessly, but the issues at stake are scarcely discernible, and their quarrels change nothing fundamental.

The phenomenon of economic boom, such as the one that attends Macondo with the advent of the banana plantation is another possible reason why a cyclical view of history predominates in Latin American writing. All over the continent there have always been booms of this kind—rubber booms, nitrate booms, gold booms, silver booms—which have provided a cycle of momentary prosperity inevitably followed by one of depression, because the mineral has run out, or foreigners have invented a cheaper synthetic alternative, or world markets have sunk.

There are, finally, many *natural* justifications for a cyclical vision of history in Latin American literature, and many of them are paraded in this novel. Natural disasters such as floods, droughts, and, not least, cyclones impose perpetual cycles of destruction and reconstruction on Macondo. Like Alejo Carpentier (and in a style that sometimes seems to be parodying his) García Márquez describes the tenuously equal battle man must fight against nature when in the tropics. Perpetual vigilance is necessary in order to keep vegetation from enveloping a house, and to keep on the right side of 'the age-old war between man and ant'.[29] It is significant that in the end, the last infant Buendía is devoured by ants a few hours after he is born and a few minutes before the cyclone destroys Macondo. Man's presence in Macondo,

[28] *Cien años*, pp. 284–5.    [29] p. 345.

his history there, has turned out to be desperately fleeting. Only
nature is permanent. Ultimately it is the cyclical rhythm of nature
that predominates.

The cycles imposed by nature invalidate historical development, make history all the more an illusion, a fiction. Like Vargas
Llosa's novels, *Cien años de soledad* is, as we have seen, full of
the *appearance* of historical action, of apparent movement
through time. Throughout the novel—on every page almost—
we indeed meet adverbial phrases that suggest temporal progres-
sion: 'thirty years later', 'it was then that', 'afterwards'. Yet then
we ask ourselves 'thirty years later than what?' 'when is "then"?'
For this movement through time always withers in the novel's aura
of timelessness: it is an illusion that only temporarily distracts
from the fact that nothing changes.

Like Vargas Llosa's heroes, even the most active Buendías are
ultimately charging at windmills. For their often hectic actions
are not only meaningless in the face of the cyclical labyrinth that
envelops them, but also fleeting and doomed to be effaced even
from memory. Thus only a few decades after his death, no one
has ever even heard of Coronel Aureliano Buendía in Macondo,[30]
despite the thirty-two rebellions he perpetrated in his heyday!

Latin America of course need have no monopoly on cyclical
time: it is possible to be a Borges and suspect that things repeat
themselves *everywhere*. Indeed the cycles that Macondo travels
through have deliberate biblical reverberations, as though to
imply that it has all happened before, that these repetitions have
been repeated elsewhere. Thus José Arcadio Buendía commits a
*crime* as a result of which he and his wife are *banished* and go in
search of a new world. They then *found* a *dynasty* and a city
which, after decades of progress, is destroyed by a *flood*. Of course
the Latin American reverberations of this mythical sequence are
as obvious as the biblical ones: many of the early colonizers left
Spain under a cloud in the hope both of escaping from the past
and of laying the foundations of a future in the New World.
But the first colonizers had several things in common with the
inhabitants of the Book of Genesis. For instance, they too were
faced with the basic task of *naming* flora and fauna that they had
not hitherto encountered. This task is re-enacted in *Cien años de
soledad*: 'At that time Macondo was a village of twenty adobe

[30] p. 329.

houses. . . . The world was so recent that many things lacked names, and in order to indicate them it was necessary to point.'[31] Again, we are reminded of how relative historical time is in Latin America. For it is possible for people to be living at the beginning of History there in the twentieth century. And time is cyclical, therefore, not only because a given society may be trapped in temporal cycles but also because the historical processes of one society may be repeated in another centuries later.

Like other mythical dynasties, the Buendía dynasty is tribulated by the fact that its founding pair was incestuous: the first José Arcadio and the first Ursula were cousins. The Buendías believe that the issues of incestuous relationships are born with the tail of a pig, and although the children of José Arcadio and Ursula are born clear of this symptom, generations of Buendías throughout the novel are warned that such is the consequence of incest.

Incest is indeed a recurring concern of the novel, and it is a constant temptation for the novel's characters despite its supposedly terrible consequences. José Arcadio's son, José Arcadio, marries a woman, Rebeca, who is supposedly his cousin, although no one knows why. The first José Arcadio's daughter, Amaranta, is quite stubbornly incestuous: she first of all earns the love of her nephew, Aureliano José, who had never imagined one could marry an aunt until he heard 'some old man tell the tale of the man who had married his aunt, who was also his cousin, and whose son ended up by being his own grandfather'.[32] Although they do not marry, Amaranta, undeterred, later experiences sexual desire even for her little great-great-nephew, José Arcadio, every time she bathes him.[33]

Yet none of these incestuous relationships have issue. It is not until the end of the book that an incestuous pair have a child when the Aureliano who deciphers the Sanskrit text and his aunt, Amaranta Ursula, end up by producing the dreaded monster, the final Aureliano, who is born with the tail of a pig.

The incest taboo is of course normally thought to exist in primitive societies because incest precludes communication between various groups of kin, and is therefore a hindrance to social cohesion. If women are kept in the family for sexual ends and not offered as wives to other groups of kin, the opportunity is

[31] p. 9.          [32] p. 132.          [33] pp. 236–7.

lost of cementing an alliance with another family through a binding marriage contract. Now it should not be forgotten that the novel is, as the title reminds us, a novel about one hundred years of *solitude*, and therefore it is about a failure to communicate, a failure to establish social relationships that bedevils all of its characters. Every single character in the novel is a victim of appalling loneliness, and many of its characters end their lives in total isolation: *locked* for years in a room, *tied* for years to a tree, or long *forgotten* in a deserted house. What is the cause of this loneliness? Not to forget the obvious, one reason can be found for it in the isolation of Macondo itself, in the isolation of a forgotten Colombian backwater. Yet why then is there no solidarity at least *within* Macondo? And what part does incest play herein?

In the case of Amaranta, incestuous leanings certainly spell an especially bitter fruitlessness and loneliness, for it is hard for her to share her passions with anyone. José Arcadio, married to Rebeca, commits suicide, and Rebeca lives out her lonely widowhood in an empty house. Interestingly, neither Rebeca nor Amaranta can somehow bring themselves to marry an Italian outsider, Pietro Crespi, who courts each in turn and with whom either one might have been far better fulfilled. They reject him for wholly mysterious, but clearly compelling, reasons. And it is the careless *introspection* of the final incestuous pair, Aureliano and Amaranta Ursula, that enables nature, attended by the final army of ants, to take over. In this instance, incest quite clearly precipitates social breakdown. For it is the pair's lack of interest in anything but each other that causes them to be overrun by their environment.

Yet normal marriages are no more successful, tending to have claustrophobic effects on those who embark on them, and it is free love that turns out to be most fulfilling. This is particularly the case of Aureliano Segundo's relationship with one Petra Cotes (to whom he regularly escapes from his wife): every time they copulate, their livestock miraculously multiplies. It is as though the book were implying that sexual liberation heralded progress and prosperity. Conversely, it is the Buendía's rigid prohibition of female sexual freedom that indirectly precipitates the final destructive incest. Aureliano, the son of Renata Buendía, has been *hidden* from the world throughout his life because he was conceived out of wedlock with an unsuitable outsider. The family hide him because they are ashamed of him, and dispatch his mother to a convent. Brought up in secret in the Buendía mansion, Aureliano is never told of his origins, and Amaranta Ursula, who is his mother's sister, never learns of them either, because the guilty secret is kept even from members of the family. Although Aureliano and Amaranta Ursula *suspect* that they are related, it can be argued that their incest is indirectly caused by their family's taboo on female sexual freedom: for if they had not brought up Aureliano in isolation he might have achieved contact with other females, and if he had known for certain who he was, he might have stayed clear of his aunt.

Incest ultimately would seem to be just the extreme symptom of the real force behind the Buendías' failure to communicate: their claustrophobic introspectiveness. For the Buendías are one of those dominating, demanding, self-contained, and self-centred families you often find in Latin America, one of those families whose autarchic nature makes contact with anyone outside almost impossible. The family's irresistible magnetic power is frequently depicted in the novel: we remember José Arcadio's blood which, when he dies, trickles relentlessly round corners until it returns to the family fold, more precisely to the matriarch, Ursula. Coronel Aureliano has seventeen bastard sons during his campaigns: all inexplicably find their way to Macondo. The tragedy of each of the characters is that he cannot break away from the family fold: whenever anyone does, he compulsively returns to it.

If Latin America were made up of strings of introspective, uncommunicative families like the Buendías, it would not be surprising that the social cohesion necessary for a constructive history should not come about. I am not sure if the novel is trying to make this perhaps rather questionable and perhaps even absurd point. I think is is certainly a novel about the failure of Latin American history, and certainly a novel about the loneliness that a claustrophobic family results in, just as it is a novel about reality and a novel about writing. It may be foolish to attempt to tie everything in it together and perhaps more sensible to be merely grateful not only that it contains so many richly disparate ingredients but also that it weathers them with such entertaining fluency.

Readers of chapter 8 will wonder if there could have been a

*Cien años de soledad* without Borges. I doubt there could have been. The novel's built-in reminders that what one is reading is a fiction, its disturbing suggestions that life may be no less of a fiction, its vision of the world as endless repetition, its deployment of messages to other writers, particularly of messages that deliberately confuse 'fact' and 'fiction', its conversion of writing into a sort of 'reading' of other literatures—all these things are Borges's familiar stamping ground. Yet García Márquez is no plagiarist, not only because his novel, in its every detail, *feels* so different from Borges's work, there being little similarity between García Márquez's Caribbean exuberance and Borges's rather English understatements, but also because though García Márquez follows Borges very closely, he somehow modifies him and throws fresh light upon him. As he does with contemporary literature of fantasy in general, he provides him with a very Latin American context. *Cien años de soledad* is a very Latin American *reading* of Borges, for it discovers Borges's relevance to Latin America —the relevance of his cyclical vision of time to the cyclical nature of Latin American history, the relevance of his sense that life is a dream, a fiction, to the dream-like nature of Latin American politics, the relevance of his sense that the past is inseparable from the fictive words that narrate it to the tragic fact that Latin America's past is inseparable from the deliberately distorted words that have claimed to record it, the relevance, finally of Borges's demonstrations that our perceptions of things depend on our previous assumptions about them to the fact that in a continent shared by so many cultures there can be no common continental perception of anything.

# 11
# Guillermo Cabrera Infante (Cuba, 1929–   )

GUILLERMO CABRERA INFANTE is the Cuban author of one novel, *Tres tristes tigres* (1967, 'Three sad tigers') which is maybe the most original work of fiction to have been written in Latin America, and also the funniest. Yet we must first of all consider an earlier book, *Así en la paz como en la guerra* (1961, 'In peace as in war'), a collection of short stories of considerable distinction, though in an idiom so very different from that of the novel that they scarcely seem to belong to the same man.

Most of the stories in *Así en la paz como en la guerra* were written in the 1950s, during the Batista dictatorship, and with deep commitment to the revolutionary cause. The stories add up to a fairly coherent whole, not only because they present a picture of Cuban life that is always coloured by the author's sense of its injustice and corruption but also because interspersed between the stories there are fifteen linking sketches which describe the repressive violence that was displayed against Batista's opponents. Although the stories were probably written at random they are consequently given a coherent structure, their proposition 'this is Cuba' being counterpointed by the proposition 'this is how it is falling apart' offered by the terrorist sketches.

The Cuba that threatens to fall apart is not an edifying one, although the author never strains to spell the fact out. Neither revolution nor repression is mentioned in the straight stories, yet a subtly suggested sense of menace permeates them. Sometimes, for instance, a placid, almost idyllic situation is almost imperceptibly disturbed on the story's last page. Thus, in 'En el gran ecbo' ('In the great echo'), a wealthy young couple visit an Afro-

Cuban dance ritual. The spectacle is merely a piece of diverting after-lunch exotica for them, 'barbarous, remote, and alien, as alien as Africa',[1] until an old black woman approaches them and asks to speak to the girl alone. For reasons not disclosed either to the girl's boy-friend or to the reader, the black woman's words, whatever they are, have a devastating effect and separate the couple. It is as if middle-class culture were too feeble, too vulnerable to withstand the most modest encounter with the Afro-Cuban foundations that lie beneath its respectable facades.

More enigmatically, we are presented, in 'Abril es el mes más cruel' ('April is the cruellest month') with the spectacle of an idyllic sun-drenched seaside honeymoon foundering when the bride, for no apparent reason, throws herself eighty-two metres down a cliff.

The middle-class security which is made thus to seem so fragile in some of the stories is of course wholly overthrown in the hair-raising terrorist sketches interposed between them. They read like a litany, almost, of brutal relentless death, correcting any illusion one might have that anything in Batista's Cuba could be there to stay. A group of revolutionary prisoners is hanged,[2] one hundred mutinous sailors are shot,[3] a man is buried alive,[4] another is treated to anal torture.[5] Now and then the scene opens on an apparently peaceful street. As though out of nowhere, violence erupts, and a man crossing the street fails to reach the other side.

These sketches have, I think, had a great deal of influence on contemporary Cuban writing, although few people in Cuba would admit it now in view of Cabrera Infante's current disfavour there. There is a school of young Cuban writers like Norberto Fuentes, Jesús Díaz, and Eduardo Heras Leon who have derived from him an unrepentantly aggressive language for the depiction of revolutionary or counter-revolutionary violence. Like Cabrera Infante, they write dead-pan, uncensored stories in which no apology is made for meticulous descriptions of the most gory details of violent death. In Cabrera Infante's case, experience as a medical student may have helped to provide the detailed information he lavishes upon us about, for example, the exact effect a bullet produces when it enters a brain.[6] Indeed, nearly

[1] *Así en la paz como en la guerra*, Montevideo, 1968, p. 141.
[2] p. 39.        [3] p. 71.        [4] p. 24.
[5] p. 82.        [6] p. 58.

every one of these sketches is expert at capturing the pathos of the detail of every death recorded.

Take the following description of the shooting of a young man: 'The fat, pale youth half closed his eyes, wheeled round, and fell to the ground into the most improbable posture: his right cheek on the pavement, his right arm beneath his body, and his left arm thrown backwards, the palm face upwards. The blood spurted suddenly, ran down his face and his hair, and stopped beneath his head, making a puddle.'[7]

These interposed sketches are not only studies of the unique pathos surrounding the death of each individual revolutionary; they are studies too of the effect repressive power has on its executors. Very rarely can one of Batista's assassins restrain himself from using several more bullets than are necessary in order to kill a man, continuing to empty out his machine-gun long after death has occurred, and treating the corpse, afterwards, to the odd kick in the face for good measure. These brutal gestures earn Batista's soldiers quick promotion. Who can argue that there was no social mobility in Cuba before 1959?

In another vein Cabrera Infante describes the wretched poverty that he himself was brought up in. Thus a child watches his impoverished mother be humiliated by a wealthy Dickensian uncle in 'El día que terminó mi niñez' ('The day my childhood ended'), and in another story, 'Un rato de tenmeallá', a little girl uncomprehendingly watches her sister prostitute herself in order to pay the family rent.

The stories are skilfully told, and have the air of agile professionalism. There is always a good final twist, very little of the narrative feels redundant, and a vision of what it must have been like to live in Cuba in the 1950s is presented which always rings true. Yet despite this, and despite the fact that Cabrera Infante's aggressive, unembellished style has set a precedent for some of the best young writing in Cuba today, neither *Así en la paz como en la guerra*—nor indeed any of the young Cuban writers mentioned—remotely approaches the unprecedented excellence of Cabrera Infante's novel *Tres tristes tigres*.

Now it will be noted that a gap of six years (1961–7) separated the publication of the two books. This is not surprising, in view of the fundamental changes that Cabrera Infante underwent dur-

[7] p. 156.

ing the period. For it was during this period that Cabrera Infante quarrelled with the Cuban Revolution and became an exile.

Cabrera Infante's quarrel with the Cuban Revolution was the result both of disagreements on general principle and of personal harassment by envious bureaucrats. It started, as far as one can tell, in 1961, when a magazine he was editing called *Lunes de revolución* attempted to campaign against the censorship of a film, *PM*, made by Cabrera Infante's brother, Sabá Cabrera, about a black female singer of *boleros*. No doubt the authorities thought the film too uncritically hedonistic; at any rate they punished the magazine's support of it by closing it. Later, in 1965, Cabrera Infante was sacked without explanation from his post as Cultural Attaché in Belgium, and somewhat rudely harassed during a trip to Cuba at the time. Cabrera Infante thereupon asked for permission to leave Cuba for two years, and he was granted it. He has not since returned.

In general, the institutionalization of culture implies the danger that cultural bosses will exercise their new-found power in a personal, maybe even vindictive way. Certainly, the institutionalization of culture in Cuba formalized the private enmities that all literary establishments relish in, and to which Cuban literary life was no exception. Cabrera Infante seems to have been the victim of such enmities, and to have suffered from the fact that one or two writers who disliked him on personal grounds achieved greater power in the cultural bureaucracy than he did, and then used it without discretion. He can hardly be blamed for having become embittered, and even if many of his admirers may feel that he has now gone too far in his condemnation of the Cuban Revolution, one fact must be recognized, namely that it would have been much easier for him to aquiesce, to keep quiet. A great many Latin American novelists are finding that a healthy revolutionary image is a great boost to sales. Cabrera Infante is too honest for such an image to come easily to him, too honest to escape the consequences of the destruction of his early revolutionary ideals.

Cabrera Infante's politics are indirectly relevant to *Tres tristes tigres*, for the book underwent a significant transformation between 1964 and 1967. When the book won the prestigious Biblioteca Breve prize in Barcelona in 1964, it was called *Vista del amanecer en le trópico*. In this first, as yet unpublished version, descriptions of Havana night-life before the revolution—the world of the forbidden film *PM*—were counterpointed with descriptions of revolutionaries who were seeking to eradicate the corruption or at any rate the unconstructive hedonism which the night-life implied. In the words of Cabrera Infante himself,

There was an area of the book that somehow criticized and objectivized the lives of all those people who lived by night, who were thus contrasted to what you could call the 'exemplary' lives of certain individuals or certain groups of individuals who were trying to change them. ... The book at that point had somewhat Sartrean pretensions, Sartrean in the sense not of *L'Être et le néant* or *La nausée* but rather of *Qu'est-ce que la littérature?* ... in fact it was, I am sad to say, very much of a socialist realist novel. Why? Because it contrasted exemplary positive lives to exemplary negative ones It had not been my intention to repeat the judgement against *PM* by other means, yet this is what I was really doing ...[8]

Cabrera Infante appears to have discovered in himself a schizophrenic attitude to his subject in the novel. On the one hand he wanted nostalgically to record the world of *PM* before it was irrevocably forgotten; on the other hand, a 'politically opportunist superego' in him felt obliged to condemn it. One is reminded of novels written in the heyday of the Spanish Inquisition, such as *Guzmán de Alfarache*, where the bawdy adventures of the *picaro* hero are periodically followed by a bout of Catholic moralizing, although the adventures are described with such relish that it is not hard to see where the author's heart lies.

In the end at any rate Cabrera Infante decided to revise his manuscript. He decided to shed his superego, to plump wholly for the hedonistic night, to suppress the positive heroes altogether, and finally to change the title from one that promised dawn in the tropical night to one that is defiantly ridiculous, being the beginning of an old Latin American tongue twister. The result is the definitive *Tres tristes tigres*, and it is this book we must now turn our attention to.

There are so many ways of reading *Tres tristes tigres* that it is hard to know where to begin. Superficially it is a novel about the day-to-day, or rather night-to-night experiences of a group of young Cubans, all of whom are friends of each other, and each of

[8] *Mundo nuevo*, No. 25, Paris, July 1968, p. 49.

whom takes up the narrative to describe his own activities and those of the others. Códac, a young photographer, records his discovery of Estrella Rodríguez, a vastly fat Negress who sings *boleros* and who is modelled on the woman of the film *PM*. Eribó, a *bongosero* or drummer, tells us of his interest in Vivian Smith-Corona, the typewriter heiress. And at the core of the novel Silvestre, a writer, and Arsenio Cue, a television actor, tell us about each other, and in particular talk endlessly about such topics as literature, metaphysics, and women. Finally, there is Bustrófedon, who scarcely appears in the novel but who leaves, when he dies, tape-recordings of his literary experiments among which are long lists of puns, anagrams, and palindromes, and most notoriously, seven descriptions of the assassination of Trotsky in the style of seven different Cuban writers. Nearly everything described occurs at night, in pre-revolutionary Havana, in every variety of bar, café, cabaret, or brothel that hedonistic city had to offer.

On one level, indeed, *Tres tristes tigres* functions as a documentary of pre-revolutionary night-life, and of Havana in general. The city is meticulously mapped out. We learn, for instance, that if you walk from the Havana Hilton to the Pigal (*sic*) and cross N street you will see pine trees near a car-park that faces the Retiro Médico skyscraper. The novel will, to paraphrase Robbe-Grillet, be useful to the archaeologist in some centuries time who chooses to reconstruct Havana in 1958. It will also be useful to a student of the city's leisure culture, of its 'cabarets, nightclubs, strip-joints, bars, *barras*, *boîtes*, dives, saloons, *cantinas*, *cuevas*, *caves*, or caves'.[9] Such a student could learn of the subtly different connotations of each of these types of place. He could learn of the vast gap that separates, say, a night-club like the Tropicana, the centre of high-class tourist *kitsch*, from the after-hour *chowcitos*, where people sing spontaneously, for no fee, and improvise dances: the world of La Estrella in fact, a woman who can lavish real feeling upon the most commercial song, yet who would probably not be appreciated by 'all those people who like artificial

flowers and satin dresses and nylon-covered furniture'.[10] If the
novel has a soul, it can probably be found in the *chowcito*. There
you might find a splendid mulatta dancing the *rumba* as though
she were inventing it, as though she were inventing dance itself
for the first time. There, a wholly unpremeditated solidarity
develops among the clients, the *familia* as the cashier calls them,
who have a genuine sense of sharing a popular culture which
they themselves have contributed to invent and which indeed they
are continuing to invent.

*Tres tristes tigres* is mostly about a Havana that the American
businessman, over for a weekend overdose of *daiquìris* and professional sex, never got to see, a private, almost secret Havana,
dedicated to Afro-Cuban rhythms and to the sound of the *bongos*.
Readers who know nothing about Cuban music, and who do not
know Havana, will of course miss a great deal in the novel, which
in many ways is a local novel—Cabrera Infante has even stated
that he wonders how it could be understood in Luyanó, ' a suburb
on the outskirts of Havana',[11] so restricted are many of its points
of reference to the very centre of the city, to La Rampa, where
most of the action takes place. Yet even at its most local, *Tres
tristes tigres* has the widest possible implications.

In the first place, although all local worlds differ greatly from
each other in detail, they have one thing in common: the spirit
of localism itself, a sense of belonging to and sharing a restricted
area of reference. An Irishman who knows and feels his local pub
is probably undergoing emotions and satisfying needs that are
not all that different from those of a man who frequents a
*chowcito—Ulysses* when apparently at its most local is ultimately
no more local than *Tres tristes tigres* is. Localism is a condition
which, though its guises differ in time and place, is fundamentally
a perennial one. Now when a local situation is observed in a
novel from the outside, presented by an outsider and for an outside readership as exotic *local colour*—the case of most of the
Latin American 'regionalist' novels of the twenties and thirties—
then indeed we are left with nothing but its specific trappings. In
such a case a novel cannot hope to have any but a local interest,
cannot hope to be more than *informative* about the local context
it has set out to catalogue. When on the other hand the local

---

[10] p. 294.                    [11] *Mundo nuevo*, No. 25, p. 42.

context is seen from the inside, when it is merely the world in which the novelist happens to live, the world he writes *from* as well as *about*, then something very different occurs. For one the local context will carry conviction, because the author knows about it, is inside it—he does not see it as exotic, as colourful, he takes it for granted. Most important, in *Tres tristes tigres* there exists a sense of belonging, of being 'inside', of *sharing* something which all the characters have and which the reader is able to feel despite his possible ignorance of the specific context. For he too may have experienced a similar sense of belonging and of sharing, albeit in a wholly different context. It is one of the trade-marks of *Tres tristes tigres* that it conveys the fundamental sense of what it is like to belong to and to recognize as familiar *any* local situation. And as such it is also very much a novel about friend-ship, about how friendship is sustained by the existence of a very few, very specific things in common, by the fact that you belong to a group, and that a few local names such as 'Club 21' or 'Tropi-cana' and a few first names such as Silvestre, Eribó, Arsenio, or Códac *mean* something, are immeasurably significant, have im-mediately rich reverberations.

*Tres tristes tigres* offers a very complex vision of friendship, and of the nature of private communication. Nowhere can it be better observed than in the section known as 'Bachata', narrated by Silvestre, which is the record of an almost interminable conversa-tion with his friend Arsenio Cue through one long night. Their conversation is based on what they share in their belonging to a particular group: a common literary heritage, a common cine-matic heritage, for they have been brought up on the same films, a common knowledge of the subtle implications of such names as 'Club 21', 'San Michel', 'Las Vegas', and 'El Sierra', their favourite night-spots, and the fact that they are both intellectuals on an underdeveloped island.

Silvestre and Cue furnish each other with a relentless display of wise-cracks, inventive puns, and very private jokes of very private reference. Yet in the end what are they able to communi-cate? Certainly not many things that matter a great deal to them. Each one, for instance, is longing to communicate to the other one very intimate thing: Cue wants to tell Silvestre that he is thinking of joining Fidel Castro in the Sierra, and Silvestre wants to tell Cue he is going to marry a girl called Laura. In each case, this one bit of important information simply does not get across. There is too much resistance to it. They are in the end too afraid of discussing what really matters to them, for they have become too accustomed to keep the truth about themselves at bay through the deployment of wit.

— There's only one solution to my problems. The one and only.
— What is it then?
He came surfing on alcohol waves to whisper in my ear:
— I'm going to the Sierra.
— It's very early for the late-night and very late for the early-morning. It won't be open.
— To the sierras not to the Sierra, *madre*!
— The John Huston film?
— No, damn you, to the Sierra Maestra! I rise up in arms—I'm going to join the *guerrilleros*.
— What!
— I'm going to join Fffidel.
— Brother, you're drunk.[12]

Silvestre and Cue are great friends, but there is very little about each other that they really know. It is only during this long night for instance that they discover that they both come from villages only 32 kilometres apart from each other. In the end, the same yearning for intimate, sensitive communication that was suppressed in the novels of Vargas Llosa by the characters' need to adopt a tough, *macho* posture is suppressed in *Tres tristes tigres* by the obligation to be witty. Cue quotes Nietzsche as saying that 'you can't talk about things that are really important except cynically or in baby talk.' Throughout Cue's and Silvestre's exchanges, one can feel their fear of the *embarrassment* of seriousness. Their verbal ingenuity is funnier and more inventive than anything comparable in Latin American fiction hitherto, but we do not miss the pathos of what it is desperately endeavouring to conceal, of what it leaves unsaid. As Silvestre remarks of Bustrofedon, 'when he made a pun a pain was hidden':[13] the same can be said of Cue when he does an imitation of Gary Cooper, when he suddenly breaks into a Texan accent, or when he speeds across El Vedado at eighty miles an hour in his Ford convertible. His witty conversation is one of the many forms of exhibitionism he

[12] *Three Trapped Tigers*, p. 375.        [13] p. 388.

adopts in order to wage a sort of holding campaign against a hidden anguish.[14] It is significant that when their vastly long, noisy session is over, and Silvestre returns home to face silence ('in silence I took off my shirt and my shoes in silence and in silence I went to the *escusado* and pissed and I took out my smile in still more silence ...')[15] he retires to bed and has a nightmare. It is indeed significant that the recording of nightmares is a recurring feature of the book, for it is in sleep that the characters' willed display of hectically exhibitionist but uncommunicative conversation must inevitably break down, and it is in sleep that the image that they project for their group, for their local *fiesta*, must be jettisoned. Indeed, much of the gaiety of the novel, for all that we relish it, is the gaiety one wears in company, the gaiety one forces out of oneself at a party. *Tres tristes tigres* is indeed one long party, one long drinking-bout or dance-session after another, following, as Emir Rodríguez Monegal has pointed out, a tradition of the cinema, where the theme of the party has long been a central one.[16] But the party must end with a hangover, the hangover of self-recognition that occurs when one's social mask is dropped.

Much of the pain that Cue's and the others' puns are holding off is social. Quite unobtrusively, the novel indeed grapples with social realities as eloquently as any socialist realist novel could, more eloquently I think because just as the feel of a local context comes across much more strongly when conveyed from the inside, so does the feel of social injustice when it is an automatic part of what the author is writing *from*, when it is not something he is strenuously attempting to demonstrate for the sake of propaganda. In the first chapter, the only one published of *Cuerpos divinos*, a novel Cabrera Infante is now writing, the narrator gives the following portrait of what we can assume to be Cabrera Infante's own background. After being referred to as a 'bourgeois intellectual' by a cultural commissar who is wearing a Jacques Fath tie, he ironically muses:

I am a bourgeois who lived in a town—the statistics were published in *Carteles* in 1957—where only 12 per cent of the population eat meat, and this bourgeois was not among them until at the age of twelve

---

[14] No doubt Cue would say he was waging a campaign against his camp pain.

[15] p. 480.  [16] *Mundo nuevo*, No. 25, p. 43.

he emigrated to the capital. Physically, spiritually, and socially under-developed, his teeth rotten, with no clothes other than those he had on, with cardboard boxes in place of suitcases, he lived in Havana during the ten most important years of his life, his adolescence, in a miserable room shared with his father, mother, brother, two uncles, a cousin, his grandmother (it's almost like Groucho's cabin in *Monkey Business*, but it was no joke then) ... at twenty he couldn't dream of having a girlfriend because he was too poor for such a Western luxury; he studied with books that had been lent or given him ... he lived for seven years with his consumptive brother whose illness destroyed his promise as a painter, while his father, wholly dedicated to the Communist ideal, allowed himself to be exploited not by the *Diario de la Marina*, that epitome of the bourgeois press, but by *Hoy*, the paradigm of socialist realism ...[17]

This is part of the pain which the characters endeavour to sup-press, but which all too often rises to the surface in *Tres tristes tigres*, as when Cue first arrives in Havana so hungry that he nearly eats a drawing-room ornament because it looks like marzipan; or such as when a girl tells her psycho-analyst of how she recognized an old friend from her home village in the house of her rich fiancé—her old friend was the maid; or such as when Ribot asks his opulent boss for a rise, since he is getting only twenty-five pesos (twenty-five dollars) a week:

*Viriato Solaún y Zulueta, Senator for life of the Republic, man of affairs, honorary president of the Centro Basco and of the Rotary Club, founding member of the Havana Yacht and Country Club, lead-ing shareholder of Paperimport and managing director of Solaz Pub-lications Co. Ltd.*, who together with his sons, daughters, and daughters-in-law, grandchildren, nephews, and great-nephews took up an entire page in the Social Register of Havana (illustrated), spoke again and at last, alas:
— Twenty-five a week? Goodness me, Ribot, but that works out to be a hundred pesos a month![18]

The private relationships, moreover, that take up so much of the novel, are all the more poignant because they are often seen in terms of the class nuances that underly them. The fact that the novel is narrated by each in turn of the main characters has much the same effect as the similar (if far more formally complex) technique has in Vargas Llosa's novels: we are able to see how

[17] Ibid., p. 65.     [18] *Three Trapped Tigers*, p. 46.

one person is several different people depending on who is perceiving him and the perceiver's impressions will of course depend a great deal on his class relationship with the man perceived. We are able to see too how in a relationship between two people one party can be coldly indifferent whereas the other (of an inferior social status) might be sycophantically involved. Thus Eribó is obsessed with Arsenio Cue, whereas Cue only alludes to Eribó once. He mentions him only when Silvestre asks what he thinks of Eribó's chances with Vivian Smith-Corona: '... she'd *never* sleep with him because he's a mulatto ... what's worse, because he's poor. Don't you know that Vivian Smith-Corona comes from one of the best families?'[19] Vivian Smith-Corona is, indeed, an almost symbolical creature in the novel, a sun-tanned nubile beauty whom Silvestre and Cue long for as much as Eribó does. For all of them, and not only for Eribó, she is the epitome of all that is sexually and socially unattainable. The novel is full of social nuances, full of vulgar social climbers and fragile social cast-offs, full of racial nuances too, and not devoid of snide remarks about Batista and his band of henchmen-assassins which, though very infrequent, are none the less (and perhaps all the more) eloquent.

There is one scene that ties up a great deal of what I have said about the novel so far. It takes place during the 'Bachata' sequence, where Arsenio Cue and Silvestre are roaming around Havana by night in Cue's car, visiting one bar after another and getting progressively more drunk, not only on the *daiquiris* and the *mojitos* and the *Cuba libres* they consume but also on their own verbal eloquence. They then pick up two girls, Beba and Magalena, drive them round in the car, and baffle them with their sophisticated wit.

Silvestre and Cue come from a background that is not all that different from that of the girls, but they are now 'intellectuals', and the gap that separates them is unbridgeable. Occasionally they break into English, and Beba complains: 'would ya quit talking English without subtitles.' The girls are not even amused when Cue regales them with a catalogue, or *cuetalogue*, of the inventions of Rine Leal, Cuba's only inventor, among whose discoveries are 'a rubber road made for cars with wheels made of concrete or asphalt ... an accidental discovery to end all accidents',

[19] p. 469.

'the car which doesn't need gas. It's worked by gravity. All you need is to build roads that slope downward. Shell will discover that its pearl is only a cultured one', or a windproof candle ('Every candle has the words Don't light! printed on it in red ink'). So defiantly absurd a joke about technological underdevelopment is lost on the girls who probably have not heard of underdevelopment anyway. Yet when a fat man is nearly run over by Cue and only saves himself by performing a deft somersault the girls roar with laughter.[20] Even what we laugh at is, alas, socially determined.

For the reader of this sequence, the joke is at first sight on the girls' ignorance:

... Abbot and Costello.
— Who's that?
— The American ambassador. It's a double-barrelled name. Like Ortega y Gasset.
— No kidding.[21]

Yet the joke is on Cue and Silvestre too. For one, their 'culture' is an ignorant one. Their conversations often constitute a merciless satire on the pretensions of Latin American intellectuals, of those dead-serious metaphysical discussions that Julio Cortázar exhibited, alas without irony, in *Rayuela*. Take the following effusion of Silvestre's: 'The sea is another time or it is visible time, another clock. The sea and the sky are glass bubbles of a water clock: that's what it is, an eternal metaphysical clepsydra'.[22] The joke is on Silvestre and Cue also because in the end they talk themselves out of the good chance they had of laying the girls. Indeed, masturbation is a recurring theme of the book, and to *masturbate* and to *masturdebate* turn out to be much the same thing. As Cue says with despair at one point, 'Silvestre isn't interested any longer in my wit which becomes as intimate as masturbation: playing a private part.'[23]

To play a private part of course is to preclude communication, whether sexual or social, to preclude the communication all the characters yearn for yet are embarrassed of, so afraid are they of the truth, so anxious are they to stave it off with humour, such as when Códac tries to knock the pain out of his friend Bustrófedon's death by punning on it: 'to think that all this, all this ... has died up there in the opera, operating theatre, where he

[20] pp. 415–22.      [21] p. 426.      [22] p. 333.      [23] p. 141.

deceased to exist.'[24] And what are the movies which all the characters are obsessed with but a form of masturbation? References
to the cinema pervade the whole book. Girls imitate actresses when
they move or dress, Cue imitates Gary Cooper. Yet what are these
models but 'borrowed dreams'? 'What's to be done, then? Stay
with Kim Novak?' asks Silvestre, after Cue has advised him to
avoid involvement and action, because they lead to disaster. 'But
doesn't masturbation lead to disaster too?'[25]

It may not be accidental that although *Tres tristes tigres* is a
euphorically sensual novel—Cabrera Infante is never happier
than when describing the sexual attractions of each one of the
many splendid women that parade his book—the sensuality is, it
would seem, only for the looking, like those legs of the *rumba*-
dancer that are described by Códac in what reads like an ode to
*mulatta* sexuality: 'and she stretched out a leg sepia one moment,
then earth-brown, then chocolate, tobacco, sugar-coloured, black,
cinammon now, now coffee, now white coffee, now honey-glittering
with sweat, slick and taut through dancing, now in that moment
letting her skirt ride up over her round polished sepia cinnamon
tobacco coffee and honey-coloured knee, over her long, broad,
full, elastic, perfect thighs ...'[26] It makes the mouth water, all
that cinnamon, sugar, honey, and chocolate, but it does not often
get to be swallowed. Cabrera Infante can do more with teeth than
Henry Miller can do with the most recondite sectors of the anat-
omy ('She stripped her lips to show off teasingly her lovely teeth')[27]
but it is, it would seem, precisely to tease that the teeth are there.

We have seen that *Tres tristes tigres* admirably documents the
leisure culture of Havana before the revolution. It depicts the
hopes and failures of friendship. It investigates the nature of
local worlds, and shows how they are as limited as they are joyful,
because the image each man opts for as a precondition for fruitful
participation in them also precludes the revelation of a deeper,
truer self. But the novel has many other functions. It is an exercise,
for instance, in passionate nostalgia, for it tries to 'fancy what the
flame of a candle looks like after the candle is blown out',[28] tries
to rekindle that very flame (not light a new one), tries to rekindle
the now extinguished Sierra, the Club 21, and so on, even the

[24] p. 289.          [25] p. 450.          [26] pp. 61–2.          [27] p. 447.
[28] The quotation is from the novel's epigraph, taken from Lewis Carroll, one
of Cabrera Infante's acknowledged masters.

Tropicana, perhaps, and rescue them from oblivion. In particular it endeavours to rescue La Estrella from the oblivion to which the Cuban authorities wished to consign her. As Códac says of her 'within two years at the most she will be completely forgotten ... and this is the most terrible thing of all because the one thing I feel a mortal hatred for is oblivion.'[29] *Tres tristes tigres* is a novel about the relentless ingratitude of oblivion, and it is a novel therefore about time, about how time abolishes the many complex ecstasies that make up a day: drinking a cup of coffee, downing a *mojito*, laughing heartily at a *particular*, unrepeatable remark, glaring happily at a 'cinnamon leg', catching one of La Estrella's inimitable cadences. It is a novel that endeavours to rebel against the manner in which time can abolish a whole epoch that once seemed so significant, a whole local world that was once so rich in associations. No doubt many critics have made or will make any number of sarcastic comments about a man who can feel nostalgic about *Batista*'s Cuba. They will of course be crassly missing the point, and not only because *Tres tristes tigres* is a novel about social injustices too, as we have seen. But mainly because Cabrera Infante's nostalgia is directed at the fragile *strategems* people improvise again *adversity*, at the rich detail of those perhaps trivial and absurd stratagems people have at some point mounted against injustice, but in particular against such fundamental problems as loneliness, mediocrity, and boredom.

*Tres tristes tigres* is finally, and most importantly perhaps, a novel about language and about literature. For one the novel is, according to a prefatory note, 'written in Cuban'. This does not mean that Cabrera Infante has emulated the unfortunate linguistic efforts of the regionalist novelists of the twenties and thirties. *Tres tristes tigres* is not written in Cuban in the sense that Güiraldes's *Don Segundo Sombra* is written in rural 'Argentinian'. There is no hectic piling on of dialect vocabulary for exotic effect. A situation is not created where a non-Cuban would have to read the novel with the aid of a glossary. For Cabrera Infante records the Cuban that he himself speaks, not a Cuban patronizingly imitated from the outside. Like Vargas Llosa, but more so, he seeks to establish a natural, spoken language as the proper language for literature, seeks to rid Latin American literature of its 'literariness', to free the Spanish language from the pomposities of its con-

[29] p. 309.

ventional written forms, from that obligation that writers of a previous generation seem to have felt to *write* a language outlandishly different, so solemnly pompous was it, from the one they spoke.

The novel in short aims to demolish 'literature', where literature means, as it often has done in Latin America, mere vacuous embellishment and solemnity. As Cabrera Infante has said, 'There can be no distinction for me between the language of a writer and the language of a bus-driver, because for me there is no essential difference between a bus-driver and a writer.'[30] Hence his aggressive attempts to satirize precisely that sort of writing that seeks to mark itself off from the bus-driver by deploying a tortuously embellished syntax and vocabulary. Take Bustrófedon's parodies of seven Cuban writers describing the assassination of Trotsky. In each case, the assassination itself is shown to be merely a tenuous pretext for each writer to show off what he thinks is 'beautiful' writing, what he thinks is 'literature'. For José Martí, it is a flowery *modernista* style; for José Lezama Lima, an almost impenetrable Gongorism, a hectic attempt to make Spanish sound like Latin; for Nicolás Guillén, the 'Afro-Cuban' poet, an equally hectic attempt to make Spanish sound like Yoruba. Each writer has a posture to exhibit. None can bring himself to call a thing by its name, to restrain himself for instance from saying 'the lands of the Aztecs'[31] instead of 'Mexico'.

Many of the jokes displayed in the parodies will be missed by readers unfamiliar with the Cuban writers concerned. Yet the parodies raise questions about literature which are not merely local. The proof of it is that they play an important, easily graspable role even in the English translation of the novel. Thus a parody in English of, say, Virgilio Piñera, who has scarcely been translated into English, is of interest because it still tells us a great deal about literature: in this case about how a writer's self-indulgence can be so spectacular (and his sense of the ridiculous so undeveloped) that he can quite seriously digress into a discussion of Louis XIV's halitosis while describing Trotsky's assassination.

It is not only in the parodies that the novel manages to debunk literary self-indulgence. Throughout the book literary excesses are subjected to merciless ironical contemplation. Gorky cannot

[30] *Mundo nuevo*, No. 25, p. 45.    [31] *Three Trapped Tigers*, p. 242.

be forgiven for writing that 'the sea laughed', Faulkner is mocked for writing that August 'like a languorous replete bird winged slowly toward the moon of decay and death'.[32] There are occasional, unannounced parodies of Hemingway, Proust, and Borges, and other passing parodies of such literary panaceas as the perspectivist novel and the psycho-analytical novel.

Now we have said that *Tres tristes tigres* is an attempt to capture the spoken language of Cuba, 'to capture the human voice in flight', as the prefatory note puts it. Yet what happens when just that is done? What happens when Cabrera Infante tries to record, say, a telephone conversation between two ungrammatical girls whose speaking voices are the essence of popular Cuban? When such a conversation is written down literally, just as it is spoken, the same thing happens as when Raymond Queneau writes down spoken French literally: the visible *written* word looks funny although it was not funny when spoken: ' Tu sabes que acmitieron a mi marío en el Vedadoténis. Sí muchacha sí. Bueno no les quedó otro remedio que hacerlo. Fue el chif el que hizo presión con dos ministros que son socios fundadores y tuvieron que acmitirlo como tu lo-o-yes ... Anoche, para selebrarlo, nos metimos en Tropicana. No, niña con *ene* no con eme. Que mal pensá tú eres hija.'[33] Such mispronounciations as *acmitirlo* or such 'Cuban' words as *chif*, or others that appear elsewhere like *yonderstán* ('do you understand?') and *emcí* ('master of ceremonies') reveal themselves, when transcribed on the page, as a joke —and a sophisticated one at that, for the joke would probably not be shared by those who uttered them. Of course, the spoken word would be restored were such passages to be read aloud,

---

[32] p. 333.

[33] p. 35. 'You know, they're making my man Cipree a member of the club. But darling, the *only* club on earth, the Yatch Club. Well, no, the yatch or yacht is strictly for non-members, darling, we members call it simply the club. How dya like that? Well darling, to tell ya the truth and nothing but, they simply couldn't of done otherwise. *The* general shot the works and threatened two ministers, no names mentioned, who are founder members, that they were going to be shot for real if they didn't comply. So they just don't have any choice but to let him, *us*, in ... Last night, the old bugger took me to the Tropicana to celebrate. No you dumb blond. Tropick not Toprick. What a filthy mind you got, darling ...' The English version here is definitely weaker than the Spanish original, but it provides some idea of how the translators have re-created the novel in English.

heard not seen. But novels are more often read privately than recited. And part of the excellence of *Tres tristes tigres* lies precisely in the fact that we learn from it that spoken words acquire very different implications when written down, that for all that we ought to avoid the excesses of a Lezama Lima, speaking and writing *are* very different things.

Cabrera Infante is indeed constantly reminding us that his novel is *not* a tape-recording but a book. Our attention is frequently directed to its bookish status: 'and it takes me longer to write what he did than he took doing it';[34] 'you who live on the other side of the page';[35] 'after this season—(translating from French, if you'll permit me and I don't think you can stop me), this vacation in hell ...'.[36] In the end, the 'human voice' that Cabrera Infante attempts 'to capture ... in flight' must be filtered through his typewriter, find its way onto a page, and become transformed into something not quite the same as a human voice: a written fiction.

A clue to the novel's reflections on the nature of language can be found in its use of the pun. The novel is rife with puns, sometimes at the rate of several per page. Like everything else in the novel, the puns are often just funny, gratuitously, defiantly stupid, part of the book's frequent enterprise to be plain ridiculous for the sake of it, a refreshing one in view of the fact that so much Latin American writing has scarcely been notable for its avoidance of pretentious solemnity. Thus Cue says things like 'Romans, countrymen, lend me your lire', then sees two blondes in the street and says 'the blonde leading the blonde'.[37] The great inventor Rine invents a space coach worthy of 'H. G. Wells Fargo'.[38] Silvestre and Cue meet a girl who announces that her name is *'Mircea Eliade*. What? Silvestre and I both start up in disbelief at the same time. *Mirtha Aleada*, she repeats.'[39] The joke in the final example is of course once again one about what happens when Cuban pronunciation is written down, as when Cubans pronounce the names of famous writers such as Shame's Choice or Andre Yi (the distinguished Chinaman). There is a great deal of playing on famous names in the book, and again one can I think see it as part of a healthily irreverent campaign against solemnity. Thus Bustrófedon's Fuckner and Scotch Fizzgerald and Julius

---

[34] p. 405.  [35] p. 373.  [36] p. 438.
[37] p. 137.  [38] p. 227.  [39] p. 141.

Seizure, 'and the philosopher avec le savoir-faire De Sartre (also called Le Divan Maquis)',[40] or his Famous In Books (or In Famous Books), among which are

> Crimes and Puns, by Bustrofedor Dostowhiskey
> Under the Lorry, by Malcolm Volcano
> Comfort of the Season, by Gore Vidal Sassoon
> In Caldo Brodo, by Truman Capone
> Ruined Vision, by Stephen Spent
> The Company She Peeps, by Merrimac Arty[41]

Yet Cabrera Infante's puns are more than just gratuitous comic effusions. Puns are words that dramatize the extent to which an author can never be in full control of language, because they demonstrate the extent to which a word can be unpredictably complex. Not only does the spoken word unexpectedly acquire a different significance when written down: the written word itself has implications and associations beyond the control of the man *writing* it. We all know what the word Bach means. Yet Bustró-fedon can make an entire dictionary of it: 'Bach, Bachata, Bach-anal, Bachelor, Bachillus (which are found in the air interrupting the spatial continuum of a Bacuum), Bachalaureat, Bacharat, Bacations....'[42] Language has its own logic, words have their own secrets. In the end, *phonetic* connections between words often predominate over connections between the ideas the words were designed to express, and these phonetic connections direct a man's thought on a course that he has not premeditated because that course must follow a relentless logic of *language*. Thus the streams of consciousness we are offered in this novel usually develop, like those in *Ulysses*, by *phonetic* association rather than by association of ideas. Take the case of the following stream of consciousness that Silvestre indulges in, not forgetting that Silvestre is a *writer*, more likely than others to weigh the implications of each word, to recognize the complex range of phonetic association in each word:

There's a Konzert and Emma Filippi will be going to battle with her harp, waltzing plus que lente. A cuntcert then. Cut that sex out! Ouch! It hurts. Shit, it's Ravel, a famous asexual. He only wrote boleros, you know. Though I don't know what he was up (or down) to in

Antibes. Remember that Ida Rubinstein danced on a table. Big deal. Idadown? *Ida* means to go in Spanish. So what? Just because you go it doesn't mean you come. Harping in the dark. Ina? Inna? In her? No, Edna asking for More by Salzedo, making harpwaves in the Seltzedo water, celestial lyre-player (liar-plier) who in the syrinx (rhymes with sphinx, like in sphinxter) makes it a celesta, an Arp. Arp? Is that how it's *spelled?*[43] Then it should be Hans Harp. What are women who play the harp called? Harpies[44] ...

The associations are in part directed by an underlying sexual obsession—a sort of schoolboy 'dirty mind'—yet often they are purely phonetic. It is as though Cabrera Infante were saying that not only is a writer not fully in control of the language he is using: any man's thoughts have directions that are motivated as much by the internal logic of language as they are by the logic that he would wish to impose upon them. For a writer in the end language is a measure of his freedom—we have seen how Cabrera Infante has liberated himself from literary cliché, from vacuous sonority, from self-indulgent embellishment, and from taboos about 'what can be said'—but it is also his master, for no word can be pinned down, no word can be neutralized and made to function innocently in a given context, without it pointing to another context, without it escaping in many other different directions.

All this the pun dramatizes eloquently. So does that other per-petrator of verbal 'alchemy', the anagram (of which Bustrófedon is an enthusiastic collector: 'Anon/Onan, navel/venal, late/tale'), in particular those anagrams that slip so effortlessly into their opposites, as if the most delicate balance, so easily disturbed by a slip of the finger on the keyboard, where holding a word in its place (casualidad/causalidad, alegría/alergia, alineado/alien-ado),[45] or those anagrams that read so differently when read back-wards, or in a mirror (live/evil, diaper/repaid, reward/drawer, drab/bard).[46] Words therefore are tenuous and slippery things, the possessors of an arcane inner life. Maybe none are more mysterious, more likely to turn us into cabbalists, than palin-

---

[43] My italics.

[44] pp 392–3. Note the deliberate bookishness of the stream of consciousness Silvestre is supposed to be having mentally in a motor-car. It is when *written down* that language most eloquently reveals its secret jokes.

[45] p. 216.          [46] p. 224.

dromes, of which Bustrófedon, again, is a master: 'Tit, eye, nun, kayak, level, sexes (everything starts with these three), radar, civic, s.o.s. (the most helpful), gag (the funniest), boob'.[47] In the words of Bustrófedon, a dictionary is 'better than Hitchcock'— for suspense, for mystery, for adventure. Like the hero-victim of a Hitchcock film, a man who uses words is grappling at something of a disadvantage with the elusive.

Silvestre's (the *writer's*) last word in the novel is *tradittori*. The novel indeed contains a long parody of the hazards of translation from English into Spanish,[48] an important instance in Cabrera Infante's enterprise to lampoon the cultural heritage of Latin America, since so many Latin Americans are brought up on hair-raising translations of foreign books. But the word *tradittori* refers too, I think, to the problem of writing in general, to the act of treason that language perpetrates against the writer, to the treason perpetrated by the writer against the spoken word when he jots it down, to the treacherous gap, in short, that separates a writer's intentions from the writing that emerges on the page. The *logicus ad absurdum* is Cue's project for a wholly aleatory literature. The reader would be provided with:

a list of words that wouldn't have any order at all. ... Along with the book the reader would be provided with an anagram to make a title out of and a couple of dice. With these elements anyone would be able to make his own book. If he throws a 1 and a 3, then he can look for the first and third words and even for a word number 4 or even for the thirteenth word—or for all of them together, and these could be read in an arbitrary order so as to abolish or increase the element of chance. The arrangement of the list of words would also be arbitrary, and both this and the reader's rearrangements would be decided by the dice.[49]

Where the writer's intentions, the writing itself, and the reader's reading of it are three different things, can there be a more logical course for literature to take? Every word, in the end, is in a state of flux, in a state of ceaseless alchemy, transformed perpetually by time, by the context in which it is read, and by the reader's

[47] p. 223.
[48] 'Historia de un bastón y algunos reparos de Mrs. Campbell'. This sequence also parodies the perspectivist novel. In the English translation, it has been turned into a splendid parody of translations into English from the Spanish.
[49] p. 357.

subjectivity. So what worse a medium indeed could there be than language to rescue La Estrella's Havana from oblivion? What is that Havana we read about in *Tres tristes tigres* in the end but a zone of a book, a paper Havana like the paper tiger of Borges's 'El otro tigre'? *Tradittori!*

# Epilogue

THE last few decades have furnished what is frequently referred to as a 'boom' in Latin American literature. Certainly, poets like Vallejo, Neruda, and Paz, novelists like Vargas Llosa, García Márquez, or Cabrera Infante, and above all, perhaps, the splendid Borges have shown that, though still underdeveloped socially, Latin America is no longer underdeveloped culturally.

There are of course many Latin Americans who feel this to be a scandalous, not a welcome anomaly. What right, they argue, have Latin American intellectuals to indulge in puns, palindromes, and Borgesian cerebral puzzles when a significant portion of their countries' populations are still underfed and unhoused? In many circles, one can indeed discern a reaction against the Latin American 'new novel', and in the past two or three years those novelists such as Vargas Llosa or García Márquez who live in self-imposed exile in Europe have had a rough reception during visits to Latin America, in particular from students. Moreover, it seems that a majority of manuscripts now being submitted to the most prestigious literary prize competitions are revealing a return to topics of social concern, the favourite being guerrilla warfare.

However, many of the most talented younger Latin American writers would probably still agree with the following opinion of the young Argentinian novelist Manuel Puig: 'The need for change is so obvious in Latin America that it is not necessary to have novels spelling the fact out. I doubt if anyone who hasn't already been converted to the cause ever will be by peaceful means. It seems to me anyway that serious journalism is far more successful than literature in politics.... One mustn't forget that it takes about two or three years to write a novel. At the rate that things develop nowadays in Latin America a novelist cannot hope to keep pace.'[1]

Most young Latin American writers are politically committed, and nearly all of them are militantly left-wing. But they are most of them still aware of the fact that a novel or a poem is a more complex affair than a political pronouncement. Maybe Mario Vargas Llosa's *Conversación en la Catedral* will prove to be a workable model for Latin American committed writing, for in that book Vargas Llosa has demonstrated that it is possible to be politically concerned yet conscious of complexity and diversity at one and the same time. For comparable reasons, the most helpful model for young poets may continue to be Vallejo for some time to come. Like Vallejo, the most successful poets of the generations that have emerged in the last two decades have made politics just one component of a varied and complex field of reference. This is the case of such poets as Enrique Lihn (Chile, 1929), Marco Antonio Montes de Oca (Mexico, 1932), José Emilio Pacheco (Mexico, 1939), Carlos Germán Belli (Peru, 1927), and many others. In Cuba, the pressure to be politically committed has, not surprisingly, been greater. But even there poets such as Pablo Armando Fernández (1930), Roberto Fernández Retamar (1930), and the sadly harassed Heberto Padilla (1930) have impressively filtered the revolution through highly personal sensibilities, and their work is as genuinely creative as that of their contemporaries in other Latin American countries.

The most encouraging recent arrival on the Latin American literary scene has been that of Manuel Puig. His two novels, *La traición de Rita Hayworth* (1969)[2] and *Boquitas pintadas* (1970, Painted Little Mouths) see to express the ethos of the provincial middle classes, an enterprise that has not been successfully attempted before in Latin American writing. His characters are usually rootless sons of immigrants who, for lack of a viable tradition of their own, have relied on what to many may seem a curiously eclectic range of cultural models: the Hollywood film, the local woman's magazine, the *radionovela*, and the lyrics of the

---

[1] *Marcha*, Montevideo, 14 July 1972, p. 29.
[2] Translated into English as *Betrayed by Rita Hayworth* by Suzanne Jill Levine, New York, 1971.

tango and the *bolero*. Puig expresses the ethos of the so-called *cursi*, the middle-class *parvenu* who lives according to the rules of what he imagines to be elegant in order to be thought elegant himself, but who is able only to display a grotesque imitation of the real thing.

Like *Tres tristes tigres*, Puig's novels are very funny while at the same time deploying an underlying pathos: the pathos of having to project a borrowed identity, the pathos of being forced by admen to compete according to arbitrary norms, the pathos of being sensitive and intelligent, like Toto, the young hero of *La traición de Rita Hayworth*, amidst a disapproving environment concerned only with such 'normal' pursuits as material gain.

Above all, Puig has captured the language of his characters. He has recorded the gap that separates their public language from their private language, and the gap that separates their written language (a grotesque *performance* whose sole aim is to impress) from their more spontaneous spoken language. There is no distance separating him from the voices he records, moreover, for they are the voices that he was brought up with himself, and he is able to reproduce them with perfect naturalness, and without distortion or parodic exaggeration. That is not to say that his novels are not very polished and very professional. Like all the best Latin American novels that have been discussed in this book, they are structured deliberately as fictions. But the authenticity with which they reflect a very real environment cannot be questioned. Like *Cien años de soledad*, Puig's novels can be read on a complex level but are capable also of wide appeal: they are no doubt accessible to the secretaries, cooks, shop-assistants, and policemen that appear in them. *Boquitas pintadas* alone has sold more than 100,000 copies in Argentina. That is proof enough that Puig has achieved a successful balance between sophistication and accessibility.

It would be rash to predict what course Latin American writing will take in the next decade—as rash as to predict what course Latin American society will take. Whatever does happen to Latin American society, Latin American writers have at any rate certainly now acquired the skill and imagination necessary to express it.

# Selected Bibliography

The following is intended as a selective guide to further reading. It comprises the principal texts described in the book, some useful anthologies and editions of complete works, translations into English, and important works of criticism.

GENERAL

Alegría, F. *Historia de la novela hispanoamericana*. 1965.
Anderson Imbert, E. *Historia de la literatura hispanoamericana*. 1961.
Caracciolo-Trejo, E. (ed.) *The Penguin Book of Latin American Verse*. 1971.
Cohen, J. M. (ed.) *Latin American Writing Today*. 1967.
Franco, J. *The Modern Culture of Latin America*. 1967.
—— *An Introduction to Spanish American Literature*. 1969.

CHAPTER 1

Altamirano, I. *El Zarco*. 1901.
Bello, A. *Silvas americanas*. 1823.
Blest Gana, A. *Martín Rivas*. 1867. (*Martin Rivas*. Tr. by Mrs. Charles Whitham. 1916.)
Echeverría, E. *El matadero*. 1871.
Fernández de Lizardi, J. J. *El Periquillo Sarniento*. 1816.
Hill, E. J. *The Odes of Bello, Olmedo and Heredia*. 1920.
Isaacs, J. *María*. 1867.
Machado de Assis, J. M. *Memórias Póstumas de Brás Cúbas*. 1881. (*Epitaph for a Small Winner*. Tr. by W. L. Grossman. 1952.)
—— *Quincas Borba*. 1891. (*The Heritage of Quincas Borba*. Tr. by Clotilde Wilson. 1954.)
—— *Dom Casmurro*. 1899. (*Dom Casmurro*. Tr. by Helen Caldwell. 1953.)
—— *Esaú e Jacó*. 1904. (*Esau and Jacob*. Tr. by Helen Caldwell. 1965.)
Mármol, J. *Amalia*. 1851–55. (*Amalia; a Romance of the Argentine*. Tr. by Mary J. Serrano. 1919.)

Sarmiento, D. F. *Facundo; civilización y barbarie*. 1845.
Villaverde, Cirilo. *Cecilia Valdés*. 1839–82. (*Cecilia Valdes; a Novel of Cuban Customs*. Tr. by S. G. Gest. 1962.)

CHAPTER 2

Brotherston, G. (ed.) *Spanish American Modernista Poets. A Critical Anthology*. 1968.
Darío, R. *Obras completas*. 5 vols. 1950–5.
Henríquez Ureña, P. *Breve historia del modernismo*. 1954.
Huidobro, V. *Poesía y prosa*. 1957.
Pontiero, G. *An Anthology of Brazilian Modernista Poetry*. 1969.
Rama, A. *Rubén Darío y el modernismo*. 1970.
Salinas, P. *La poesía de Rubén Darío*. 1948.
Videla, Gloria. *El ultraísmo*. 1963.

CHAPTER 3: VALLEJO

*Los heraldos negros*. 1918.
*Trilce*. 1922.
*Poemas humanos*. 1939.
*Literatura y arte* (Textos escogidos). 1966.
*Novelas y cuentos completos*. 1967.
*Sus obras poéticas*. 1967.
*César Vallejo: an Anthology of his Poetry*. Ed. by J. Higgins. 1970.

CRITICISM

Coyné, A. *César Vallejo y su obra poética*. 1950.
Higgins, J. *Visión del hombre y de la vida en las últimas obras poéticas de Vallejo*. 1970.
Monguió, L. *César Vallejo (1893–1938)*. 1952.

CHAPTER 4: NERUDA

*Crepusculario*. 1923
*Veinte poemas de amor y una canción desesperada*. 1924.
*Residencia en la tierra (1925–1935)*. 1935.
*Tercera residencia*. 1947.
*Canto general*. 1950.
*Odas elementales*. 1954.
*Estravagario*. 1958. (*Extravagaria*. Tr. by A. Reid. 1972.)
*Cien sonetos de amor*. 1959.
*Memorial de isla negra*. 5 vols. 1964.
*The Heights of Macchu Picchu*. Tr. by N. Tarn. 1966.
*Selected Poems*. Ed. by N. Tarn. 1970.

CRITICISM

Aguirre, M. *Genio y figura de Pablo Neruda*. 1969.

Alonso, A. *Poesía y estilo de Pablo Neruda*. 4th ed. 1968.

Reiss, F. *The Word and the Stone: Language and Imagery in Neruda's 'Canto General'*. 1972.

Rodríguez Monegal, E. *El viajero inmóvil: Introducción a Pablo Neruda*. 1966.


CHAPTER 5: PAZ

POETRY

*Libertad bajo palabra*. (Obra poética. 1935–58.) 1960.

*Salamandra, 1958–1961*. 1962.

*Sunstone*. With a translation by P. Miller. 1963.

*Ladera este*. 1970.

*Configurations*. Tr. by Charles Tomlinson *et al.* 1971.


ESSAYS

*El laberinto de la soledad*. 1950. (*The Labyrinth of Solitude*. Tr. by L. Kemp. 1961.)

*El arco y la lira*. 2nd rev. ed. 1967.

*Corriente alterna*. 1967.


CRITICISM

Céa, C. *Octavio Paz*. 1965.

Phillips, R. *The Poetic Modes of Octavio Paz*. 1972.


CHAPTER 6

Alegría, C. *El mundo es ancho y ajeno*. 1941. (*Broad and Alien is the World*. Tr. by Harriet de Onis. 1941.)

—— *Novelas completas*. 1959.

Amado, J. *Pais do Carnaval*. 1932.

—— *Cacau*. 1933.

—— *Suor*. 1934.

—— *Terras do Sem Fim*. 1942. (*The Violent Land*. Tr. S. Putnam. 1945.)

—— *Gabriela, Cravo e Canela*. 1958. (*Gabriela, Clove and Cinnamon*. Tr. J. L. Taylor and W. L. Grossman. 1962.)

Arguedas, A. *Raza de bronce*. 1919.

Gallegos, R. *Doña Bárbara*. 1929. (*Doña Barbara*. Tr. R. Malloy. 1931.)

—— *Canaima*. 1935.

Güiraldes, R. *Don Segundo Sombra*. 1926. (*Don Segundo Sombra*. Tr. Harriet de Onis. 1948.)

Icaza, J. *Huasipungo*. 1934. (*Huasipungo*. Tr. Mervyn Saville. 1962.)

Lins do Rego, J. *Menino de Engenho.* 1932.
—— *Doidinho.* 1933.
—— *Bangüê.* 1934.
—— *Plantation Boy.* Tr. Emmi Baum. 1966. (Includes the above three novels.)
Ramos, G. *São Bernando.* 1934.
—— *Angústia.* 1936.
—— *Vidas Secas.* 1938.
Rivera, J. E. *La vorágine.* 1924. (*The Vortex.* Tr. by Earle K. James. 1935.)

CHAPTER 7

Arenas, R. *Celestino antes del alba.* 1967.
—— *El mundo alucinante.* 1968. (*Hallucinations.* Tr. G. Brotherston. 1971.)
Arguedas, J. M. *Los ríos profundos.* 1958.
Asturias, M. A. *El señor Presidente.* 1946. (*The President.* Tr. Frances Partridge. 1963.)
Bioy Casares, A. *La invención de Morel.* 1940.
—— *El sueño de los héroes.* 1955.
—— *El gran serafín.* 1967.
—— *Diario de la guerra del cerdo.* 1969.
Carpentier, A. *Los pasos perdidos.* 1953. (*The Lost Steps.* Tr. Harriet de Onis. 1956.)
—— *El siglo de las luces.* 1962. (*Explosion in a Cathedral.* Tr. J. Sturrock. 1963.)
Cortázar, J. *Los premios.* 1960. (*The winners.* Tr. E. Kerrigan. 1965.)
—— *Rayuela.* 1963. (*Hopscotch.* Tr. G. Rabassa. 1966.)
Fuentes, C. *La región más transparente.* 1958. (*Where the Air is Clear.* Tr. S. Hileman. 1960.)
—— *Las buenas conciencias.* 1959.
—— *La muerte de Artemio Cruz.* 1962. (*The Death of Artemio Cruz.* Tr. S. Hileman. 1964.)
—— *Cambio de piel.* 1967. (*A Change of Skin.* Tr. S. Hileman. 1968.)
Guimarães Rosa, J. *Grande Sertão: Veredas.* 1956. (*The Devil to Pay in the Backlands.* Tr. J. Taylor and Harriet de Onis. 1963.)
Lezama Lima, J. *Paradiso.* 1966.
Lispector, Clarice. *A Maça no Escuro.* 1961. (*The Apple in the Dark.* Tr. G. Rabassa. 1967.)
Onetti, J. C. *La vida breve.* 1950.
—— *El astillero.* 1961. (*The Shipyard.* Tr. R. Caffyn. 1968.)
—— *Juntacadáveres.* 1965
Puig, M. *La traición de Rita Hayworth.* 1968. (*Betrayed by Rita Hayworth.* Tr. S. J. Levine. 1971.)

—— *Boquitas pintadas.* 1970.
Sarduy, S. *De donde son los cantantes.* 1967.

CRITICISM

Fuentes, C. *La nueva novela hispanoamericana.* 1969.
Harss, L. *Los nuestros.* 1966. (*Into the Mainstream.* 1966.)
Lafforgue, J. (ed.) *Nueva novela latinoamericana.* 1969.
Rodríguez Monegal, E. *Narradores de esta América.* 1962.
—— *El arte de narrar.* 1969.

CHAPTER 8: BORGES

*Discusión.* 1932.
*Historia universal de la infamia.* 1935.
*Historia de la eternidad.* 1936.
*Otras inquisiciones.* 1952.
*Ficciones.* 1956. Tr. Anthony Kerrigan. 1962.
*El Aleph.* 1957.
*El hacedor.* 1960.
*Obra poética.* 1923–67.
*Elogio de la sombra.* 1969.
*El informe de Brodie.* 1970. (*Dr. Brodie's Report.* Tr. by N. T. di Giovanni in collaboration with the author. 1972.)
*Labyrinths.* Selected Stories and Other Writings. Ed. by D. A. Yates and J. E. Irby. 1964.
*A Personal Anthology.* Ed. by A. Kerrigan. 1967.
*The Aleph and Other Stories.* Tr. by N. T. di Giovanni in collaboration with the author. 1970.
*Selected Poems, 1923–1967.* Ed. by N. T. di Giovanni. 1972.

CRITICISM

Barrenechea, A. M. *Borges, the Labyrinth Maker.* 1965.
Christ, R. *The Narrow Act.* Borges's Art of Allusion. 1969.
Rodríguez Monegal, E. *Borgès par lui-même.* 1970.

CHAPTER 9: VARGAS LLOSA

*La ciudad y los perros.* 1962. (*The Time of the Hero.* Tr. by L. Kemp. 1967.)
*La Casa Verde.* 1965. (*The Green House.* Tr. by G. Rabassa, 1969.)
*Conversación en la Catedral.* 1970.

CRITICISM

Boldori, R. *Mario Vargas Llosa y la literatura en el Peru de hoy.* 1969.
Oviedo, J. M. *Mario Vargas Llosa: la invención de una realidad.* 1970.

CHAPTER 10: GARCÍA MÁRQUEZ

*La hojarasca.* 1955.
*El coronel no tiene quien le escriba.* 1961. (*No One Writes to the Colonel.* Tr. by J. S. Beenstein, 1971.
*Los funerales de Mamá Grande.* 1962.
*La mala hora.* 1962.
*Cien años de soledad.* 1967. (*One Hundred Years of Solitude.* Tr. by G. Rabassa. 1970.)

CRITICISM

Gullón, R. *García Márquez o el arte de contar.* 1970.
Oviedo, J. M. *et al. Aproximación a García Márquez.* 1969.
Vargas Llosa, M. *García Márquez. Historia de un deicidio.* 1971.

CHAPTER 11: CABRERA INFANTE

*Así en la paz como en la guerra.* 1961.
*Tres tristes tigres.* 1967. (*Three Trapped Tigers.* Tr. by D. Gardner and S. J. Levine in collaboration with the author. 1971.)
*Un oficio del siglo veinte.* 1969.

CRITICISM

A. Sánchez-Boudy. *Tres tristes tigres y la nueva novela latinoamericana.* 1971.

# Index

Latin American literature is now generating considerable interest and excitement, particularly in the United States and Western Europe. Yet until recently, the figures and forces behind this fabulous, rich art have remained, for the most part, relatively unknown and unexplored. Filling the need for a critical guide to this currently acclaimed body of poetry and prose, the present book traces its development since 1810 and assesses in particular the work of seven important writers: César Vallejo, Pablo Neruda, Octavio Paz, Jorge Luis Borges, Mario Vargas Llosa, Gabriel García Márquez, and Guillermo Cabrera Infante.

The author has focused on writers of the last four or five decades on the grounds that it is only since about 1920 that Latin American literature has matured and become significant in its own right—not merely interesting for those who are already concerned with its context. While most contemporary